Adventures of a Travelling Monk

Praise for *Adventures of a Travelling Monk*

Adventures of a Travelling Monk illustrates a soul's search for meaning, purpose and bliss. Everyone's journey looks different, but this book will give you the courage to walk yours.

—Jay Shetty

Indradyumna Swami is one of the most amazing people to be roaming our planet. The places he goes to, the people he meets and the intriguing experiences he encounters are filled with incredible suspense, hope and humour. His story reveals the magic of life, wherein joy, faith and love can be dynamically discovered in a world often defined by confusion, suffering and conflict. *Adventures of a Travelling Monk* is a long-awaited publication wherein Indradyumna Swami shares the spiritual treasures of his extraordinary heart. Let us now join him on an unforgettable adventure.

—Radhanath Swami

An intrepid modern-day sadhu takes his readers along for the journey as he carries the wisdom of India to all corners of the globe. I couldn't put this book down. It is a remarkable story of a remarkable life.

—Gauranga Das

Adventures of a Travelling monk

A memoir

INDRADYUMNA SWAMI

HarperCollins *Publishers* India

First published in India by HarperCollins *Publishers* 2024
4th Floor, Tower A, Building No. 10, Phase II, DLF Cyber City,
Gurugram, Haryana – 122002
www.harpercollins.co.in

2 4 6 8 10 9 7 5 3 1

P-ISBN: 978-93-5699-860-5
E-ISBN: 978-93-5699-717-2

Typeset in 11.5/16 Adobe Jenson Pro at
Manipal Technologies Limited, Manipal

Printed and bound at
Thomson Press (India) Ltd

MIX
Paper | Supporting
responsible forestry
FSC® C010615

This book is produced from independently certified FSC® paper
to ensure responsible forest management.

*To my long-standing friend, companion and advisor,
Sri Prahlada Dasa. The adventures we shared together
travelling throughout the world for over fifteen years
will remain forever dear to my heart.*

The detailed notes pertaining to this book are available on the HarperCollins *Publishers* India website. Scan this QR code to access the same.

Contents

Introduction

Indradyumna Swami is one of the pre-eminent teachers in the International Society for Krishna Consciousness (ISKCON) popularly known as the Hare Krishna movement. He will tell much of his story himself in the coming pages, but for the purpose of this introduction: He became an initiated disciple of A.C. Bhaktivedanta Swami Prabhupada the founder of ISKCON in 1971 at the age of twenty-one, after a short spell of service in the US Marines. Eight years later, at twenty-nine, he entered the sanyasa (renunciate) order; this is a formal acceptance of a monk lifestyle dedicated to travelling and sharing spiritual teachings with others. As of 2023, Indradyumna Swami had about 7,000 initiated disciples across the globe.

Beginning in the early 1990s, Indradyumna Swami began writing an account of his travels for his students and friends who were interested in where he was, who he was meeting and what he was up to. He wrote about the interesting people he talked to, the places he visited (often places exotic to many of his readers), the festivals he organized and attended and the pilgrimages he undertook with friends and students. His readership gradually increased, especially with the advent of social media, as more and more people became interested in his travels and the spiritually enriching reflections and lessons he shared from the road. Posted on his social media channels and his website, travelingmonk.com, his articles were read, liked and shared by thousands around the world.

This volume includes twenty-one of Indradyumna Swami's best articles selected by a panel of his friends and disciples. The chapters cover the length and breadth of the globe, and the full fifty years of his active service as a travelling monk. Beginning with his account of how he first met his spiritual master (Chapter 1), he takes readers from post-war Sarajevo (Chapter 4) to Bali (Chapter 9) to the Baltic Sea coast (Chapter 5) to the Himalayas (Chapter 19). The final chapter, Chapter 21, is set in Vrindavan, India, the birthplace of Lord Krishna, where Indradyumna Swami spent the two years of the Covid pandemic. After fifty years on the road, he found himself confined to a single dwelling, but he continued to travel virtually by lecturing three times a week to his students over those two years. The volume concludes with an epilogue that sees Indradyumna Swami again taking up the mantle of his travelling service as the world emerged from its Covid dormancy. At seventy-four years of age, he continues to travel widely, while retaining close ties to the holy land of Vrindavan which he regards as his eternal home.

—Mandala White (Mandira-Mani dasi)

1

USA

Finding My Spiritual Master:
A Story of Two Lives

The Life I Was Saved From

This is the story of my life. Or better yet, the story of two lives: the one my spiritual master saved me from, and the one he gave me. Both concern the same person, but one life was transient and full of confusion, while the other is eternal and full of knowledge and bliss. This is the story of a miracle, for me at least. It is the story of how I was given a life of service and joy.

You could say my story begins with my birth. But I now know it goes back many lifetimes to a past too distant for me to know or understand. If cameras had existed that long ago, I imagine we would see on these pages photos of kings and paupers, animals and humans, the famous and the infamous, all being born, dying and then being born again.

But this chapter of my story begins, like all life stories, from the day I was delivered anew into a new life with a new family. I was born in Palo Alto, California, into an affluent and somewhat unusual family—or at least the generation before my parents was unusual. My paternal grandfather, bent on seeking adventure and escaping a life in the American suburbs, left for Tahiti on a sailing ship before my father was born. The man I thought of as my grandfather was my grandmother's fifth husband, and he made millions of dollars from inventing the floating lids used on petroleum tanks. My grandfather was generous with his money and supplemented the income my father made in advertising.

Although we never wanted for anything, I found out quickly how tough life could be. At the age of four, I contracted spinal meningitis. I remember seeing my mother cry when they told her what I had. All I knew was a raging fever and lonely months in the hospital as the doctors tried to save my life. I remember once hearing nurses whispering about my inevitable death. Anxious for shelter, I wondered, 'Where is my mother? Why can't she help me?'

After some months the medicines proved effective. I left the hospital a little wiser. I was only four, but I knew more about what to expect. Life wasn't going to be a fairytale.

When I was six, Old Yeller died. He was the neighbourhood hound, the best friend of all the boys on the block and our constant companion until the day he crossed the road a little late. The car that hit him didn't even stop. Some of the boys ran after it throwing rocks. The rest of us cried at Old Yeller's side as we watched his life ebb away. We pleaded with Mr Franklin, who came by in his ice cream truck, to save Old Yeller. He just stood motionless, because it was too late. Again, the thought came to mind: 'Who can we turn to for help?'

As I grew, school seemed irrelevant and I became disillusioned quickly. Even as a young child, I was aware that death, sadness and conflict marred the shiny, affluent world in which we lived. When I visited my friends' houses I noticed that their parents were always fighting. My mother's best friend took matters into her own hands. She left her unhappy marriage and her children behind to pursue a new life with her lover. At school, boys would get into fist fights over girls. The day my mother's father died, I watched her crumble and didn't know what to do. Once there was a suicide in our neighbourhood. People all around me were suffering, but nobody seemed to want to or be able to address it.

There was no talk of spirituality or God in my family home. My parents, both Stanford graduates, were not inclined towards religion. They spent their time painting, reading philosophy, poetry, pulp fiction and scientific publications and arguing with each other. My best friend was a Mormon and one day he and his family invited me to their church. But I didn't trust the priest and I didn't like the dark environment.

None of it made any sense because everyone told me that life was supposed to be happy. I went to my grandfather for help. 'Grandpa, isn't there something more than all this?' I asked as I gestured to his mansion. We were sitting on the back porch overlooking his expansive garden.

'Sure there is, Brian,' he said. 'Do your mom and dad not talk to you about heaven?'

'Never,' I answered.

'Well, there is a heaven and if you live a good life, you can go there when you die.'

'But what is heaven like?' I asked.

'Heaven,' he said, 'is a place where all the girls stay beautiful forever and you can smoke cigars and drink as much as you want. I sure am looking forward to going there!'

My grandfather died shortly after this conversation, and though I was sad, I was also happy for him because he had told me where he was going and that he wanted to go there. Somehow leaving behind the confusion of the world to go to a better place seemed like a good deal.

Not only people, but animals too were suffering. I was always very affected when I saw dead animals on the side of the road. When I was twelve years old, my teacher asked us to draw what we would like to see on the table at the upcoming Thanksgiving feast. I drew vegetables; no turkey or meat. My classmates saw it as hilarious, my teachers thought it odd.

My father initially resisted my interest in vegetarianism. The day I refused to eat meat he figured I was downright impolite and sent me to bed without supper. But later, some people moved into our neighbourhood who were keen on healthy living, they exercised a lot, ate yogurt and practised a vegetarian diet. My father got to know them and became a vegetarian himself. At fifteen, I was not a strict vegetarian. My father organized a visit to a slaughterhouse. When I saw the workers shooting cows and cutting their throats, I vomited and became a committed vegetarian on the spot.

My father was concerned about me. Some weeks after my unpleasant experience at the slaughterhouse, he pulled me aside for a quiet word. 'I'm worried about you, Brian,' he said. 'You don't seem to be interested in anything. What do you want to do when you finish school?'

'I just don't know, Dad.'

'Okay, son,' he said. 'You need to find something—a hobby or a passion of some sort. I think you should try some kind of sport.

What I'm going to do is write a list of sports and you can choose which you'd like to do.'

I closed my eyes and put my finger on the list he wrote. It landed on 'swimming'. By my freshman year of high school, I was captain of the swim team and on track for the Olympics. In my senior year I followed the new fashion and grew my hair long. I refused to cut it when my coach demanded it and he kicked me off the team.

I started swimming elsewhere. I surfed the waves at Stinson Beach just north of San Francisco, with my friends. Out there I felt I was coming close to something satisfying—we were free and moving and in touch with something bigger than ourselves. But always at the back of my mind, there was an awareness of my vulnerability: 'What if something goes wrong out here? Is anyone looking after me?'

That summer we packed up our gear and headed south to Mexico in search of the perfect wave. At San Blas we were thrilled when we caught waves that gave rides more than a kilometre long. But the real challenge was around the point at Rodgers Bay. There the waves broke in perfect formation. The curl was flawless—you could ride through the tube! But there was one problem: the waves broke onto a coral reef.

I don't really know what compelled me to paddle towards the reef that day. Some boys challenged me, others pleaded with me not to go. Perhaps I was desperate.

I caught the wave with ease. It was big, beautiful and long. I quickly turned left, crouched, and suddenly found myself racing into the tube. I was thrilled, exhilarated! This was it! But in my excitement, I lost my concentration and slipped right into the deadly reef. I remember screaming for help as the coral tore into my skin. Again, the same thought returned: 'Who can help me now?'

I rolled and tumbled across the rocks and landed close to the beach. Some villagers came and pulled me out. I was fortunate; except for a large gash on my left leg, I had mostly minor cuts and bruises. But my surfboard was finished, and so was my search for the perfect wave.

Back in the States, I reflected that though I couldn't save myself maybe I could save others. In January of 1968, I enlisted in the United States Marine Corps, America's top fighting unit, alongside eight of my closest friends. We had been all the way through school together, had played football and were on the same swim team in high school. All of us wanted to help our country by stopping the spread of communism in Vietnam and what better way to do it than to fight as a team of brothers? We knew each other through and through and we knew we could make a difference together. I thought if we could win in Vietnam, perhaps we could bring peace and happiness to the world.

My unit shipped out to Vietnam in early summer of 1968, but I was ordered to stay back for advanced weaponry training in underwater demolition. A few days later in the middle of training, I was pulled aside by my senior officer and told to go immediately to see the Commanding Officer, a serious-looking man in his sixties. He directed me to a chair in front of his imposing desk.

'Lance Corporal Tibbitts, thank you for coming in,' he said. 'I'm afraid I have some bad news. Your platoon came under heavy artillery and rocket fire during combat and all the members of your platoon were killed. I'm sorry. We're going to give you some time off training.'

I didn't know whether to turn right or left when I stumbled out of the Marines training facilities. My life, as I knew it, was over.

I ended up living with six friends in a rented house in Kentfield, California.

One evening, the phone rang.

'I'll get it,' said Jonny in a resigned voice. He put his beer down and dragged himself off the sofa and into the kitchen. 'The damn phone rings all day long, and it's never for me.'

Sure enough: 'It's for you Brian,' he called to me.

'Who is it?'

'Dunno, I didn't ask,' Jonny said. 'But the guy sounds official.'

'Thanks, man,' I said, taking the receiver from him. Into the phone I said, 'Hello, this is Brian. Can I help you?'

'Is this Lance Corporal Tibbitts?' asked a commanding voice. I immediately realized it was a Marine Corps official.

'Sir, yes sir! It's me.'

'The captain of the local duty station is requesting that you come to see him at zero-eight-hundred tomorrow morning,' he said.

'What's it about?' I asked.

'That's classified, soldier.'

'Sure. Okay,' I said. 'I'll be there.'

It had been nearly three months since I'd been asked to take leave. A few weeks earlier, I'd been to a three-hour review at the naval base. Though the official wouldn't tell me over the phone, I suspected that I was being called in to resume service. I had been in the Reserves since taking leave and had attended compulsory training one weekend per month ever since my friends had been killed. I was trying to hold myself together. It wasn't easy, but I thought I'd done a pretty good job of not letting it show.

The next morning, I arrived in full uniform at the Marine Corps centre on Madison Avenue in San Rafael. Once more I found myself standing in front of a large shiny desk before a solemn, older man in uniform, his chest adorned with medals.

'I have the report of your meeting with the naval doctors last week in Oakland,' he said. 'Son, on the advice of those physicians, we're discharging you from the Corps, effective immediately. An honourable discharge.'

I felt my stomach drop. 'But why?' I blurted out. 'I thought I was on my way to Vietnam!'

'The doctors have determined that the death of your high school friends has had a major effect on you,' the captain said. 'We don't deem you fit for combat.'

'But I'm over it,' I said in a bigger voice. 'I'm ready to go.'

'Not according to what I have here in front of me,' he said, tapping the pages on his desk. 'Your father's deceased?'

'Yes sir. Last year. It was sudden.'

'It says here he was on the aircraft carrier USS Cabot in World War II in the South Pacific. Says that he was injured and that he received a Purple Heart.'

'Yes sir,' I said, surprised. 'He saw action there. It was his dying wish that I join the armed forces.'

'Has your mother remarried?' the captain asked.

'No sir.'

'Are you helping her out financially?'

'Yes sir, I am.'

'Son, we've taken all that into consideration. Your discharge papers will be mailed to you within a week.'

'But sir—'

'That will be all, soldier.'

'But I'm not a soldier anymore,' I said, standing up.

'You gave a good year to your country,' he said. 'You can be proud of that.'

When I got back to the house, I shared the news with my friends. They all jumped up and down for joy, but I was despondent.

'Come on, man!' Steve said. 'Be happy! You know how many guys wish they could get out of going to the war in Vietnam?'

'You know my story, Steve,' I said. 'Harvey, Jerry, Paul and all the others died in combat while I was stateside. They're gone and I'm still here. I don't feel good about that.'

The mood in the room changed abruptly. Craig, the most spiritually minded of my friends, looked concerned at my words. He was like a big brother to me. Tall, freckled and with a full head of red hair, he stood out in a crowd. He had done well in school until the drug culture hit and he had started missing classes. Intelligent and inquisitive by nature, he had recently started showing an interest in Indian philosophy.

'Everyone has their karma, Brian,' he said. 'Try not to feel guilty. Karma is a law of nature. What you do, good or bad, comes back to you. It wasn't your time to die then, and it isn't your time now either.'

Searching for Meaning

With my time in the Marines behind me, I gradually found myself on a personal quest for answers, a spiritual journey. I had left behind the disciplined life of a soldier and was wandering in search of meaning. One day I took a walk to try to clear my head. I went into the church on the corner of my street and sat awkwardly in the pews with folded hands.

'I can't remember ever having come into a church,' I said out loud. I wasn't sure who to talk to so I directed my words towards the cross on the altar. 'My parents weren't religious, and I guess neither am I. But what can I say, God? I'm struggling with a few issues and honestly I don't know who to turn to. If you're there, if you're real, can you give me a sign? Some direction?'

It was quiet in the church. I sat a few minutes and when nothing happened, I stood up and left, grabbing a free copy of the Bible from the Bibles kept at the entrance on my way out.

A few weeks later, I wandered into a local alternative bookstore. Browsing through the section on Eastern philosophy, I picked out a book I thought might help. It was called *The Tibetan Book of the Dead*.[1]

I stopped in a park on the way back to the house and read the first few chapters. I was confronted by a concept totally foreign to me: the theory of reincarnation, the idea that there was life after death.

'It helps a little if you believe in reincarnation, I guess,' I thought. 'If it's true, it means the guys are probably doing okay somewhere else.'

When I got back to the house later that afternoon, Craig was sitting on a couch. He could see I was upset even without me saying a word. 'Hey, Brian,' he said. How about we sit and have a talk? How are you?'

'I just don't know where to turn from here,' I confessed.

'I think you should look to the East,' he said. 'Like India. The Beatles went there. They stayed in an ashram for a few weeks. Look, yesterday I was in San Francisco, in the Haight-Ashbury, visiting some friends. Someone gave me an invitation to a big event that's happening tomorrow in Golden Gate Park.'

'Yeah, what kind of event?'

'It's a big parade with a gigantic chariot from India,' he said. 'A spiritual gathering. People dress up like in India. They're gonna sing songs and burn incense. Stuff like that. It's the talk of Haight-Ashbury. All the hippies in San Francisco are going.'

'What's it all about?'

'I'm not completely sure,' Craig said. 'But there's going to be a vegetarian feast at the end, so I'm going. You wanna come with me? It's free!'

'I guess so,' I said. 'I don't really feel like going to a big celebration, but I guess I'll go if you're going.'

'Hey, but it's not just a celebration,' Craig said. 'Maybe you can find the answers you're looking for.'

'Yeah, sure. Okay,' I said. 'Where shall I meet you?'

'I'll meet you at the event,' Craig replied. 'Just drive over Golden Gate Bridge and take the second exit into the park. We can meet at noon next to the big chariot.'

The next morning I got up late and rushed through the traffic towards Golden Gate Bridge, which was an hour from where we lived. There was a long line of stationary cars backed up for at least a kilometre at the toll gate. 'Reports are just coming in of a bad accident on Golden Gate Bridge,' the newsreader announced on the radio. 'The California Highway Patrol says to expect a delay of several hours.'

I gave up after two hours. 'Must be my karma,' I thought, remembering Craig's explanation for unfortunate reversals. The next day Craig came bursting into the kitchen where I was having breakfast. 'Hey, Brian,' he said. 'What happened, man? I looked for you everywhere at the parade yesterday.'

'Sorry,' I said. 'There was an accident on the bridge. I waited for hours and just gave up.'

'Man, you really missed out,' Craig said. 'It was far out! There were literally thousands of people. The chariot was huge! We all pulled it through the park on ropes for three miles down to the beach. Then we had a feast of rice pudding, fruit salad and sugar balls. The food was so delicious! But you know what impressed me the most?'

'What?'

'The guru! He's the spiritual teacher of the people who organized the event. He's from India. He rode on the chariot with statues of their gods. His speech was super cool. He began by telling us he was going to sing a song by an incarnation of God who lived 500 years ago. At the end, he encouraged us to sing, dance and eat the food.'

'Wow. Sorry I missed it.'

'Yes, but listen to this,' Craig continued. 'I was thinking of you as he spoke. Everything he said seemed to resonate with what I know about you. I mean, he was talking about finding the answers to the questions of life. And how we're struggling in this world but that there's a spiritual way out. Stuff like that. And when he said his practice includes singing and dancing, I thought, "Yeah, that's Brian when he's doing good." Because you like to sing and dance. And you know what?'

'What?'

'I'm convinced he's your guru. I mean seriously, man. One day you're gonna be his student!'

'No way, Craig,' I said. 'I'm not even looking for a guru.'

'I get it. But if you ever do want a guru, he will be your guru. Believe me. I'm gonna write down his name for you.'

Tearing off a piece of newspaper that was lying on the couch, he wrote down each letter of the guru's name and handed it to me. 'They call him Srila Prabhupada,' he said.

I took the scrap of paper and crammed it into a pocket in my jeans. That night before going to sleep I emptied out my pockets onto my bed and found the piece of paper. I stuffed it into the cover of my *Sgt. Pepper's Lonely Hearts Club Band* record album by the Beatles. For a few weeks, I mused over Craig's advice that I look to the East for the answer as to why my friends died in the war and I didn't. My discharge from the Marine Corps, though honourable, weighed heavily on my mind. I finally decided to leave the house I was living in with my friends, leave California, and leave the United States of America (henceforth, the US) altogether.

'For now,' I thought, 'I'll go to Europe and experience different countries and different cultures. I'll meet all kinds of people. Maybe I'll find some answers to my questions.'

In September 1969 I boarded a flight for Europe with a friend. We visited England, Denmark, France, Germany and Greece. While we were in Germany I met Ilene, an American girl who was also travelling and searching. She joined us as we travelled farther to Turkey, Egypt and Lebanon. We were thinking of going on to India when unforeseen circumstances forced me to return to the US.

Back in America, Ilene and I got married in a small backyard ceremony at our friends' house. I wore jeans and she wore a sundress and we all ate ice cream for our wedding breakfast. Together, we started to follow Craig's advice in earnest by attending lectures of various yogis and spiritual teachers, most of whom had travelled from India with their teachings. We weren't overly impressed with any of them. Many of them had acquired wealthy followers and were embracing the materialistic lifestyle of America, while continuing to talk about spirituality. I sensed a lack of genuineness in most of those I met.

Ilene was intellectually brilliant and she went back to university soon after we got married. While she was studying, I earned a little money to support us by making cement birdbaths for three dollars an hour. Then in December 1970, Ilene was accepted to study at the University of Michigan at Ann Arbor. I found a job doing gardening on campus.

The Life I Was Given

One afternoon when I had finished my gardening duties, I wandered into a museum on the University of Michigan campus hoping to forget my troubles by browsing through antiquities. An exhibit on India's culture and traditions caught my eye. As I surveyed the paintings and artifacts, my eyes fell upon a beautiful painting called *Krishna and His Milkmaids*. The scene captivated my attention, and

I moved closer to read the text that went with it: 'This scene depicts heaven, where God enjoys eternal life.'

'Yes,' I thought, 'that's what I'm looking for: eternal life, a place beyond the highs and lows of the world. But could it be like this? Who is Krishna, and what is a milkmaid anyway?'

I looked around for someone to explain the painting in more depth. But a guard announced that the museum was about to close. Disappointed, I walked out the main entrance and there on the lawn before me were orange-robed monks singing and dancing with large staffs in their hands. A group of about 200 students had gathered around them. When the singing stopped, one of the monks stepped forward to speak. And, unbelievably, he started speaking about the person in the painting I had just seen: Krishna.

'Thank you for listening,' he said in a clear voice. 'This chanting of the Hare Krishna mantra is a transcendental sound vibration coming down from the spiritual world.' The students started drifting away, after a few minutes only a few remained. But I stood dumbfounded by the whole experience, captivated by the young monk's presence and by the atmosphere they had created. Another monk came over to me. 'My name is Vishnujana Swami,' he said. 'What's yours?'

'Brian,' I replied and added, 'Tell me more about what you're doing. Tell me about Krishna.'

'Okay, but first let me tell you about my guru,' he said. 'One can only understand Krishna by the mercy of the spiritual master.'

'Who is your guru?' I asked.

'His Divine Grace Srila A.C. Bhaktivedanta Swami. He is affectionately known by his students as Srila Prabhupada,' he replied.

The name was familiar, but I couldn't figure out why.

'My guru, Srila Prabhupada,' he said, 'is a genuine sadhu—a genuine spiritual teacher. I know this because he has full control of mind and senses. What I mean is, he thinks about God, he talks about God, and all his actions are dedicated to God. And he is not making anything up or inventing anything to serve his own ego or senses. He comes in a line of disciplic succession.'

'What does that mean?' I asked.

'It means that my guru has his own guru. And his guru has a guru. And that line of teachers and students extends all the way back through history to Krishna. The philosophy Prabhupada teaches comes from the Vedas, the ancient scriptures of India. And the most important text from that literature is the Bhagavad Gita, which was spoken by Krishna Himself! No one can find fault with Prabhupada. He is someone who loves Krishna! He actually loves God and has dedicated his whole life to Him! Five years ago, he came to America by ship because he wanted to teach Americans how to love God too.'

'He came on a ship. Like a yacht?' I asked, recalling the wealthy Indian gurus I had met.

'No! On a freight ship,' Vishnujana Swami replied. 'And he came with just a few dollars in his pocket and a trunk of the books he had written. He came because his spiritual master asked him to come way back in the 1930s, and because he felt compassion for others. Tell me, did you ever feel like it was wrong that life in this world is temporary? Or that people suffer?'

'Yes,' I confirmed.

'Right! And it is wrong. Because we are spiritual souls and we are by nature eternal and full of bliss and wisdom. No one wants to die; everyone wants to live. Even a cockroach. I saw one the other day running around trying to get away. Everyone wants to live and everyone wants to be healthy. That's why we spend millions of dollars on hospitals every year. And naturally, nobody wants to be miserable—we want to enjoy ourselves. We want to be eternal and full of knowledge.

'But we left the spiritual world, where everything is eternal and joyful, to come here to the material world to try to enjoy ourselves separately from the divine. And the paradox is that the more we try to enjoy and become masters of the world around us, the more we suffer. Why is that? It's because we have forgotten our eternal spiritual identity as servants of God. We might think that being a servant sounds dull and demeaning. But we are tiny spiritual beings, and God is the greatest spiritual being, so it is natural for us to serve Him.

'The first teaching of yoga is that this body is only a vehicle; it's not really us. I'm not black or white, pretty or ugly, man or woman, young or old, American or Indian, rich or poor. These are bodily designations; these are the things that keep us apart from each other, aren't they? These are the things that wars are fought over. Let's free our consciousness from these designations. The only way we're going to actually be able to live together very peacefully and intimately is if we realize the beautiful thing in one another. That thing which makes us all equal, that thing which makes us equal with the plants, the trees, the animals and everything else. And that's consciousness.

'This is the warm invitation in Krishna consciousness, that you realize that beautiful nature of yourself as spirit. Prabhupada's mission is to help us realize this.'

'Yes, but how does he do that?' I asked.

'There are lots of different ways to achieve spiritual perfection, depending on the time and place,' he said. 'But the easiest and most powerful way right now in the age we are living in—it's called the age of Kali, and it's the winter season in the cycle of ages—is to chant the names of God, as you just saw us doing. We chant the names Hare,

Krishna and Rama; we do it together congregationally and on our own as a meditation practice every day. Because Krishna is absolute, everything about Him is also absolute. You as a person are different from your name—Brian—but Krishna's name is non-different from Him. Therefore, when we chant Hare Krishna, we are connecting directly to the divine. Chanting enables us to reawaken our spiritual identity.

'If you would like to get out of this ocean of birth and death, this ocean of old age and disease, and enter into our real atmosphere— eternity, knowledge and bliss—all you need to do is chant, to dance, to feast. You don't have to necessarily join our religion, shave your head or put on robes like I wear. It's not about that. It's about giving your love to the Absolute and all living beings.'

'Can your spiritual master be my spiritual master too? Can I be his disciple like you?' I asked.

It wasn't long before I was. Within a year, I was an initiated disciple of Srila Prabhupada and was following his example by dedicating my life to reawakening my true spiritual nature. And so my new life began, my life as a disciple of my spiritual master and as a devotee of Krishna. The day when I met Prabhupada's disciples at Ann Arbor was the day I started the spiritual journey that continues today, fifty years later.

I had long forgotten the short exchange I'd had with Craig after he attended the chariot festival in San Francisco. But ten years after meeting Vishnujana Swami, I went to visit my mother in California, where I went through some of the possessions I had left with her when I went to Europe. When I picked up my *Sgt. Pepper's Lonely Hearts Club Band* album, a tiny piece of yellowed newspaper fell out from the cover. There, written in Craig's handwriting, was Srila Prabhupada's name.

If I could show you all that's happened since then, you'd see many images of singing the holy names and dancing with unbridled joy. You'd see images of feasts and festivals, of travels in far-distant lands, and of illuminating discourses too numerous to capture or explain adequately. Suffice to say that the day I met devotees of Krishna, I started home again, beyond the dualities of birth and death, to the shelter of the eternal realm, a shelter that I try to share with others, including you, through the pages of this book.

Learn from the wise with submission, inquiry and service. The self-realized souls who have seen the truth will give you knowledge.
—Lord Krishna in the Bhagavad Gita (4:34)

2

USA and UK

'Here Comes Srila Prabhupada!'

We Visit our First Hare Krishna Temple

It had been six months since I had met Vishnujana Swami in Ann Arbor. Now he and the other monks with him were visiting Detroit and had nowhere to stay, so I invited them to come and stay with me and Ilene at our house.

By the time they left five days later we felt our lives had been transformed, but as they neglected to communicate clearly that Hare Krishna temples were sprouting up across North America, I had no idea that there was a temple less than an hour away in Detroit. However, as my friends all knew that I had met Vishnujana Swami, one said that he'd seen some men with shaved heads and little ponytails wearing orange robes in downtown Detroit.

So we spent time driving around Detroit looking for them, convinced by my friend's sighting that there must be more monks like the ones we had met. Another friend had stumbled upon a house where devotees were living, but there was nobody there when I visited. When I knocked on the neighbour's door, the woman who answered told me that they had just moved and she gave me their new address.

And so, after much effort, we finally visited our first Hare Krishna temple in 1971. Situated on East Jefferson Avenue, the temple was in a prominent home in a once well-to-do area in the heyday of Detroit's automobile manufacturing period. Escalating racial tensions and the rise of the Japanese car had seen a downturn in Detroit's flagship industry throughout the 1960s. By the time the Hare Krishna devotees arrived on East Jefferson, the area was neglected and impoverished—which was why they could afford to live there. Most of the other people living in the area were poor African Americans.

We turned up on the temple doorstep just in time for what they called the Sunday Love Feast—a gathering for devotees and newcomers that consisted of chanting, philosophy, and a vegetarian feast. The devotees handed out large plates of freshly cooked rice, dal, samosas, chutney and halva to the guests, and even bigger plates to the devotees. It wasn't long before I was getting a devotee-sized plate and only a couple of months before we moved in.

About fifty devotees lived in the temple. The young men and women lived in separate ashrams within the building and the few married devotees, including Ilene and I, had a room per couple. Nobody was over twenty-five years of age. We did everything together: we rose before the sun for our earliest prayers and japa (chanting) meditation, we studied the handful of Srila Prabhupada's books that we had, we cooked and offered all our food to Krishna, eating together morning and evening, and during the days we went out into our neighbourhood and into the city in our robes to hold kirtan—congregational chanting of God's names. Accompanied by mridang (drum) and kartal (cymbals), we chanted: 'Hare Krishna,

Hare Krishna, Krishna Krishna, Hare Hare; Hare Rama, Hare Rama, Rama Rama, Hare Hare.' We handed out books and magazines about Krishna consciousness to whoever would accept them.

In short, we were like a loving and supportive family and Srila Prabhupada was our father. Most of us had never met him, but we felt that we had a relationship with him already from reading his books and hearing about him from those who had met him. Everything was focussed on him and mystically we felt his presence.

I Meet My Guru, Srila Prabhupada

We prepared for his arrival for months. We repainted the temple building inside and outside, and manicured the garden. The seat on which Prabhupada was to sit to lecture was freshly upholstered and we purchased new pots and cooking utensils for the temple kitchen. We let the press and various dignitaries throughout the city know that the Founder Acharya of the International Society for Krishna Consciousness would be making his first visit to Michigan.

Now, finally, the day had arrived. The whole temple community—men, women, and children—gathered in the driveway to welcome our spiritual master.

'Here comes Srila Prabhupada! Here comes Srila Prabhupada!' The calls reverberated throughout our Detroit temple accompanied by the blowing of conch shells, heralding the much-anticipated arrival of our spiritual master.

The car pulled up outside the temple and our temple president stepped forward to open the front door for him. Srila Prabhupada emerged from the car, beaming as the devotees showered him with fragrant rose petals. I noticed that everyone around me was crying, especially those who had met Prabhupada before.

Prabhupada was small in stature, but to me he seemed larger than life. He made his way towards the temple door along a path lined with devotees on either side. Each devotee handed Prabhupada a flower and as his hands filled with the brightly coloured blooms he handed them back to others further down the line.

We had arranged a reception for him in the temple room which seemed lit up by his presence. He sat on his raised seat and folded his hands in humility as a devotee placed a white and red rose garland around his neck. But as soon as he began to speak, he commanded an authority of timeless wisdom, quoting verses from Bhagavad Gita and other ancient scriptures. I was so mesmerized by seeing him in front of me that I could hardly focus on what he was saying, but one statement stuck with me.

'Our first proposition,' Prabhupada said, 'is that you are not this body; you are spirit soul. Some way or other, you are in contact with this material world and you have got this material body and under illusion you are accepting something which you are not.'

I had read many times in Prabhupada's books that we are not our temporary bodies. But when he leaned forward slightly and said those words, I felt them enter my heart and I was convinced: 'Oh, yes, I'm not my body, I'm a spirit soul.' If I had any doubts about my choice to dedicate my life to Krishna consciousness before his arrival, they were all dissipated in those few minutes of his association.

Srila Prabhupada's visit lasted a week. He came to the temple every morning and evening to lecture. As one of the many new devotees I did not expect that I would speak to him personally, and simply appreciated my good fortune to be able to hear directly from him every day. The day before he departed there was an initiation ceremony at which he accepted twelve devotees as new disciples. I was broken-hearted that I was just one month shy of being qualified to sit in the ceremony (devotees had to be part of the community for twelve months prior to initiation). I was twenty-one at the time and I already understood the rewards of becoming Srila Prabhupada's disciple were great: freedom from karma, liberation from birth and death, and ultimately, awakening love of God, love of Krishna, within my heart.

The day after the ceremony, all the devotees gathered outside the temple to bid farewell to our spiritual master. With a burst of inspiration, I ran upstairs to my room and tore a piece of paper from my notebook. 'Dear Srila Prabhupada,' I wrote, 'I want to thank you for coming all the way to Detroit and spending the week here with us. I am sad that I couldn't become your initiated disciple this time. I will miss you so much and I want to give you this small donation towards your book trust. Your servant, Bhakta Brian.' I thrust some of the only money I had—a $10 bill—into an envelope along with the letter. Then I ran downstairs. Prabhupada was just getting into the car that would take him to the airport.

'Srila Prabhupada!' I cried. 'Please wait! I have something important for you!'

Prabhupada looked directly at me. I ran forward and handed him my letter and, smiling at me, he put the envelope into his pocket. Then he got in the car and was gone.

Two weeks later, a letter arrived in the mail from Srila Prabhupada. Whenever a letter from him arrived, there was a great deal of excitement in the temple. The letters were almost always to the temple president or to devotees who had spent time with Prabhupada. 'Who's the letter for? Who's it for?' one of the devotees asked the temple president.

'It's for Brian,' he said, handing me the envelope. 'For me?' I said incredulously. I carefully tore open the envelope and read aloud to those gathered around:

My dear Bhakta Brian,

Please accept my blessings. I want to thank you for your letter
and kind words, along with a donation of 10 dollars to my
newly created book fund. I have information from the temple
authorities there in Detroit that you are doing nicely in Krsna
[Krishna] consciousness. Please continue to chant your rounds
and follow all the rules and regulations. Please also always
follow in the footsteps of advanced devotees and in due course
of time I will accept you as my duly initiated disciple.
I hope this meets you in the best of health.

Your ever well-wisher,
Bhaktivedanta Swami

P.S. I appreciate your feelings of separation. I am also feeling
separation from my Guru Maharaja, but I always feel that he is
watching over and protecting me.

As the months went by following Prabhupada's visit, I indeed felt he
was watching over me. I studied his translations and explanations of
Bhagavad Gita and Srimad Bhagavatam, and though he was far away
I felt his presence in his words of wisdom. His words became even
more significant to me six years later when he left this world, the final
paragraph becoming a great source of solace and relief. His words
have accompanied me throughout my life since I was twenty-seven
years old, assuring me that even in his absence he is watching over
and protecting me.

About six months after Prabhupada visited Detroit, another letter
arrived from him confirming with our temple president, Bhagavan

das, that we could now be initiated. In his absence, Bhagavan was to officiate at the traditional fire yajna ceremony. The letter read:

My dear Bhagavan das,

Please accept my blessings. I beg to acknowledge receipt of your letter dated 22 November 1971, along with beads and letters from several devotees at Detroit temple. I am very glad to accept these students as my duly initiated disciples and their names shall be as follows:

Brian Tibbitts / Indradyumna das
Ilene Tibbitts / Kripamayi dasi
Heidi Paeva / Harisakti dasi

These are all very nice boys and girls, and I have very much appreciated their attitudes of devotion and surrender as displayed in their letters to me.

We had a ceremony in which each of us vowed to chant for two hours per day and refrain from meat eating, intoxication, illicit sex and gambling. Bhagavan read out our names given to us by our spiritual father, and we threw ghee-soaked grain into the yajna as we repeated sacred mantras he chanted.

A few days later, Bhagavan das called a meeting letting us know that Prabhupada had requested him to leave Detroit to start a temple in Paris. He asked if there was anyone interested in joining him in the venture. My hand immediately shot up. When I looked around, nobody else had raised theirs.

'Do you speak French?' Bhagavan das asked.

'No, I don't,' I said.

'If you don't speak French, how can you help in Paris? Do you have any qualifications at all?'

'I don't,' I admitted. 'But in the Bhagavad Gita, Krishna says: "*Jayo 'smi vyavasayo 'smi, sattvam sattvavatam aham.* I am victory, I am adventure, and I am the strength of the strong." I may not speak French, but I like adventure.'

Bhagavan das smiled. 'Okay, that's enough for me! We leave in one week. By coincidence, Srila Prabhupada is also flying to Europe next week. See if you can book us on the same flight.'

My happiness knew no bounds!

The next day I phoned Transworld Airlines to try to get Bhagavan das and I seats on Prabhupada's flight from New York to London. The plan was that we would spend a few days in London before moving on to Paris.

'I'm sorry,' the sales representative said. 'That flight is full and we have a long waiting list.'

'Please!' I begged. 'You have to get us on. We want to accompany our guru on his mission.'

'What's a guru?' she asked.

'A spiritual teacher,' I said. 'Our guru is named A.C. Bhaktivedanta Swami Prabhupada. He's helping us to understand who we actually are and the intimate connection we have to God.'

'I see,' she said. 'Well, that does sound quite important. Let me speak with my supervisor and see what we can do.'

She came back to the phone after what felt like forever, with good news.

'Young man,' she said, 'this must be your lucky day. As I was talking to my supervisor two cancellations on that flight came in. We decided to move you and your friend to the front of the line so that you can travel with your spiritual teacher.'

'Thank you so much!' I said, unable to believe what I was hearing.

'What did you say your teacher's name is? I'll try to seat you beside him.'

'Bhaktivedanta Swami!' I blurted out.

'Please hold,' she said. I could hear her shuffling papers. 'Yes, the seat next to him is free. I have allocated that seat to you.'

A week later, Bhagavan das and I arrived at JFK airport just as Srila Prabhupada was being checked-in for the flight. When we saw him, we bowed down at his feet in the middle of the airport terminal. We then proceeded to airport security. The security officer was a big man with a red face.

'Open that white briefcase now!' he snapped at Srila Prabhupada.

Shocked by his disrespectful attitude towards an elderly sadhu, I stepped forward and spoke to him in a soft voice. 'Sir, with all due respect, if you speak like that again to my spiritual master, I'll have to show you a thing or two.'

The officer looked taken aback. 'I thought you Hare Krishnas were non-violent!' He turned his attention back to Srila Prabhupada who was having difficulty opening the briefcase locks.

'Let me try, Srila Prabhupada,' I said, and he stood to one side while I fiddled with the locks. I had always wondered what Srila Prabhupada carried in his briefcase and when the lock suddenly popped open, I found myself face-to-face with my spiritual master's personal effects. There was his passport, a photo of his spiritual master, Srila Bhaktisiddhanta Saraswati, his reading glasses, two pens, a notebook, some Ayurvedic medicines, and a newspaper clipping with an article about our movement.

The security officer cleared his throat. 'I'm supposed to look at that, young man,' he said. 'Not you.' I pushed the briefcase over to him. He gave it a quick look over and glanced up at Srila Prabhupada. 'You may go,' he said in a softer voice. I felt he had realized his mistake in speaking harshly to a saintly person. As we walked to the plane, Srila Prabhupada said to me, 'Without good company, people develop unfavourable qualities. Devotees must become fixed-up in spiritual life and give their association to others.'

'Yes, Srila Prabhupada,' I said. I took note in my mind that, amongst other things, spiritual life means to share one's good fortune with others.

Once we were seated on the plane, Srila Prabhupada turned to me. 'Do we have something to eat? Some food offered to Krishna, some prasadam?'

'Um, no, I don't think so, Srila Prabhupada,' I said. 'I didn't know that it was my responsibility to bring something.'

Then I remembered I did have something! 'I have a bag of oranges, Prabhupada,' I said. I cut them up and arranged the pieces on a plastic plate supplied by the flight attendants. 'I hope this is sufficient,' I said, placing the plate on Srila Prabhupada's tray table. He seemed to enjoy them and even saved a couple of pieces for me. Remembering a statement in scripture that the remnants of food left by the spiritual preceptor are spiritually purifying, I enthusiastically bit into a piece of orange—peel and all. My eyes started burning and tears rolled down my cheeks. Srila Prabhupada looked me incredulously, his eyes wide open.

Once we were airborne, the flight attendants closed all the window blinds and a silent film of Charlie Chaplin appeared on the screen towards the front of the plane. Because I was sitting next to my spiritual master, I picked up my copy of Bhagavad Gita and began reading from it aloud, thinking that he would be impressed by me studying scripture rather than watching a movie. But then I heard Srila Prabhupada laugh. I glanced away from the page and saw he was watching the movie. So, I put down my Bhagavad Gita and I watched the film and laughed along with Srila Prabhupada.

But once the film finished, I realized how confused I was. I said, 'Srila Prabhupada, I thought we weren't supposed to watch movies because they distract us from our spiritual life.'

He replied, 'Krishna is the source of everything, including humour. I was appreciating Krishna's original humour in the antics of Charlie Chaplin. What were you seeing?'

I was too embarrassed to reply, realizing that I had just been seeing Charlie Chaplin. But I marvelled at the pure devotee's ability to see the Lord in every aspect of His creation.

We arrived in London, and collected our bags from the luggage carousel. The arrival terminal was a passenger-only area, but I could hear a roaring kirtan taking place somewhere close by. It sounded like there were hundreds of devotees just beyond the frosted glass doors. Bhagavan das checked the bags over and realized that one was missing.

'Indradyumna can stay to find this bag,' Srila Prabhupada said. 'It is very important this bag is not lost. In it are the commentaries of the acharyas on Srimad Bhagavatam—Srila Sridhara Swami and Srila Visvanatha Chakravarti Thakur. I must have these for my writing. Very precious.' He turned to me. 'You must make report with the airlines.'

'Yes, Srila Prabhupada,' I said softly. 'I will try to find the bag.' Inside I was heartbroken. I wanted to join the kirtan I could hear, and to be there as Srila Prabhupada was received at the London temple. There was even a rumour that George Harrison would be there at the temple. He had produced the *Radha Krishna Temple* album earlier that year, one of the tracks of which had peaked at number twelve on the UK charts. I didn't listen to the Beatles anymore, but I was still excited at the prospect of being there when one of them greeted my spiritual master. I was also feeling weak and exhausted because all I had eaten since leaving New York were the oranges.

I heard the devotees cheer as Prabhupada entered their midst. I, meanwhile, found the missing baggage counter and began filling in what felt like endless forms. Feeling I had done everything I could, I made a move to leave, but the gentleman behind the counter advised me to wait a little longer because sometimes missing bags appeared on the baggage carousel even several hours later.

'Several *hours* later?' I asked.

'It's worth a try,' he said, shrugging.

Reluctantly, I waited around and sure enough several bags did indeed appear on the carousel ninety minutes later. To my relief, one of them was Srila Prabhupada's missing bag.

'The guys down below sometimes get a bit distracted and lose stuff,' an airline worker quipped, seeing me seize the bag.

Outside the terminal, the rain poured down, welcoming me to London. I hailed a taxi, my light cotton dhoti almost soaked to the skin. 'What's up, young man?' the taxi driver asked me, as I slammed the door shut. 'You get up on the wrong side of the bed?'

'Nope,' I replied. 'I just got separated from my guru.'

Like the Transatlantic Airlines representative I had spoken to on the phone the week before, the taxi driver wasn't familiar with the word.

'What's a guru?'

'It means "spiritual teacher",' I replied. 'Just as we require a teacher in any field of knowledge, we need a teacher to learn about spiritual knowledge.'

'I never thought of knowledge in relationship to religion,' he said.

I remembered something Srila Prabhupada had said when he visited Detroit. 'My spiritual master has taught me that religion without knowledge is sentimental and knowledge with religion is simply speculation.'

'Wow!' he said, 'that's a good one!' We continued to discuss the philosophy of spiritual life all the way to central London. I remembered Srila Prabhupada's instructions to me in the airport to share my good fortune with others.

The temple was a five-storey building sandwiched between two other buildings on a quiet street near the British Museum. The bottom storey was painted yellow and there was a big sign that read 'Radha Krishna Temple' over the front windows. Exhausted, weak, cold and dehydrated, I dragged the heavy suitcase from the taxi up to the door of the temple. Inside the temple, I found a large group of devotees sitting in front of plates that had obviously just been emptied of their contents.

'Hey, Prabhu, welcome to London!' one of them called. 'You missed an ecstatic reception and an incredible feast!'

'I'm glad to be here at last,' I said. 'Is there any prasadam left?'

'No, sorry! Nothing's left. Probably because it was such super-excellent prasadam!'

I was dismayed. 'Okay,' I said. 'But can any of you help me carry this bag up to Srila Prabhupada's room?'

'That's up four flights of stairs!' another devotee said, 'I can't possibly move!' Everyone else agreed that they were too full to help.

Resigning myself, I picked up the bag and started up the stairs. By the time I reached the second floor I thought I was going to pass out, but I persevered and eventually found myself before a door with a brass plaque that read, 'His Divine Grace A.C. Bhaktivedanta Swami.'

I was so exhausted and disoriented that I didn't even knock. I just turned the doorknob and backed into the room, pulling the heavy bag. Before I knew what was happening, Srila Prabhupada's servant called out, 'Prabhu! Watch out! You're going to bump into Srila Prabhupada!'

Horrified, I turned around to find Srila Prabhupada standing just centimetres from me. I immediately fell to the floor before his feet and began reciting a prayer: 'I offer my obeisances to my spiritual master, who gave me beautiful kanthi mala, effulgent tilak, the beautiful form of a devotee, and who offered me his shelter. In one of his hands, he is holding my hand, and with his other hand he is holding the lamp of knowledge, which helps me to cross over the dark ocean of the material world. My guru deserves the greatest respect, because only he can rescue one in the blinking of an eye. I bow down to him again and again.'

Suddenly I felt a sharp slap on my back. I heard Srila Prabhupada speak some words and then walk away. By the time I stood up he had entered another room, but his servant was standing with his mouth open in amazement. 'Srila Prabhupada slapped you on the back in firm appreciation,' he said. 'I never saw him do that before!'

'And what did he say?' I asked. 'I heard him say something!'

His servant replied slowly, relishing the moment. 'He said, "So much endeavour in the material world, but when I take you back home to the spiritual world, everything will be easy and sublime".'

I couldn't believe my good fortune! For the menial service I had performed, I had received a most wonderful benediction: my spiritual master had said he would take me back to the spiritual world!

'My life is yours, Srila Prabhupada,' I said under my breath. 'For now, and for eternity.'

Two days later, as we were getting ready to depart for the station to catch our train to Paris, Srila Prabhupada called us to his office. We sat submissively before him as he explained the importance of our mission and gave some practical advice as well. 'As you make French devotees,' he said, 'find some amongst them who know English well and begin to translate my books into French. My spiritual master, Srila Bhaktisiddhanta Saraswati, very much wanted the teachings of Lord Krishna to be shared all over the world.'

He reached into a dresser drawer next to where he was sitting and pulled out a chaddar shawl for me. 'Take this,' he said. 'A gift from a Vaishnava is a very special thing.'

Then, in one of my life's defining moments, Srila Prabhupada spoke the words that would guide me throughout my spiritual life. 'Indradyumna das,' he said, 'Preach boldly and have faith in the holy names.'

'Yes, Srila Prabhupada,' I replied in firm conviction. And with those two instructions engraved within my heart, I left to serve my spiritual master, fearless and ready for any challenge I might confront in Paris or on any adventure throughout the world in the decades to come.

Once you have received the truth [from a self-realized soul] you will never again fall into illusion, and you will see all living beings in Me, the Self of all.

—Lord Krishna in the Bhagavad Gita (4:35)

3

USA and Poland

My Brother's Search for Shelter

In August 2004, my younger brother Pete decided to take his own life. We had last seen each other six years earlier at our mother's funeral in America. I had not heard from him since.

After leaving our childhood home as young men in the late 1960s, our lives had gone in very different directions. Whereas I had adopted the lifestyle of a Hare Krishna devotee by becoming a vegetarian, giving up drugs and alcohol and dedicating my time and energy to helping others, Pete had embraced the prevalent drug culture of the time.

In the early 1980s, I was managing the Hare Krishna temple in Paris. I knew Pete was in trouble, so I invited him to France to spend a few weeks with me. It was a difficult visit. We had taken walks around the city and had had long conversations, but I had problems keeping him away from drugs and alcohol during his stay. He didn't seem at all interested in what I was doing with my life. But on the last day of his visit, I saw a change in him. He was running late for his flight and I was anxiously searching the temple for him. I found him in the main temple room standing in front of the altar. I watched in surprise through a slightly opened door. He bowed his head for a long time and when he rose, he stood before the altar with his hands folded. I could see his lips moving and though I couldn't make out what he was saying, I knew he was praying. He didn't see me and I didn't ask him about it, but I had held on to that memory because I felt that he was looking for shelter.

Twenty-one years later, Pete had been a drug addict for half his life. I had tried to find him through the police, the internet and friends in America, but had no luck. I later found out it was because he had been homeless for five years. The inheritance he had received from our mother had been embezzled by a devious accountant and he was left on the street. He would curl up to sleep on a cardboard box at the entrance to a store or take refuge in the bushes near the railroad tracks in San Francisco. He got food by rummaging through garbage cans on the street. Eventually he owned practically nothing. The child-size sleeping bag he had acquired (which went only up to his waist) and the clothes he had on his back, all fit into a small bag.

He drifted from town to town, sometimes living with other addicts and sometimes living alone where no one would notice the severe bouts of depression that haunted him. He got robbed and beaten up. He watched as some of the friends he made while living on the street died of drug overdoses or exposure. Because he lived outside for years even during winter, he contracted many infections and diseases. At one point a cancerous growth on his face became so prominent that a sympathetic doctor operated on it without charge, leaving him with a disfigured nose. He sought shelter in the one thing that dulled his pain: drugs. His preference was for speed, a type of amphetamine.

Because of his casual, happy-go-lucky nature Pete always made friends easily and drug pushers supplied his habit for nothing for the most part. But the relief he obtained through drugs never lasted, and after twenty-five years of addiction he came to a point where he'd had enough. Ironically, he was in a better place materially speaking than he had been for decades. He was living in an apartment with a woman he had met several months earlier. Linda Sue had been left homeless by a divorce and she too had turned to drugs. The government had taken away her two children, but returned custody to her when she managed to rent an apartment in a San Francisco ghetto. One day she and Pete found an old computer in a garbage can on the street. They took it to a local computer shop and Pete charmed the owner into repairing it as a favour. After they got it up and running, Linda Sue was shocked to discover that Pete had ordered a bottle of pills which she knew could be deadly if taken in quantity. When she confronted him, he admitted he was contemplating suicide. Linda Sue didn't know much about Pete's history and she asked him if he had any family or old friends who could help him or to whom he would want to talk. When he told her he had an older brother, she persuaded him to try to find me.

The problem was that Pete couldn't remember how to spell my name. I had always been his big brother Brian, but for the past four decades I had gone by the name given to me by my spiritual master when he initiated me. Trying to spell 'Indradyumna', Pete typed in various combinations of letters in his internet search, and finally in the wee hours of the morning he hit upon the correct spelling. He selected the first hit and went to my travelingmonk.com website where he spent the rest of the night and most of the next day reading the articles I had written about my travels, teaching and outreach. That evening he called Linda Sue over.

'I found my big brother,' he said, 'and I'd like to contact him.'

The next morning, I found an email from Linda Sue in my inbox:

My name is Linda Sue DeLaney. Peter is my boyfriend. I met him last year. I was homeless and the government had taken my two children and put them in a foster home. Peter was also homeless. He had been living in a tent up in the hills for three years. This is where I ended up. Recently I got my children back. We live in a ghetto in San Francisco. I worry about Peter because he lived outside for so long and it was such a hard life. It is very difficult to get him motivated. He becomes depressed easily.

Recently he has talked about suicide. He found your website and showed it to me. He was very happy to be able to read about your service and travels. I encouraged him to write, but he is too embarrassed. I am taking the liberty of writing to you myself. I would be grateful if you could email or phone him. Contact with you would mean everything to him. Sincerely, Linda Sue.

I got to the end of the email, picked up my phone and dialled the number Linda Sue had supplied. It was Pete who answered.

'Pete, this is your big brother.' There was no response. I could hear Linda Sue speaking in the background.

'Pete, it's me,' I said. 'I've been looking for you for years. I never forgot you and I'm here for you now.'

I could sense he was trying to find the courage to say something.

'Pete,' I persisted.

'Hare Krishna,' he said softly. 'I'm so glad you called. I'm so glad I found you.'

'Why didn't you call me?' I asked. 'I didn't know things were so bad.'

He paused. 'I didn't even have a dime to make a phone call,' he said, 'that's how bad it was. And I didn't know where you were. And I was embarrassed.'

'I'm your brother,' I said. 'You can share anything with me.'

Then he told me his story.

'How did you tolerate it all?' I asked.

'Whenever it got really rough, I chanted Hare Krishna,' he said. 'I acted like I didn't care when I was with you in France, and in lots of ways I didn't. But I was always hearing that mantra and it stuck in my mind. I understood it was a sort of shelter because it is a spiritual sound, and I felt it protected me. For all practical purposes, I should have died a long time ago.'

'Keep chanting,' I said, 'and don't take your life.'

'I won't now,' he replied.

'It's only the beginning,' I said. 'You've been looking for shelter and Krishna has answered your prayers. And He's answered mine as well, because I found you.'

I was in Poland while all of this was taking place and I spent the next couple of days thinking about how I could help Pete from so far away. I and my team of 300 volunteers were preparing to participate in the annual Polish Woodstock festival. I wanted to be able to give Pete a chance to taste a better way of living. What better way than at a four-day festival of chanting, dancing and feasting? I phoned Pete and asked him whether he, Linda Sue and her two children would like to join us in Poland in ten days.

He was speechless, eventually saying, 'We don't have passports. We don't even have money for a bus to the passport office.'

'I can work everything out,' I replied, 'if you would like to come.'

'It's a big gamble,' my assistant Guru-Kripa das said as I hung up the phone.'He's a drug addict and so is she. It's very hard for people like them to give up drugs. It could turn out to be a waste of time and money.'

'But we have to try,' I said.'Where there's life, there's hope.'

When Pete and his family arrived in Poland, Guru-Kripa's words came back to me. As Pete and Linda Sue got out of the car, I saw their eyes were red and I thought it was probably from taking drugs.

'I'll give it my best and depend on the Lord,' I thought. I walked up to Pete and gave him a big hug.

Over the next few days, I smothered them in love and immersed them in an ocean of nectar: Krishna's Village of Peace at the Polish Woodstock festival. If they had any intention of taking drugs over the next few days, there was no time—not even a second! And why would they want to? During the festival we chanted and danced all day long, and every day was a festival. My friend Govinda Swami calls the Polish Woodstock festival the greatest show on earth: the huge tent, the vegetarian food, the cultural exhibits, the devotee bands, the people.

Everything swept up Pete and Linda Sue in a tide of love and excitement. They both stayed drug-free throughout the festival and into the next week. Their eyes became clear and they wore perpetual smiles on their faces. Then, after the festival, they accompanied our group north for two more weeks of festivals on the Baltic Sea coast. It was a blistering pace, but to my surprise they seemed to have no difficulty keeping up. Wherever we went Pete and I talked, often with Linda Sue joining in the conversations.

'I have always been attracted to India,' Linda Sue told me. 'And you know what, Maharaja? We were so down. We were suffering so much. You can't imagine how grateful we are now.' Pete and Linda

Sue had taken to calling me Maharaja, a term of respect often used in India for those who have taken a vow of renunciation.

'Maharaja,' Pete said now, 'do you think it would be a good idea if I started chanting on beads? I've seen that all the devotees have their chanting beads with them all the time. They always seem to be chanting!'

'Initiated devotees chant for around two hours every day,' I said. 'They chant one maha mantra on each of the 108 beads on their strand, and they go around the beads sixteen times a day. It's a form of meditation. Chanting the names of God is the quickest and most effective way to become self-realized and to understand our eternal relationship with God.'

'Maybe I could do just two or three per day,' he said.

'I think you should try for sixteen,' I said with a smile. 'You're fifty-three years old. You have to make up for lost time.' He looked hesitant.

'Do you remember when you were in Paris twenty-one years ago?' I asked him. 'You stood before Krishna with your hands folded, begging for shelter.'

'I don't remember,' he said.

'Well, I remember,' I said. 'And chanting Hare Krishna is the Lord's answer to your prayer.'

'Okay, sixteen rounds it is,' Pete said with conviction.

But it turned out that he couldn't chant sixteen rounds a day. He experienced so much relief from chanting, he soon found himself chanting thirty-two rounds. A few days later, he said, 'From this day onwards, I swear I'll never take drugs, drink alcohol or smoke another cigarette.'

'That's a tall order,' I replied. 'Some people say that to make it, you'll have to go through a rehabilitation programme and join

Alcoholics Anonymous. It's rare to just stop all those things in one day and not revert to them.'

Pete became serious. Holding up his bead-bag, he said with conviction, 'And rarer still to get this. My experience is that if you chant Hare Krishna, you have no need for drugs.'

At the end of the summer tour, Pete and Linda Sue went back to America, but not to San Francisco. They realized there was too much temptation there. Instead, I asked devotees in Alachua, Florida, to help them settle in the devotee community there. They kindly agreed to help them establish a home.

The sage who knows Me as the ultimate purpose of all sacrifices and austerities, the Supreme Lord of all planets and demigods, and the benefactor and well-wisher of all living entities, attains peace from the pangs of material miseries.

—Lord Krishna in the Bhagavad Gita (5:29)

4

Croatia and Bosnia-Herzegovina
Attack on the Festival of India

In the spring of 1996 I was invited to bring a Festival of India to tour Croatia and Bosnia-Herzegovina, two nations that were part of the former Yugoslavia. The entire region had been in turmoil throughout the first half of the 1990s. After the Cold War came to an end and the communist rule of eastern Europe collapsed, the Yugoslav Federation also crumbled, leaving on uncertain ground the six republics that made up Yugoslavia—Serbia, Croatia, Macedonia, Montenegro, Slovenia and Bosnia-Herzegovina. The Yugoslav Wars that followed were a series of separate but interrelated conflicts along ethnic–religious lines of division (Serbian Orthodox, Croation Catholics, and Bosniak Muslims) that included independence endeavours, genocide and insurgencies.

When I arrived in Croatia in April 1996, the country had concluded its war with Serbia less than six months earlier. I was travelling with an international team of twenty-five devotees, including the Bhaktivedanta Players, a professional theatre troupe based at the

Bhaktivedanta Manor temple in London which was donated by George Harrison in 1973. Our intention was to bring upliftment and joy to the region by holding festivals that featured singing, dancing, philosophy, theatre and vegetarian food, in the major cities of Croatia and Bosnia-Herzegovina. My experience has been that suffering—whether due to war, natural disasters or personal difficulties—leaves people with questions about life and hungry for answers that will give them relief. The festivals were to be a chance to offer the gift of spiritual knowledge.

Our initial festivals on the tour were successful. In Zagreb, the capital of Croatia, more than 3,000 people came. During my lecture, I talked about the need for spiritual education in society. For the finale, I led a rousing kirtan—the call and response singing of God's names inaugurated 500 years ago by Chaitanya Mahaprabhu, the most recent incarnation of the Lord. Festival goers enthusiastically joined in with our singing of the holy names.

But the following afternoon in Split, the second largest city in Croatia, things took an unpleasant turn that exposed the pain and trauma present as a result of years of war. A large party of both the international visitors and the local Hare Krishna devotees donned colourful, flowing clothing and took musical instruments onto the city streets to chant and sing. We chanted near Split's Saint Domnius Cathedral. Built in the fourth century as a mausoleum to Roman Emperor Diocletian and converted into a church by the early Catholics in Croatia in the seventh century, the church is regarded as the second oldest structure used as a Christian cathedral.

As Sri Prahlada das played his accordion and thirty devotees chanted and danced to the holy names in happiness, we drew a crowd of onlookers. I noted the difference between the atmosphere in Split and in Poland where my team and I chanted on the streets throughout much of the year during the 1990s. In Poland, our chanting and dancing always brought out an appreciative mood among the people and they often joined in. But in Split, the people just stared at us. I often give a little talk between singing sessions to tell people what the Hare Krishna movement is about. That day in Split, I mentioned that Hare Krishna devotees were vegetarian and that we practised ahimsa or nonviolence and wouldn't hurt an ant.

'Would you kill a Serb?' a man from the back of the crowd yelled.

It became tense as everyone looked at me for my answer. To say no would turn the crowd against us, because many had lost friends or family members in the war with Serbia. But to say yes would immediately be a contradiction of what I had just said. So I did something I rarely do: I simply ignored the question and started to speak on another subject. The tactic seemed to work until a powerfully built man in his twenties started screaming at me. We sometimes get drunks trying to shout us down while out chanting on the street, but this young man seemed particularly angry. I concluded the talk quickly and asked Sri Prahlada to start singing again. But before the kirtan could get started, the man came forward.

'Croatia is a Catholic country,' he shouted, 'and you are not welcome here!'

I looked into the crowd and saw that they were not prepared to defend us in any way. Suddenly, the man leapt up and tried to kick Sri Prahlada in the head, narrowly missing him. Then, with two more kicks he smashed the accordion. Two of the local devotees who were in the crowd in conventional clothing came forward and held him back.

But then a companion of the first man pulled a knife and urged him on. Even angrier than before, the man moved forward again. There were other friends of the movement sprinkled throughout the crowd, and a couple of them confronted the pair and dragged them away.

The incident made for a tense atmosphere and I could see the agitation of the young men in the crowd, many of whom had recently returned from the war. We kept singing for a few minutes until people started to shout and throw rocks. Everywhere I looked I saw faces full of hate and anger. Leaving as fast as we could, we were followed by young men shouting obscenities.

Although we were shaken from the experience, we went through with the public festival that had been advertised in Split the following day in the stunning historical venue of Diocletian's Palace complex. The festival was attended by 600 people, many of whom had witnessed and were appalled by the incident outside the church.

The next morning, we rose early to begin the six-hour drive to Sarajevo, the capital of Bosnia-Herzegovina, where we were scheduled to have programmes and perform street kirtan. We headed south from Split in a caravan of two vans and four cars, with a total of thirty-two devotees, along the Adriatic coastal road and past resorts destroyed by the war.

Just before the border, we stopped briefly. A Croatian soldier walked up to our car, rifle in hand, and put his head in the window. I was a bit alarmed as he engaged in an emotional conversation with Lucas, the middle-aged driver of the car I was riding in. Lucas had served in the Croatian Army as a major. The soldier seemed disappointed by what he heard and eventually shook his head and left. I enquired what the soldier had asked about, and Lucas replied that he had wanted to know the whereabouts of his friend, a devotee who had fought alongside him on the battlefield and had helped him by telling him about Krishna and chanting meditation.

Lucas and I were close because he had saved my life several months ago when I visited Croatia for the first time. We were chanting on the streets in central Zagreb when a soldier pulled out a pistol and pointed it at me as I spoke to the crowd. He screamed that he wanted to kill the 'bishop' because God had not saved his family. We later learned that the soldier's wife and six children had been killed by Serbian forces a week earlier. Crazed with grief and numbed by alcohol, he had been wandering the streets in his army fatigues when he chanced upon our chanting party. Lucas had dealt with numerous soldiers in distress before, and he approached the man and began speaking to him in a calm voice. Gradually he convinced the man that he shouldn't kill me and finally the soldier burst into tears, put his gun away and walked off.

As we now crossed the Bosnia-Herzegovina border, the stark reality of war was even more pronounced. There were strings of three or four villages in a row destroyed and abandoned. Troops from IFOR (the Implementation Force), a NATO-led international peacekeeping body, were everywhere in the populated villages.[2] It's possible to get a smile from people in most parts of the world, but here the death and destruction were too omnipresent for much light-heartedness.

After passing through mountains and over specially erected bridges, we reached Mostar. I had been there when travelling through Europe as a young man of nineteen, just before I became a Hare Krishna devotee. I remembered Mostar as a beautiful little town with a quaint thirteenth-century bridge spanning a sparkling river. But the town we entered bore no resemblance to the one I had visited years ago. Literally every house, apartment, shop and building was riddled with bullets and shrapnel. Many had gaping holes in the sides and we could see inside as people conducted their daily affairs.

Buildings had been gutted by fires and demolished vehicles were strewn here and there. The people went about their lives stepping over mangled steel or concrete and walking through bombed-out buildings. The damage was so extensive I imagined it would be many years before the town could be rebuilt. Lucas pointed out positions where Serbian gunners had been only weeks before. He was able to determine how far their artillery could fire and what damage it would have done. Such knowledge seemed to come easily to Lucas, and I understood how someone with his experience and understanding had survived.

Mostar was bad, but nothing could have prepared us for the city two hours farther up in the mountains: Sarajevo. Approaching from the west, we did not see a single building in the suburbs of the city that was untouched by the war. It was the same in central Sarajevo, the entire city had been ravaged.

One of the most startling things to me was that there were graves everywhere. Fifty-thousand people had died during the fighting and, because they were surrounded, the local population had buried their dead within the city limits. Most parks and gardens had become graveyards. Even patches of land between two buildings served as cemeteries for two or three bodies, or a single grave was marked with a cross or a Muslim tombstone on a grassy intersection.

The small Sarajevo temple was situated in the Muslim sector of the city. The fifteen local devotees greeted us with a kirtan, which was a cheerful contrast to the destruction around us. Like the rest of Sarajevo, the temple was riddled with bullet holes and shrapnel.

When Bosnia had declared its independence from the Yugoslav Federation four years earlier (in 1992), Serbia had laid siege to Sarajevo—ostensibly to protect the Serb ethnic minority, as the Bosniak majority government had ordered they be evicted from the capital. Most of the citizens—Bosniaks, Serbs and Croats— remained indoors to shield themselves from the relentless mortar attacks and sniper fire that rained upon them, venturing out only for essential items. The devotees occasionally ventured outside to distribute books and vegetarian food door-to-door or to the few people on the street. The temple became a shelter for refugees from the hills who were driven from their homes by the advancing armies. To live outside meant certain death, so throughout Sarajevo people with homes or apartments gave shelter to others less fortunate. Several families came to the temple seeking shelter, and fifteen people lived in the temple room throughout the siege.

Our plan of action while in Sarajevo was the same as it had been in Croatia: to have a large public festival in the evening and to advertise it by going out on the streets and chanting during the day. It was to be the first time that Hare Krishna devotees had sung in public since the war began. Prior to our international team's arrival, the local devotees had sought and received permission to sing in public from the local police who also agreed to send an escort of two or three policemen in case there was any trouble. The local devotees didn't expect any trouble though, because they had such good relations with the majority of their Muslim neighbours.

The morning after we arrived in Sarajevo, everyone was excited about the prospect of chanting in public again. The devotees dressed in their best clothes—the men in clean saffron or white robes and the women in colourful saris and intricate decorations painted around their eyes and on their cheeks. Many devotees carried baskets of cookies to hand out to pedestrians, and others carried invitations to our festival. Sri Prahlada began to sing with a new accordion that had replaced the one damaged two days earlier, and we proceeded along the road in twos, dancing in unison and carrying the flags and banners the local devotees had made especially for this parade.

It was a beautiful day and the singing and dancing was extraordinarily attractive against the backdrop of devastation. But from the beginning, I sensed that something was wrong. 'Are you sure it's safe to chant in public like this?' I asked a young Bosnian devotee named Edvin. 'Won't the Muslims take offence at our big kirtan party coming through their part of town?'

'Maharaja, don't worry,' Edvin said. 'They love us. We distributed free food here throughout the war.'

What I learned later was that the local devotees had failed to take into consideration something crucial—it was a holy day for Muslims, and we were enroute towards the largest mosque in Sarajevo just as the prayer hour was finishing. The war may have officially been over, but there remained feelings of hatred and desire for revenge between the diverse peoples of the region.

Oblivious to this and bolstered by the assurances of the local devotees, we danced and chanted loudly, smiling and waving to passers-by. Some people returned smiles as we went by and a few took the cookies and invitations we were passing out. But most were cautious. In retrospect, I realized that they had been through hell and the contrast of so many happy people singing and dancing would have been difficult for them to adjust to.

We wove our way through the old cobblestone streets and past some market stalls built in Ottoman-style architecture, turned a corner and the mosque was suddenly looming ahead. The moment I saw it, I wanted to turn around, but it was too late. Among the crowd emerging from the mosque, three men in their late twenties saw our procession and after exchanging a few words charged towards us, their faces twisted in hate.

One of the international members of our party, Priyavrata das (director of Food for Life Global, the movement's free food-distribution programme), was walking backwards in front of the chanting party, filming with his video camera. He didn't even see what hit him. The man leading the charge struck him full force in the head with a flying kick. Priyavrata spun forward, his camera flying and fell to the ground. The three men then plunged into our party, furiously kicking and punching the devotees.

The chanting stopped and some of the devotees fought back in defence. As one of the attackers came for me, I charged towards him swinging my cymbals over my head and he retreated. To my left I saw three devotees beating back one of the attackers, who fell into a store window, smashing it to pieces. Although we bloodied them, I noticed they seemed unfazed. Nevertheless, they were outnumbered and the three of them retreated.

We remained in the middle of the street, afraid to take another step forward, yet at the same time unsure whether to leave. A number of devotees had bloody noses and cut faces and looked as if they were in shock. We tried to assemble everyone to make a retreat, but took too long.

Suddenly, as if out of nowhere, the three attackers returned, but this time with a group of about thirty large men who I later learned were hardened killers recently returned from the war. A reporter from a local television station was filming the scene; one of the men took her camera and smashed it on the ground. On that cue, about ten of them charged through the centre of our party. We ran to either side of the street and they then cornered and attacked us, starting with those who looked the strongest. I could tell that these men knew what they were doing and they knew how to bring down those they regarded as their enemies.

The first man down was Narsimha Kavacha das, a tall Australian student of mine who was my secretary at the time. One of the thugs shoved a pistol in his face, threatening to pull the trigger but instead smashing the butt over his head. Narsimha Kavacha fell to the ground unconscious. As blood formed a pool around his head, four men began kicking him in the ribs.

One of the English theatre performers, Thakur Bhaktivinoda das, tried to rescue Narsimha Kavacha but was overpowered by the four men. I was appalled to see a fifth come at Thakur from behind and stab him in the back. In my peripheral vision, I saw devotees running. To my right, I saw Bhakta Colin, the tall Liverpudlian saxophone player with our group, overpowered and stabbed by three burly bearded men.

One of our police escorts tried to stop the fighting but was slapped in the face by the attackers and thrown to the side of the road. There was blood in pools and splatters on the street and I wasn't sure of everyone's whereabouts. Narsimha Kavacha was still unconscious on the ground twenty metres in front of me. When Edvin tried to make it to him, he was stabbed. Those of us still standing carried or dragged the wounded, backing away while the men screamed 'Allahu Akbar! Allahu Akbar!'

When we rounded the corner away from the mosque, we waved frantically to two traffic policemen who were driving past in a car. They put Thakur and Edvin into the back seat and said they would take them to a hospital. While Thakur was getting in, I was shocked to see that the back of his shirt was drenched in blood.

'There's another devotee lying in the street back there and we haven't been able to rescue him,' I told the police. 'These men were stabbed while trying to help him. And another devotee was stabbed and I don't know where he is.'

'Sir, we'll do our best to help them,' one of the officers said. 'We'll look after these two men and call for backup to look for the others and stabilize the situation. Do not go back there yourselves!'

Back at the temple everything was in total confusion as we tried to account for missing devotees, local and international. We called all the hospitals in Sarajevo to try to find out the number of wounded, where they had been admitted and, most urgently, whether Narsimha Kavacha and Colin were safe. Within an hour we had located them. A store owner had pulled Narsimha Kavacha off the street into his shop and had then driven him to the hospital, the same hospital where Thakur, Edvin and others had been taken. The driver of a car had stopped and picked up Colin off the street and then driven him to a different hospital.

Having found the injured devotees, I wanted to go and visit them. The locals suggested that it would be better for me not to go in my robes, since the men who attacked us could still be roaming the streets. But no one had any civilian clothes at hand and time was short. I had no idea whether those who had been attacked were dead or alive.

One of the local devotees named Bhakta Mirza offered to drive me. Approaching the hospital where Colin was being treated I saw that like most buildings in Sarajevo, it was partially destroyed. Sections were bombed out. The entire building was riddled by machine-gun bullets and many parts were blackened by fire. Initially, the security at the hospital gates refused us entry. The authorities had stopped allowing visitors long ago, because the 'visitors' were often soldiers dressed as civilians trying to enter the hospital to kill their enemies. But eventually they agreed to let us in, mainly because they trusted me on account of my robes.

The first thing I noticed was all the patients in the wards and the waiting areas were lying on stretchers and beds very low to the ground. Then I noticed the bullet holes along the walls at waist height and above where snipers had shot through the walls; the low-lying beds were an attempt to keep patients safe from those aiming to kill or maim them from outside the building.

When I reached the main floor of the hospital I was introduced to Mr Nakash, the head surgeon. He was a large man with a big moustache and his eyes had deep black circles under them. Nakash was known internationally for his work during the war when he performed operations for days at a time with little sleep or food, often when the hospital was under artillery and rocket attack. His work was complicated by the fact that there was no electricity or water, and during the entire period he operated without anaesthesia.

He raised his arms when he saw me. 'In the name of Allah,' he said, 'please forgive what has been done to you. The people of Sarajevo are with you. Only some maddened soldiers have done this. Come now. I will take you to see your friend.' Then he added, 'I have your Bhagavad Gita. It helped me during the war.'

Colin was asleep, his chest and stomach covered with bandages.

'I have done a preliminary examination of him,' the surgeon said. 'He has broken ribs and bruises from being kicked. But most concerning are his stab wounds. His lungs are slowly filling with blood. It's vital that we release the liquid that is filling the places where he has been stabbed. I will operate on him within an hour.'

Colin stirred when I asked if he would be okay. He grimaced and barely opened his eyes, but I thought he knew I was there.

'He's in pain,' I said. 'Can you give him something for the pain?'

'We have very little anaesthetic, only local, not general,' Nakash said. 'I have to save what little we have for the operations. He will have some when I open him up.'

'Colin,' I said, 'I'm here. Can you hear me?'

'Maharaja,' he said, his words slurring, 'you have to get me out of here. I need to be discharged so I can get home.' Then he passed out.

'He will be here for a few weeks,' the surgeon said. 'I've talked to the consultant at the hospital where the other three victims are and it seems he's in the worst shape of those injured.'

I wanted to get to the hospital where the other three were, so we made our way along the strange, bullet-pocked hallways towards the exit. I heard screaming coming from one of the rooms and saw a woman thrashing around in a bed with hospital staff trying to calm her. A man in a wheelchair looked at us darkly as we passed and muttered something in Bosnian under his breath.

'What did he say?' I asked Mirza.

'He said what happened was our own fault,' Mirza said, 'and that we should have stayed in our own countries if we didn't want to be attacked.'

At the second hospital, there was no one to ask for directions. We walked through the place room by room and eventually found Narsimha Kavacha on an operating table with doctors stitching up his head. One of the doctors pushed me out of the operating room and told me to wait outside.

As I waited in the hall to speak to the surgeon, my eye caught two men approaching from the other direction. They appeared to be Muslims and were looking at me with the same look of hate I'd seen in the eyes of the attackers. I braced myself for trouble.

'You are not welcome here,' one shouted. 'Leave this hospital or I'll kill you! Get out of our country!' He spat in my face.

The door burst open and the surgeon appeared. 'What's going on?' he asked, taking in the situation. He addressed the two men in a raised voice. 'Hasn't the war spilled enough blood? Our citizens' blood has soaked the soil of this country and now you want to spill foreigners' blood too?' He pointed to the door. 'Leave! Now!'

Looking chastened but angry, they retreated. Shaking, I found a washroom to clean my face and when I came back the surgeon was still there waiting to give me a report on Narsimha Kavacha.

'Your friend's condition could be serious,' he said. 'His concussion is severe and he has no memory of anything more recent than five days ago. He got off lucky, being hit over the head with a gun. If he'd been shot—and he easily could have been—who knows if he would have survived?'

'Where are Edvin and Thakur?' I asked.

'Thakur is the British man?' he asked. I nodded. 'We are still assessing him. We're unsure about the extent of his injuries, but we are optimistic. Edvin is about to go into surgery. He's going to be okay.'

Back at the temple, the devotees were afraid that the attackers would come to find them, especially given that the temple was situated in a Muslim neighbourhood. The police came to take statements from those who had been present at the attack and they promised to guard the temple over the next several days. They had somehow obtained the video from the journalist whose camera had been smashed and wanted us to watch it to identify the attackers. As the video began many devotees started crying, having to relive those moments so soon after the event. The police asked us to identify the attackers. It wasn't difficult. You don't easily forget someone who has tried to kill you.

The following day, the whole city was talking about the attack and the fact it had occurred during Sarajevo's first few months of peace. The leading newspaper in Sarajevo, *Vecernfe Novosti*, published a front-page headline: 'Bloody beginning to the Festival of India'. The article described the attack in detail. It mentioned how the parade to promote our festival was violently and brutally attacked by thirty men and how we had fought back 'like lions'.

The reporter went on to say it was shameful that foreign blood was being spilled on Snipers' Alley, a name given by citizens to the street we were chanting on where many had been killed by snipers. I later learned the news had gone international with reports in England, Switzerland, France, Australia and India.

The Police Chief of Sarajevo apologized for the incident on national television, saying it did not represent the feelings of most Sarajevans towards the Hare Krishna movement. Several Islamic publications, though, accused us of provoking the attacks and threatened that further action would be taken.

Despite these threats and feelings of shock that sat with a lot of the devotees, we decided to proceed with the Festival of India as planned. The police provided thirty armed guards who stood at every entrance. The people of Sarajevo, many of whom wanted to express their sympathy, came in droves. More than 1,500 people attended the festival, including ambassadors from several countries, members of IFOR, the United Nations and the Red Cross, as our reduced team performed on stage, some adlibbing multiple roles to cover for those too injured to perform.

The day after the festival, most of the international visiting devotees left Sarajevo, including two of those who had been attacked and were deemed well enough to make it back to London. Edvin had been discharged too, but Colin remained in hospital for several weeks. I asked the local devotees to help him, and they did. They took him fresh vegetarian food every day and later took him to the British Embassy which, in turn, helped him get back to Britain. I later heard that the lives of the devotees who had been attacked had been saved by their doctors in more ways than one: not only did they mend their wounds, they also stopped the attackers from entering the hospital to finish what they started.

Our Festival of India in Sarajevo is an example where our endeavour was not successful in bearing the desired fruit by external measures. Although our intention for the festival was to bring some cheer to a region that had seen so much pain and hardship over five years of war, and although the festival itself had been well received overall by the local people, we had also managed to provoke hostility in a still-sensitive environment and paid a heavy price with the serious injuries born by our team. In such situations, I take solace in the understanding that in serving by doing good work, even when it is not met with success externally, the process itself is also meritorious and purifying and is thus its own reward.

You have the right to work, but not to its results. Do not be attached to the fruits of work, or to not working.
—Lord Krishna in the Bhagavad Gita (2:47)

5

Poland

Golden Days

Editor's Note

O f the numerous countries that Indradyumna Swami has
visited, Poland is the most important. It is the site of his most
significant project, the Festival of India (organized in cooperation
with the Viva Kultura Foundation), which has been touring Poland's
Baltic Sea coast for just over thirty years.

Indradyumna Swami first visited Poland in 1990. The plan was to
spend the summer in several eastern European countries—Poland,
Czechoslovakia, Hungary, Yugoslavia, Bulgaria and Romania—all of
which had emerged from communist rule just months earlier. The
first stop of the two-month tour through eastern Europe was Poland,
where Indradyumna Swami visited Krishna devotees in three Polish
cities and towns.

In Wroclaw, a city in western Poland, the devotees organized a
small public event that included kirtan, a short introductory talk on

the Hare Krishna philosophy, and vegetarian refreshments. The event was filled to capacity with people who were relaxed, participatory and eager to know more—they chanted and danced in the kirtan, they listened to the lecture with attention and they had more questions than could be answered in one evening. Indradyumna Swami was enlivened by his first experience with the Polish public. He asked the organizers if they could arrange events in other Polish cities.

He stayed in Poland for the rest of that summer. Devotees hired halls across the length and breadth of the country, and a small team of volunteers travelled with him to advertise the event through street kirtan on location during the day and then help to host the festival in the evening. The facilities were sparse—one devotee had a car, and everyone else hitchhiked. In every location, the Polish people joined in, dancing with devotees along the cobbled streets during the days and participating at the public events that went late into the night. The convoy of travellers increased as more and more people, especially youth, asked whether they could travel on to the next destination with Indradyumna Swami and his team.

The following summer, in 1991, Indradyumna Swami returned to Poland and has continued to do so for thirty more summers since. In the early years the festivals were indoor events attended by 150 to 400 ticket holders. His Polish supporters and students began to make arrangements for the tour throughout the year—hiring buses to transport the team of volunteers, finding larger venues to host the festivals and accommodation where the team would be based for the summer.

But by the mid-'90s, the festivals were held outdoors in town squares or open fields and parks close to towns or beaches. The outdoor festivals transformed both the character and the magnitude of the project. Attended by 5,000 to 8,000 people a night and held six nights a week, the festivals have become a fixture of the Polish summer experience on the Baltic Sea coast. As the years rolled by, the festival developed into a five-hour stage show inspired by and showcasing the culture and philosophy of the Hare Krishna movement and India more generally.

The stage and seating area for watching the show is now surrounded by booths and tents offering festival goers the opportunity to experience different aspects of Hare Krishna. There is a book table, a question-and-answer booth, an outdoor yoga studio, a restaurant tent, vegetarian cooking demonstrations, face painting, a tent where women can choose a sari to wear for the evening, and much more. An operation of this size requires a lot of manpower and equipment—10 tonnes of staging, lighting, amplification, marquees, seating, costumes, props, restaurant equipment and so on.

Early on, the festivals were run by a core group of Polish devotees with the help of 250 to 300 volunteers in the summer, often teenagers who were interested in the Hare Krishna movement. As the size of the project grew, help came from Hare Krishna devotees in Ukraine and Russia as well.

During the late '90s and early 2000s the success of the festival generated a backlash, in the form sensationalist media campaigns, by those concerned that the Krishna teachings and lifestyle were an affront to the Polish-Catholic identity. Over this several-year-period it was not uncommon for festivals to be cancelled at the last minute by city officials or venue providers under pressure from those with political clout. Indradyumna Swami persevered through this difficult chapter and in time the negativity and fear subsided.

In addition to holding its own annual festivals, the Polish Festival of India tour is a major part of one of the largest music festivals in the world—the three-day Pol'and'Rock festival (formerly known as

Festival Woodstock Poland) organized by Polish musician and media personality Jurek Owsiak. Pol'and'Rock was first held in 1995. It came on the heels of the Polish Jarocin festival, an anti-establishment 'alternative' event that became one of the biggest and most important music festivals in Europe during the 1980s and early 1990s.

The Jarocin festival was cancelled in 1994 as increasing aggression and anger was expressed by festival goers towards police, culminating in a riot. In contrast to Jarocin, Owsiak's Pol'and'Rock festival was explicitly 'peaceful'. It was modelled on the original American Woodstock festival held at the height of the hippy era, and its official motto was (and is) 'Love, Friendship, Music'.

In 1996, Owsiak invited Indradyumna Swami to develop an area called Krishna's Village of Peace in the middle of the Pol'and'Rock site. His thinking was that Hare Krishnas were promoters of peace, served good vegetarian food, were drug-free and could provide a clean, wholesome space in which festival goers could detox, meditate, eat well and maybe even experience a spiritual awakening. With up to 750,000 attendees and a major event on the Polish cultural calendar, the Pol'and'Rock festival has done much to establish the Hare Krishna movement as an enduring component of contemporary Polish culture.

Today the Hare Krishna Polish festival has been established as a charitable entity—the Viva Kultura Trust. People who remember the festivals from their childhood now bring their own children to have the same experience. There is much energy directed towards improving the quality of the stage performances, and many talented performers and artists join the tour to contribute their skills. The tour managers also have their eye directed internationally, with the idea of taking a more compact group out of Poland and around the world. This has already been tested in Australia and America with great success. Indradyumna Swami continues to lead the Festival of India project with vision and dedication.

Good News and Bad

'Do you want the good news or the bad news first?' Nandini dasi asked me on the way out of the airport terminal. I had just arrived in Warsaw, ready to embark upon our 2001 festival season in Poland, and had been met by Nandini and Radha-Sakhi Vrinda dasi, the festival managers. I could see they were eager to brief me.

'Okay, give me the bad news first,' I said.

'The anti-cult groups, under the auspices of the Church, are beginning their annual media campaign against us,' Nandini said. 'They know we'll soon be starting our festival tour in Lodz and that we will be along the Baltic Sea coast in the summer. There is a barrage of negative newspaper articles about us, as well as several horrific television broadcasts, all filled with false propaganda. And a booklet warning of the dangers of cults has been distributed to every teacher in every school in the country. We are the main focus. They accuse us of mind control, breaking up families, and a number of criminal activities.

'As a result of the constant barrage of misinformation,' she added, 'a recent survey revealed that 65 per cent of the population favours closing down the "cults" in Poland. We're number one on the list.'

'But how can they say we are a cult?' I asked. 'We've been registered as an official religion in this country since 1991.'

Nandini replied with an infamous quote: 'If you tell the people a lie for long enough, they'll eventually believe it.'

'Okay, now give me the good news.'

'Wherever we go,' said Radha-Sakhi Vrinda, 'we meet people who've been to one or two of our festivals since 1990. Those people are always happy to see us and many are willing to help us where they can. In another survey, 52 per cent of Polish people say they believe in reincarnation. We feel that all the book distribution, festivals and media programmes we've done have contributed to that belief. The Mayor of Zary is one of our supporters. He has just been added to a group of advisers to the Polish President. The President's personal secretary (who was also Poland's minister of Home Affairs) spoke at the opening of ISKCON's exhibition on Vedic Culture at the Warsaw Museum.

'Plans for the Woodstock festival are continuing without opposition,' she added. 'Jurek Owsiak told us he is counting on the Hare Krishna Village of Peace being there. He said to tell you he wants our presence to be even bigger and more colourful than last time.'

'How is that possible?' I replied. 'The tent we rented from Germany was bigger than an American football field. It held 10,000 kids for four days!'

The discussion continued once we arrived at the festival office. It looked like the headquarters of a military operation. There were several devotees poring over maps, considering when and where we would hold festivals in the area chosen for the spring portion of our tour. Phones were ringing and faxes were coming in and going out.

The room buzzed with information about where we would purchase the 22 tonnes of food we needed for distribution at Woodstock, about the arrival of 130 devotees from eastern Europe and Russia, about the three buses we would be using for the next three months, about insurance policies for devotees and volunteers, and about security arrangements for the festivals.

I met briefly with our public relations group, ICP, and asked if they had any information as to what steps the anti-cult groups would take. (The Duke of Wellington said, 'The whole art of war consists of guessing at what is on the other side of the hill.') To my surprise, they told me that ICP's Achintya dasi had recently gone to a meeting of some of the biggest anti-cult groups in Poland. More than a hundred people were present. There were the usual speeches about the dangers of cults and our movement was mentioned several times.

One speaker warned that the Hare Krishna movement had made inroads into public schools. To the audience's horror, she told the story of a schoolteacher who mentioned to her students in class that the Hare Krishna movement was actually not a cult but an ancient spiritual tradition that had been practised in India for thousands of years. One of her students spoke against her and an argument ensued during which the teacher defeated the student. When the other students applauded the teacher, the student who had objected walked out in frustration.

As more speakers vilified the Hare Krishna movement, Achintya gathered her courage, stood up and boldly identified herself as a devotee. Immediately there was silence, all eyes were upon her. With her audience captive, she defeated each of the accusations that had been made against ISKCON. At the end of her presentation, she fielded questions for two hours, the meeting finishing only when the main organizer realized that his objective of discrediting our movement had been unsuccessful.

On the day of the first festival the dawn revealed a beautiful clear sky, one of the most important factors for a successful outdoor event. When I went downstairs, devotees were already busy loading our 24 tonnes of festival paraphernalia into three large trucks. This included the huge sound system (capable of addressing over 100,000 people), fifteen large tents with displays on various aspects of Vedic culture, and our large restaurant equipped to serve splendid vegetarian food to large quantities of people throughout the entire five-hour programme.

There was an air of excitement as the 140 devotees concluded their duties before boarding the three buses to the festival site. Last-minute touches were being made on the twenty exquisitely beautiful large puppets for our new theatre production, 'Krishna in Vrindavan'. Devotees were busy rehearsing kirtan for the stage show. Dancers from South Africa were checking their ankle bells and outfits for their premiere performance with us. Everyone was again looking forward to a season of fifty consecutive festivals.

By 9 a.m., a caravan of assorted trucks, buses and cars was rumbling along the road to the festival site in Tomaszow, thirty-five kilometres away. We planned a short street-kirtan parade before setting up at the site. We were more than a hundred devotees strong, and on the day of our first festival everyone was happy and enthusiastic.

As we danced and chanted through the streets, we handed out invitations to the festival that evening. The people graciously accepted the invitations by the thousands and promised to attend. I was feeling the greatest happiness at the possibility of sharing with the people the wonderful world of Hare Krishna.

However, not all was well. I have chanted on city streets for decades and have become attentive to the nuances of people's responses. Initially I noticed a few people standing still as we passed, their eyes riveted on our kirtan party. One or two looked angry. I then noticed that all the posters we had put up the night before were covered with bright stickers that read: 'Attention! Sect! Festival cancelled!' Then a few antagonistic young men shouted obscenities at us. I wasn't sure, but I sensed that there may be some kind of effort being made to stop our festival, and that the angry young men we encountered were somehow connected.

After the Harinam (the congregational chanting of the Hare Krishna mantra) we proceeded to the festival site and worked hard for the next five hours, setting up our spiritual village. Our semi-trailer truck, once unloaded, folds out into a professional stage, complete with a set of thirty-six bright lights. Around the perimetre of the festival site, we have tents that include displays on vegetarianism, reincarnation, Vedic art, spiritual science. We have a restaurant tent, a book tent, and a question-and-answer tent. We also have a tent where festival goers can choose one of 250 saris to wear for the evening.

An hour before the festival started, there were already several hundred guests milling through the shops and eating in the restaurant. We officially opened the festival with a kirtan and a short introduction that included a message of appreciation for all the mothers present because it was Mother's Day. Then our South African dancers bedazzled the crowd with a spectacular Kathak Indian classical dance.

As it was their first performance for us, I stood among the crowd to watch. Out of the corner of my eye I noticed some of the same angry young men who had shouted at us during the day and realized that they weren't watching the entertainment but seemed to be checking out things. I called a member of our security team over and asked them to keep an eye on the young men.

The stage performances went smoothly one after another. People seemed to love the new puppet show, which was designed specifically for children. Several times I walked around the festival site visiting booths. One area was so crowded I could hardly move. The local police later told Nandini they estimated the event had attracted more than 4,000 attendees.

The crowd was full of people wearing bindis, saris and traditional Indian face painting. Many people approached me to sign their copies of Bhagavad Gita and the other books they were purchasing at our bookshops. During the middle of the festival, I gave a short lecture from the stage on the basic tenets of our philosophy. I remarked that the festival atmosphere was special and many people smiled and nodded their heads in agreement. When I pointed out that thousands of people were enjoying themselves despite the fact that we served no alcohol at the site, everyone laughed.

As evening fell many of the families began to go home and the festival crowd changed to young people eager to hear our reggae band, Village of Peace. The band is well known, partly because it plays at Pol'and'Rock every summer. By the time night fell, the band was halfway through its repertoire. The kids were loving it and the musicians were in top form. Hundreds of youngsters were chanting and dancing and many of us felt it was one of the band's best concerts.

Then just as they were beginning their last song, chaos erupted. I was standing beside the sound tent when I saw a large canister sail over the heads of the audience and land in the middle of the crowd standing in front of the stage. It exploded when it hit the ground, releasing a cloud of pepper gas. The kids started gagging. Within seconds, a group of twenty young men attacked the crowd. They were dressed in black, had shaved heads and wore big boots and bandanas over their faces. Swinging baseball bats, iron bars and chains, they began to beat devotees and guests indiscriminately.

One of the first to be hit was a twelve-year-old girl who fell to the ground, her head bleeding. Before our security team could respond, several people had been injured. My student Premaharinam das from Bosnia sustained a heavy blow to the forehead. Another devotee was struck with a baseball bat in the face, and when he fell the skinheads pummelled him into the ground. Guests were falling left and right as the skinheads, screaming neo-Nazi slogans, viciously beat them. Three members of our security force descended on the attackers with fury, while other devotees fought the skinheads with chairs and tables. Many of the women ran for the shelter of the buses parked nearby.

Outside the melee, people called the police on cell phones. As more people joined the fight, the skinheads retreated only to reassemble and attack again. One of them jumped into the gift shop, where the devotee behind the counter picked up a chair and smashed him with it with all her might.

Then as suddenly as they appeared, they dispersed. There was blood everywhere. Five devotees were injured, as well as a number of guests. Ten minutes later an ambulance arrived and took the most seriously injured to the hospital.

A long twenty minutes later the police arrived. They had been only two blocks away, but somehow did not arrive in time to help the situation. They did not seem very interested in making a report on the attack, and informed us that they couldn't offer us any protection for the rest of the night as they had only three men on duty in the entire town. Their blasé attitude led us to believe that they were connected with the attackers. We even suspected that the local Church might be involved. We didn't have any proof, but people milling around after the attack told us that they had been called by local priests and warned not to attend the festival.

To my surprise, people stayed at the festival site after the attack. They were angry that such a peaceful event had been so brutally disrupted. I heard people discussing religious intolerance and discrimination, a common enough topic in Poland. I appreciated their support, but I was nervous that so many people had remained behind. What if the skinheads returned to finish the job?

We had been scheduled to hold a second festival at the same site the following evening, but after some deliberation we decided to pack up and cancel the event. It was too risky to remain, as our security force was not prepared to deal with so many well-armed men. It had taken the help of our guests to repulse the attackers.

Fortunately, no one was seriously injured; the wounded required stitches and were then discharged. That night the women returned to our base, while all the men stayed behind to protect the crew who were dismantling the festival. Several carloads of skinheads arrived two hours later, but we made a show of force and they retreated. We arrived back at our base at 4 a.m.

After a few short hours of sleep our management team met to discuss strategies for dealing with such attacks. We decided to prepare a report for the media, as our opposition could easily turn the issue to their favour by saying that our presence provoked the incident. Most importantly, we concluded that our own security would be unable to deal with such a scene again. We decided to employ a professional security group to protect our festivals in the future.

A Change of Heart

'Over my dead body! Never! Not in a million years will I rent my school to you!'

As I walked through the door to our makeshift office, I heard a woman screaming these words at Nandini through the phone.

'Gosh. Who was that?' I asked.

'That was the director of a school near the Polish Woodstock site,' said Nandini. 'She's refusing to rent it to us. It's a problem because we need accommodation for our 400 volunteers.'

'Can't we just rent the three we used last year?' I asked.

'We can only get one of those,' Nandini said. 'The other two are being renovated. I ask this lady every year to rent us the school and I always get the same response. She thinks we're a cult.'

'I guess we'll just have to look further,' I said.

'There really aren't very many more big schools to try in the area,' Nandini said. 'But I have one more idea for this school. I'm going to ask the mayor of that town to speak to the director. He's our friend, so maybe he can persuade her.'

The next afternoon when we were chanting on the beach, I got a call from Nandini.

'We got the school!' she shouted.

'She agreed?' I said, somewhat surprised.

'Not exactly,' said Nandini. 'The mayor told her she could lose her job if she didn't. It wasn't pleasant, but it worked.'

Several days later, our festival group of 250 devotees left the Baltic Sea coast and headed southwest towards the Woodstock festival site. Within days, 150 more devotees joined us from Ukraine, Russia and other European countries.

Having been part of Polish Woodstock from the beginning, our crew was experienced and had finished setting up several days before the event. Our seventy-metre-long tent, along with twenty smaller ones, stood tall and impressive on our half-hectare site.

On the first day Polish Woodstock organizer Jurek Owsiak invited us onto the main stage for the official opening, along with our colourful group of fifteen dancers from India. When we arrived, we saw a crowd of 250,000 young people stretched from in front of the stage to the perimeter of the festival grounds. We positioned ourselves as close to the stage as possible.

As several dignitaries walked by us, my godbrother Patita Pavana das noticed Lech Walesa and shook his hand. Walesa had been instrumental in bringing democracy to Poland and later became president of the country.

'I'm from America,' Patita Pavana said. 'In San Francisco they've named a street after you.'

Walesa seemed pleased. As he continued forward, the line momentarily slowed down and he stopped in front of me. I had heard that he was a staunch Catholic and not favourable to our movement, so I took the opportunity to talk to him. 'Mr Walesa, it was a brave thing you did, standing up to the communists. Your courage helped bring about democracy and freedom of religion in this country. On behalf of our movement, I would like to personally thank you.'

He looked a little surprised, but after a moment he relaxed and smiled. 'You're welcome,' he said.

Owsiak then took the stage to a roar from the crowd. 'It's going to be a very special Woodstock this year,' he shouted. 'I'd like to introduce you to Michael Lang!' He put an arm around an older curly-haired man standing next to him. 'He's the one who organized the first-ever Woodstock event in America forty years ago!' More cheers erupted from the crowd. 'And this will be the fifteenth year of Polish Woodstock!' Walesa spoke next, followed by another man I didn't recognize.

'Let's get this party started!' Owsiak shouted after the speeches, and a rock band roared to life behind him. As the dignitaries filed off the stage, I put out my hand to the man who spoke after Walesa. 'Hare Krishna,' I said. 'Thank you for your nice talk.'

To my surprise, the man pulled me close and kissed me on the cheek. 'I know who you are,' he said, 'and I'm aware of the work you're doing. I want you to know I love you for it and I'm grateful.'

There was a lot of commotion because so many people were leaving the stage. I grabbed a stage technician and pointed to the man who had kissed my cheek. 'Who is that?' I asked.

He said a name, but I didn't catch it. 'Who?' I asked again.

'One of the best-known film producers in Poland,' he said.

'Oh well,' I thought, 'the film producer appreciates us. Perhaps Krishna will bring us together again.'

Each day we opened our village at 10 a.m. Within minutes huge lines formed in front of the Food for Peace tent where we were serving vegetarian food that was delicious and freshly prepared. On the first morning I was helping with the serving when one of the visiting devotees from Russia came over to me.

'Maharaja,' he said through a translator, 'there's a young man in line who doesn't have any money. He keeps showing me this old piece of laminated paper. He insists he can eat as much as he wants.'

I took the paper and was surprised to see it was in my handwriting. It was dated 18 August 2004. It read: 'Dear devotees, this boy is my friend. He swept the road in front of Lord Jagannatha's chariot for hours today during the ratha-yatra. He loves to sing Hare Krishna and dance in ecstasy. He has no money, so please allow him to eat as much as he wants throughout the festival for free. Indradyumna Swami.'

'I wrote it five years ago,' I said.

'I told him that,' the devotee said, 'but he says you told him the ratha-yatra parade is eternal and therefore the paper is good forever.'

I laughed. 'Okay then,' I said, 'he can eat this year and every year.'

As in previous years, we held a ratha-yatra parade in which we pulled a chariot holding deities of Krishna and His brother Balaram and sister Subhadra. This lasted several hours each day and took place on a road that cut through the centre of the large field. At one point the road was so crowded it took an hour to go just thirty metres. We didn't mind, we simply chanted louder and danced more enthusiastically. And the kids joined in.

On the second day of the Polish Woodstock, we heard that Owsiak was making announcements across all forms of media asking that no more people come to Woodstock. I turned on the radio in time to hear his announcement. 'There are over 450,000 people here now,' he said. 'We don't have the infrastructure to accept more. Stay home and hear about it later.'

'That must be why so many kids are coming to eat,' I said to Nandini. 'It's the largest crowd I've ever witnessed at Woodstock. I've never seen such huge lines. The cooks estimate we'll distribute well over 130,000 plates.'

'Actually, there's another reason so many kids are coming to our food tent,' said Nandini. 'They're boycotting all the other food stands. When the owners of the stands realized how many more people had come this year they raised the prices, and of course nobody likes that! The word is out that Krishna's Village of Peace is the best place to eat and it's not expensive. Lots of people are either eating here or walking three kilometres into town to buy groceries.'

As always, we provided entertainment. In our small tents there were yoga classes, face painting, books, astrology, shops, and a questions-and-answers booth. In the evening, various bands played on the stage in our main tent. Six-thousand festival goers crammed into the tent to hear Madhumangala das and his punk band, Gaga, from the early '90s. He got them all chanting Hare Krishna and dancing. And each night, Govinda Swami and his Silk Road Bhajan Band performed in the mantra rock tent. His kirtans are legendary at Woodstock, so each evening the tent was crowded with devotees and non-devotees alike.

For me, one of the sweetest parts of the evenings was watching people walk by and be drawn inside by his melodious singing.

On the first evening I noticed three middle-aged women standing at the entrance to the tent scoffing and ridiculing the kirtan. Govinda Swami was leading an explosive kirtan as 300 people chanted and danced around the tent.

The next night the women came just as Govinda Swami had everyone swaying to a light and joyous melody. Mesmerized by the beauty of it all, they were drawn into the tent. They stood and watched for hours. On the third night, they came early and stood in the middle of the crowd as the singing started. They looked up on the wall of the tent where we had a banner displaying the Hare Krishna mantra, and I was surprised when I saw them start chanting along with everyone else. Later in the evening I saw them dancing wildly with the crowd.

On the fourth and final night the women were the loudest chanters and the wildest dancers of all. Because of their age, they caught the attention of onlookers who passed by the tent. The kirtan went on until midnight. I couldn't keep my eyes off them, they danced with abandon, their arms raised high in the air chanting Hare Krishna at the top of their lungs.

As the kirtan was coming to an end, I went to find Nandini and her husband Jayatama das. They had both worked hard to organize the festival and I wanted them to see how happy the devotees and the kids were in Govinda Swami's kirtan. I motioned for them to come up on the stage.

'Isn't this wonderful, Nandini,' I said. 'This is the essence, the very heart of our festival.'

'So true,' she said.

I pointed to the three middle-aged women singing and dancing up front. 'Just look at those women,' I said. 'They've been with us every night. They love kirtan.'

'I know,' Nandini said. 'I know them.'

'How do you know them?' I asked.

Nandini smiled. 'You see the one in the middle? That's the director of the big school we're staying in, the one who refused to rent to us for so many years. The other two are her secretaries.'

'How is that possible?' I asked. 'She was so antagonistic towards us.'

'She came to speak to me this morning,' Nandini said still smiling, 'and told me she came to our village the first day to find reasons that she shouldn't have to rent the school to us next year. She was noting what she considered so many faults, but she said that something happened when she was standing outside the mantra rock tent. Listening to Govinda Swami's kirtan, she had a change of heart. At first, she didn't want to admit it, but something drew her back again the next night. She said the singing was the most beautiful thing she'd ever heard and she was transfixed.

'The next night she wanted to experience it for herself, so she and her secretaries stood right in the middle of the tent. When the kirtan began they saw the mantra on the wall and started chanting. Suddenly, one of our girls pulled them into the kirtan. They've been completely transformed. She said we could have her school next year and even begged me to take it.'

As the kirtan came to an end, I saw the director and her two secretaries standing with their eyes closed, swaying slowly back and forth. When the kirtan finished none of them moved. They just stood there as if savouring the sweetness of chanting the holy names.

'The Polish Woodstock really was special this year,' I said to Nandini, 'but this woman's transformation is the most special thing of all. How fortunate we are to have seen it!'

A Path Revealed

I nodded off to sleep on the way to one of our last festivals along the Baltic Sea coast in the summer of 2019. I woke just as Guru Kripa das was parking behind our large ratha-yatra chariot at the festival site.

'I'm so tired I don't even know what town we're in,' I said laughing.

'The name of the town isn't so important,' said Guru Kripa. 'What's significant is that this is our forty-sixth festival of the summer!'

'Forty-six festivals, one after another,' I thought. 'And with the Polish Woodstock in the middle. No wonder I'm exhausted.'

But there was no time to dwell on the tiredness of my tiredness. Hundreds of excited people were already taking their seats on the benches in front of our stage. The restaurant was packed with guests ordering prasad. Numerous tents depicting various aspects of the Krishna-conscious lifestyle were overflowing.

'If it wasn't for Nandini,' I said to Guru Kripa, 'none of this would be happening today.'

'Why is that?' he asked.

I told him how some high-placed people on the political right convinced the local mayor and the city council to cancel our festival on the grounds that we made too much noise. They requested Nandini to come to their weekly meeting so that they could officially inform her and cancel the contract. Despondent but eager to argue our case, she drove to the town hall on the day of the meeting. In the parking lot, she happened to see the previous mayor who had been in office for many years and was an old friend of hers. She asked for his advice on how to handle the situation.

'My advice?' he said. 'I'm going in with you!'

The previous mayor was a powerful orator and he spoke in our defense for thirty minutes in front of the city council. Nandini didn't say a word, neither did the city councillors who sat looking thoroughly chastened. When he finished, he picked up the contract and waved it in the air.

'It still stands,' he said. 'Are we all in agreement?'

The city councillors nodded.

As he and Nandini were leaving the room, he said over his shoulder, 'And what's more, you should all come to the festival. It's one of the most prestigious events we hold in our town each year. It's an honour to host this event.'

There were no further complications with the festival, everything ran smoothly. The day it rained for half an hour during the stage show no one left the benches, instead a forest of umbrellas—big ones, small ones, colourful ones, patterned ones—popped up and the people stayed where they were. Then the rain stopped, the sun peeked out from behind the departing clouds and the umbrellas came down. No one missed even a moment of the show!

The actors, though, couldn't take shelter under umbrellas. Despite the rain on the stage, they kept up their performance; they had been performing for two months straight whether it was windy or rainy or hot. They were real troupers!

Walking around the festival site that evening, I bumped into an older man. 'I'm so sorry,' I said. 'Please excuse me.'

'No need to excuse yourself,' he said. 'It gives me a chance to finally speak to you.'

'Oh, you wanted to speak to me.'

'Yes,' he said. 'I was fifty-four when I first came across your festival. I'm eighty-four now. I can attest to the fact that you've been holding this festival for thirty years.'

'You don't look eighty-four,' I said.

'Of course not,' he said. 'I took to heart what you said in the first lecture I heard you give. I gave up eating meat, fish and eggs. I started practising yoga and I read the Bhagavad Gita every day. And I sing the song too!'

'You mean the Hare Krishna song?' I asked.

'Is there any other song worth singing?' he replied with a grin.

'No, no. You're right,' I said, secretly wishing I had the same conviction he seemed to possess.

'We have to sing it because someday we'll die,' he continued. 'In the fourth lecture I heard you give, you said that we can't take anything with us when we die except our love of God. And you said God is present in His name.'

'Yes, I do say that,' I said. 'Where do you plan to go when you die?' I instantly felt sorry, thinking it might be an inappropriate question to ask someone I had just met.

'With him.' He pointed to the actor who had played Lord Ramachandra and who was posing for photos with guests. 'But up there!' He pointed to the sky. 'Being with Krishna would be okay too!' he added.

The hair on my arms stood up as I watched him walk away.

'We know that old man,' a teenage girl said. She was standing nearby with her friend, both of them wearing saris. 'We see him here every year. Sometimes during the theatre performance he cries.'

'I see,' I said, feeling overwhelmed. Fortunately, the other girl changed the subject.

'We just picked out our favourite saris in the fashion booth. They said we could keep them. We plan to wear them to school this coming semester.'

'Really?' I was astounded. 'Can you do that?'

'Yes,' she said. 'If we wear saris to school, all the other girls will start wearing them. And if all the girls in our school start wearing them, then girls in other schools will also start wearing them. We plan to start a new fashion in Poland.'

'That sounds like a bit of a challenge,' I said.

'Not really,' said the first girl. 'We're beautiful and so are the saris. Just wait and see.'

'Sure, I'll wait and see,' I said with a smile.

I decided to check out the book tent, but I had only gone twenty metres when a man came up to me and placed a Bhagavad Gita in my hand.

'Can you sign this for my wife?' he asked.

'Sure,' I said. 'Should I include your name too?'

'Don't bother,' he said. 'I'm not interested. Every year my wife drags me to this event and before we leave, she asks me to buy her a Bhagavad Gita. I always refuse and we argue about it for the rest of our vacation, so I finally agreed to buy it for her. Hopefully I'll get some peace now and be able to enjoy my vacation.'

'You made the right choice,' I said handing the book back to him. 'Finding peace of mind and real happiness are two of the themes in the Bhagavad Gita.'

Just outside the book tent, another man approached me.

'I heard you talk in another town this summer,' he said. 'I bought a Bhagavad Gita afterwards. I've been reading it for two weeks. As a result, I've made a firm resolution.'

'Interesting,' I said. 'What resolution have you made?'

He stood up a little straighter and his voice took on a slightly official tone. 'I am going to put it in my will that all generations of my family who come after me will be obliged to read this book before they reach twenty years of age. I already mentioned it to my lawyer.'

A teenage girl came up to the man with a Bhagavad Gita in her hands. 'Papa, I want my own copy! And I want the man to sign it.'

Her father hesitated. They were not well-dressed, so perhaps they couldn't afford it. 'Papa!' she insisted. 'Today is the celebration of the Assumption of Mary, when the Virgin Mary goes to heaven. My name is Maria. It only makes sense that you buy the book for me today. Ave Maria!'

Her father still seemed to hesitate.

'Look,' I said, 'because this is such a special day, a holy day, I'm just going to give you this book, Maria. It's yours now. You take it.'

Hearing this, she burst into tears, and then her father started crying too. I felt my own eyes well up with tears of appreciation for the mercy of Lord Chaitanya in making Krishna consciousness so accessible to people.

One of the more popular theatre performances in our show is a drama we call, 'The Bhagavatam'. It was starting on the stage, so I turned back to the benches. The play's theme is the art of dying. In the final scene, one of the performers comes down off the stage and presents the First Canto of the Srimad Bhagavatam to someone in the audience. As the devotee descended the stairs, I motioned to her to give the book to one middle-aged woman who had sat mesmerized throughout the entire performance. The lady was overwhelmed by the gift and started crying.

'This festival is a real tear-jerker tonight,' I thought.

The woman with the book came over to me. 'I saw you directed that actor to me,' she said.

'Yes, I did,' I replied.

'But how did you know?' she interjected as tears streamed down her face. 'How did you know?'

'How did I know what?' I asked.

'Today is my fortieth birthday,' she said. 'I am all alone. My family—my husband and children—have all passed away. I woke up this morning asking God to give me a sign that He is still here for me. I prayed for Him to give me the knowledge I need not to give in to depression and to go forward in life. Then this afternoon I got an invitation to your festival and in the theatre, I found so much comfort and hope. And then you directed the actor to give me this book!'

She paused. 'How did you know?' she asked softly.

'The Lord is in everyone's heart and He alone knows our deepest desires,' I said. 'I am happy I could act as His instrument.'

'Thank you. Thank you. Thank you,' she said. 'This has been a life-changing experience for me.'

'For me too,' I said.

After the final kirtan of the night, there was an older woman waiting for me at the bottom of the stage steps.

'Do you remember me?' she said.

'Yes, of course,' I said. 'You were the mayor in this town fifteen years ago. You fought off all the opposition so we could have our festivals here.'

'Yes,' she replied with a smile. 'You had many enemies back then.'

'We certainly did,' I said. 'But you stood up for us. And we always won.'

'Yes,' she said nostalgically. 'It was a good fight.'

Again, tears came to my eyes. 'I'm such a cry-baby tonight,' I thought. Aloud I said, 'Thank you for coming this evening! You still remember us.'

'How could I forget you?' she said. She held up one of her hands. 'You gave me this ring one day after we defeated a particularly difficult opponent. You told me it was worn by your God who gives protection.

And it seems it has worked. All my friends have passed away, but I am standing.'

'We are here only because you safeguarded our mission,' I told her.

'I hope to see you again next year,' she said as we parted ways.

'It's been an extraordinary festival,' I said to Guru Kripa as we got in the van.

He smiled and replied, 'Gurudeva, you say that after every festival. In fact, you've said it forty-six times this summer so far.'

'That's true,' I admitted. 'I don't know how we're going to survive after our last festival three days from now. How will we all bear separation from these magical events? These are golden days.'

One who teaches this supreme secret [love of God] to others offers Me the greatest love, and without doubt comes to Me. No one is dearer to Me than such a person, nor on earth will there ever be one more dear.

—Lord Krishna in the Bhagavad Gita (18:68-69)

6

Azerbaijan and Russia
Nuclear Waste and Vedic Temples

Editor's Note

Indradyumna Swami has been visiting Russia since before the fall of the Soviet Union. His first visits took place in the late 1980s when he ventured into the country to encourage the thousands of underground Russian-Soviet Hare Krishnas, many of whom had been imprisoned in psychiatric facilities or prisons for their religious faith. Prior to the collapse of communism, Indradyumna Swami entered the country as part of an official tour group—the only way to legitimately visit Russia at the time—and then slipped away from the group as often as he could to attend secret gatherings organized by the Russian devotees in their homes.

When the Soviet Union and with it communism collapsed in Russia, Indradyumna Swami was in Poland. During the 1980s and early '90s he travelled with a portable radio in order to stay abreast of current affairs, and he and his team listened to the BBC's coverage of the fall of the Soviet Union as it happened. Mikhail Gorbachev was taken into house arrest in Crimea and a coup group launched a military offensive in Moscow, surrounding the parliament buildings. Boris Yeltsin famously stood on a tank and rallied the people and the presidents of the Soviet republics to oppose the regime that had held power for almost seventy-five years.

A week later, Indradyumna Swami was in Moscow, having received an invitation from the leaders of the fledgling Russian Hare Krishna movement. He participated in the first public chanting of Harinam in Red Square along with 2,000 other devotees. The blown-out windows of the parliament had yet to be repaired and there were blackened marks of explosives on the walls. There was a sense of this being an historic moment.

There followed several years of tremendous growth of the movement. In the uncertainty that accompanied the transition from communism to capitalism, there was a power vacuum which enabled the Russian Hare Krishna devotees to accomplish things that would have been difficult in more stable political circumstances.

During the 1990s the movement established major centres in St Petersburg and Moscow; the movement's publishing arm—the Bhaktivedanta Book Trust—printed millions of books in Russian and took out billboards in the subways advertising Hare Krishna literature; a radio station called Radio Krishnaloka promoted the movement and broadcast music and philosophical lectures in Moscow and St Petersburg; Hare Krishna schools sprung up to educate members' children; and a Russian chapter of the Hare Krishna food distribution network, Food for Life, distributed free vegetarian food in the war zones that proliferated in the former Soviet Union. If things in Russia tend to be big, the Hare Krishna movement was no exception.

Indradyumna Swami played a pivotal role as travelling teacher and mentor during these formative years, becoming the formal spiritual guide for thousands of Russian students. His travels throughout the former Soviet Union were coloured by the uncertainty and lack of regulation across Russian social, economic and business structures, the same forces that fostered the growth of the movement. For example, when he first came to Russia, his visa required him to stay in Moscow but the local devotees got him a student card from Moscow University which enabled him to travel throughout Russia. The planes he travelled on were dirty, sometimes without adequate seating and with ropes to slide out of the plane in case of emergency. Flights were often diverted without explanation or because of lack of fuel.

There were instances of him and his team crossing borders—once by driving through a river—without proper documentation, and their Russian translators managing to get them through checkpoints manned by armed guards. Sometimes they were driven in old Lada cars and sometimes in limousines, the latter an initiative by a mafia boss who temporarily became interested in the Hare Krishna philosophy. It is an understatement to say that the uncertainty of the environment made for uncertain journeys. Events were often left unexplained and incomprehensible to non-Russian speakers.

As the post-communist culture of Russia became more settled, the Hare Krishna movement experienced more stability but less growth. The early leaders of the Russian Hare Krishna movement were all American, because the movement's origins in America meant that most of the senior members were American. Today, the main initiating spiritual leaders of the movement in Russia are Russian. Nevertheless, Indradyumna Swami remains a pivotal figure in the Russian Hare Krishna movement, with annual visits that have continued since those early uncertain times.

This chapter explores Indradyumna Swami's experiences during his travels to Azerbaijan, Siberia and Russia, where he witnessed the preservation of Vedic culture, the impact of materialism on society, and the growth of the Hare Krishna movement. Indradyumna Swami emphasizes the importance of cultural preservation, spiritual values, empathy and compassion in a world dominated by materialistic concerns.

Indradyumna Swami touches on various themes—the history and significance of the Vedic temple, the impact of nuclear waste on the people of Siberia, the growth of the Hare Krishna movement in Russia, the impact of capitalism and free enterprise on corruption, and the destruction of historical sites during the communist revolution —in this chapter.

Azerbaijan

Arriving at the airport in Baku, Azerbaijan in 2004 I was greeted by a wave of hot desert air. Bordered by Russia, Georgia, Armenia, Iran and the Caspian Sea, Azerbaijan is a country rich in resources, chiefly oil, which is its primary industry. Security was tight at the airport. Azerbaijan was technically at war with Armenia over Nagorno-Karabakh, a large tract of land southwest of Baku claimed by both countries. In spite of a ceasefire, there were daily skirmishes in which soldiers were killed on both sides. At the time travel outside the country was restricted for men of military age, so many of my students waiting outside the airport terminal to greet me had not seen me since my last visit in 1997.

On the drive to the temple, I asked the local devotees about any changes in the country. I was surprised to hear that the government had closed down all but twenty of the 350 spiritual organizations in the country in 2002. We were one of the twenty that were accepted

and officially registered as bona fide religions. I considered this quite
a success in a Muslim country. Despite the official recognition, the
devotees could practice and preach Krishna consciousness only in
the capital, Baku, and in no other cities or provinces. And services
could be held only in the temple compound. That meant no Harinam
street-chanting and no festivals outside Baku.

When we arrived at the temple there was a large assembly of
devotees waiting in the driveway (they didn't step out of the compound)
and participating in a loud and enthusiastic kirtan. Neighbours were
peering from their windows and some children ran behind our car
calling out 'Krishna! Krishna!' Small groups of moustachioed men
watched my arrival with curiosity as they stood nearby fingering their
Muslim prayer beads. As I got out of the car, I heard loudspeakers
from a nearby mosque calling the faithful to prayer. I marvelled
how here, in a Muslim country, devotees of Krishna were living and
practising their faith.

After a couple of days in Baku, I asked whether someone could
take me into the desert to the Temple of Fire which I had visited
before. It was an ancient Vedic temple built by ascetics from India
in the outskirts of Baku. It had natural gas fires coming out of the
earth. I knew that the temple had a history that went back thousands
of years. The earliest written records of it dated back to the followers
of the ancient Zoroastrian faith which preceded Islam. These people
were mainly worshippers of the elements, and fire was their main
meditation.

In the fourth century BC, they worshipped at the site. From the
fifteenth to the eighteenth centuries AD, Baku was one of the most
important trade centres between Azerbaijan and India. Goods
were brought by traders from India and then sent by sea to Russia
and western Europe. Some historians say the Temple of Fire was

frequented by Indian sages for thousands of years. These descriptions conform to Srila Prabhupada's statement that Vedic culture once flourished all over the world. This much I had found out on my previous visit, but I wanted to know more.

'The temple has remained undisturbed for centuries,' I said to one of the local devotees, 'but how is that possible? When India was ruled by Muslims, they took it upon themselves to destroy numerous temples, especially temples of Krishna.'

'It is some distance out of Baku,' the devotee said, 'and sometimes it is covered with sand from sandstorms, so no one bothered with it. When Azerbaijan became part of the former Soviet Union and religion was restricted, the temple was indirectly protected because no one took interest in it and the site became a dump. When then Indian Prime Minister Jawaharlal Nehru came to Baku in 1960, he visited the temple. Afterwards he requested the Russian government to clean up the site and establish it as a protected historical monument, which it did.'

Entering the temple for the first time in many years, I was again impressed by its majesty. The compound was surrounded by large walls, with a main temple in the center and twenty-six other rooms around the periphery. Small fires emanated from the rock floor of each room. Ascetics used to live in the rooms, worship the fires and perform severe austerities. The Azerbaijan government decided to promote tourism there and had recently installed dioramas of yogis performing austerities in many of the rooms. In one room was a diorama of a yogi lying on limestone, a severe skin irritant. In another room, a yogi stood in heavy chains. The display board said he had vowed never to sit again. In another room, ascetics were shown fasting while meditating on the sacred flame.

These kinds of severe bodily austerities have nothing to do with bhakti yoga, which aims at awakening one's love for God through devotional activities, but it was fascinating to see the ancient site where sadhus attempted to become detached from this world of birth and death. In one of the rooms was kept a register with the names of hundreds of visitors who had visited the site over the centuries: 1671 Streis, Dutch sailor; 1733 Lerh, German traveller; 1743 Ganvey Johnas, English merchant; 1780 Reinegs, Russian scientist; 1825 Keppel, German traveller; 1879 Donovon, English traveller; 1903 Jokson, American scientist. There was also a book with references to the site from the writings of others who had visited the temple: for instance, Villot, French missionary and traveller, wrote in 1689:

Near the well was seen a volcano, erupting fire for eight or ten months. They call this place 'Ateshgah', which means the home of the fires. Even nowadays it is honoured by Hindus and herbs. They come here to worship from different places and throw silver and gold coins and even keep two dervishes to guard this sacred fire.

German traveller Kemper wrote in 1683:

Here, near the fire some were cooking for the settlement Sroganny ates-gava, called so up to this fire. Others were burning lime. Two descendants of the ancient Persian tribe, newcomer Hindus, and fire worshippers were passively sitting around the wall, built by them and prayed, gazing at that flame gushing out of the ground and worshipped.

Russian traveller I. Berjozin wrote in 1842:

> Situated in the southern part of Russia, the city of Baku
> represents many things, noteworthy of full and deep
> attention of the visitors of all kinds. But without any doubt,
> inextinguishable fire is the unique phenomenon, attracting the
> glances of travellers.

Our guide during this visit was a young woman in her late teens who
told us about the temple through a translator. She pointed out the
fire burning in the main temple in the middle of the compound. The
main temple was a simple but impressive structure. On the top was
a trident like those carried by worshippers of Lord Shiva. Nearby,
another fire was burning in a smaller structure. When the yogis
departed from this world, our guide explained, they were cremated
there and their ashes taken back to India and immersed in the holy
River Ganges.

'What surprises me,' I said, 'is that these fires are still burning after
thousands of years.'

'The present fires are from gas piped into the site,' she said. 'In
1883, the first digging for oil in this region took place nearby. As a
result of the drilling, the natural gases just under the surface of the
earth escaped and soon all the fires went out. The yogis living here
explained it differently, and maybe more accurately. They said that
by drilling, the excavators created a wound in Mother Earth's body
and the gods became displeased and withdrew their mercy—the fire.
The yogis then cursed the rulers. They said that this region would
be plagued by war and poverty for centuries. Then they went back to
India. And it's a fact. Although we produce so much oil, we are at war
and we remain poor.'

I asked her why the doorways in the temple were so low, I thought maybe it indicated that the ascetics living there were small in stature.

'Oh no,' the guide answered. 'It was a way of making people bow in humility as they entered to worship the sacred fires that came from the earth. They were practising to become saints. Your guru, Srila Prabhupada, was a modern-day saint because he taught people all over the world how to love God in a simple way.'

'She knows about Srila Prabhupada?' I asked the translator, surprised.

The translator spoke with her. 'She says she has never met him,' he said, 'but she hopes to some day. She knows all about his mission to America in the 1960s. She wants to know if he will ever visit Azerbaijan.'

My eyes welled up with tears. Here, in this remote part of the world, someone was speaking about and inquiring with such faith about my spiritual master.

'I'm sorry,' I said. 'He passed away many years ago.'

She looked visibly affected.

'How do you know about my spiritual master?' I asked.

'A friend of mine happened to have one of his books and she gave it to me,' she said. 'I learned to appreciate him from that book.'

I left the holy Temple of Fire with a deeper appreciation of Vedic history, and more importantly a greater appreciation for my spiritual master, inspired by the words of a young Muslim girl who understood him to be a genuine saint of our times.

Siberia

I tried to get comfortable on my 2006 flight from Moscow to Siberia, but it wasn't easy. The seats were small and close together and although the plane had been renovated it was still a vintage model dating back

at least twenty years. But it was midnight and we were exhausted so I
and my Russian secretary Uttama-sloka das eventually fell asleep on
the five-hour flight to Krasnoyarsk, one of the largest cities in Siberia.

Half an hour before landing the cabin lights came on. I woke up and
noticed a man across the aisle staring at me. Finally, he stood up and
came over. 'I'm curious,' he said. 'Why are you going to Krasnoyarsk?
Not many foreign tourists go there. I'm sure you're aware of Siberia's
dismal history, what with Stalin's labour camps and the deaths of tens
of thousands of political dissidents.'

'I am aware of that unfortunate history,' I said.

'The future isn't much brighter either,' he said. 'Siberia is fast
becoming the nuclear wasteland of the world. Foreign countries have
paid the Russian government billions of dollars to dump their high-
level radioactive waste around Krasnoyarsk. But the people of Siberia
never see the money. It all ends up in Moscow. There's only one thing
the people get.'

'What's that?'

'Cancer!' he said loudly. The person in the seat in front of me
turned around, looking annoyed.

'They dump the nuclear waste into gigantic holes near two towns
on either side of Krasnoyarsk. It's no coincidence that the region has
one of the highest incidences of cancer in the world.'

'Why do people live there?' I asked.

'They pay big salaries to keep people in Krasnoyarsk,' he said.
'People will do anything for money. Even die for it!'

'Gosh!' I exclaimed. 'Why are you going there?'

'I'm a doctor,' he said. 'My organization is helping to finance a
cancer clinic in Krasnoyarsk. I'm going to oversee the project. I can
see from your robes you're some kind of religious person. I hope you
can help the Siberian people somehow.'

He went back to his seat and left me with my thoughts. 'One of the highest incidences of cancer in the world,' I thought. 'I can't do much practically to help people with cancer, but I can help by giving the spiritual knowledge I have received. Life is such that even though people are suffering they still have to be reminded that this material world is a temporary place full of misery and the only alternative is spiritual life.'

It certainly had been an uncomfortable flight. After we landed, we ended up waiting in our seats forty-five minutes for buses to transport us from the tarmac to the terminal. No one said anything, not even when the captain shut off the power and we sat waiting in the dark, stuffy cabin. 'If this were Europe or America,' I thought, 'you'd hear people shouting, but here they just tolerate it all. Russians are tough, but Siberian Russians are the toughest because they live in Siberia, one of the coldest places of the inhabited world.'

Outside the terminal we were met by a large group of husky men in leather coats asking if we needed a taxi.

'It's like a scene from the 1930s,' I said to Uttama-sloka. 'Look at those old wooden buildings. The bright lights of Moscow seem far away.' We were met by my student, Guru Vratta das, and a driver.

On the way to our apartment, we saw a streetcar plough into a small car. The driver stepped out of her vehicle, blood gushing from a cut on her head. She reached into her purse and calmly pulled out a scarf which she put to the wound. Her passenger, a man in his fifties, stood next to the car in shock. What amazed me most was that people drove by without slowing down.

'It's unbelievable,' I thought. 'In most other places people would offer to help or see what happened. Here they just drive on.'

'Can't we stop?' I asked the driver.

'The police will arrive soon,' he replied. 'Better we don't get involved.'

A couple of days into my stay in Krasnoyarsk, I asked whether we could go to a Romani village I had visited two years ago. I was looking forward to seeing the people I had met again. Guru Vrata told me that several of the Romani I had met last time had died drug-related deaths, whether as users or as dealers.

'Don't the police stop them from dealing drugs?' I asked.

'The Romani village is a country within a country,' he said. 'The police have no authority there.'

Driving through the village, we quickly became an object of attention. Children stopped playing to stare at us. Women hanging laundry glanced at us and quickly looked away. In contrast, a group of men playing cards on a porch looked up and studied us intently as we drove by. I noticed several wooden stands on street corners which I learned were drug dealers' stalls. We pulled up outside a comparatively opulent house, the same house we'd had our programme in two years ago.

'Alexander, the owner of this house and a leader in the Romani community, has been following our spiritual practices since your last visit,' Guru Vrata told me. 'He's hoping to become your formal student.'

Alexander and his wife, Lena, greeted us respectfully at the door. 'Welcome to our home, Guru Maharaja,' he said. 'My friends are upstairs in the living room. They are looking forward to meeting you.'

Once I was seated, Alexander invited a tall man to come forward to speak to me.

'This is Victor,' Alexander said. 'He's just been released from jail after three and a half years.'

'I was sentenced to five years,' Victor said, 'but I was released early for good behaviour. Because I was injured when the police arrested me, I wasn't able to work in prison. I knew about the Hare Krishna mantra, and I used my time to do chanting meditation. I chanted for two hours a day and read Krishna philosophy. I told other prisoners about what I was reading, and many of them appreciated what I had to tell them. One of them was a leader of the Siberian mafia. It was so hard in jail. Sometimes there were forty men in a thirty square-metre cell. There were often fights between the prisoners. But my mafia-leader friend protected me.

'The prison authorities appreciated my behaviour and my positive influence on the other prisoners so much that they had me give classes on what I was reading on the closed-circuit prison television. In some ways I think they were sad to see me go.

'And now I'm out. But there's a problem.' I saw his eyes were filled with tears. 'I was more focussed on my spiritual life when I was in prison. I'm not chanting very much anymore. What should I do?'

'Well,' I said, 'in one sense we are all prisoners in a jail with four great walls: birth, disease, old age, and death. It's the same as an ordinary prison: everyone suffers here and it's hard to get out. Chanting the names of God is the best way to get freedom from this prison we are all in. Do you have a home and a family, Victor?'

A hush came over the room. Guru Vrata leaned over.

'His wife is still in prison,' he whispered. 'There's a code among Romani women that they take part of the blame for their husband's crimes even if they are innocent. This is so their husband's time in prison is reduced.'

I saw how uncomfortable Victor was, so I quickly tried to shift the focus. 'Where is Vadim, that handsome man with the light-coloured eyes I met last time?'

Again, the room was silent. Guru Vrata leaned over a second time.

'He was severely wounded in a knife fight last month,' he whispered. 'They took him to the hospital, but he wasn't given priority because he is Romani. But then one of the doctors saw he wore tulasi beads around his neck, and he must have known that all devotees do because he asked if Vadim was a Hare Krishna. And when he said he was, the doctor operated on him and saved his life.'

'Is he out of the hospital?' I asked.

'He's in a prison hospital. As soon as the operation was over the police arrested him for previous offences,' Guru Vrata said.

Alexander spoke up. 'I want to tell you how much my spiritual practices have changed my life,' he said. 'I used to be a drug dealer myself. I gave up my life of crime when I started chanting regularly. I now sell cars for a living. I follow all four of the principles followed by formal initiates of the Hare Krishna movement: I don't eat meat, I don't take any intoxicants, I don't gamble, and I don't have sex outside of marriage. I also tell my community about the benefits of this way of life. And many Romani are taking up aspects of it themselves.'

'That's wonderful,' I said.

'So,' Alexander said, 'I want to request that I be initiated as your formal student and that you become my teacher.'

'Yes,' I said. The room burst into applause. 'But I have one request: I would like you to ask for the approval of your community elders before the initiation ceremony in a few days. If they give their approval, I will be happy to become your teacher.'

On the morning of the initiation ceremony, we still had no answer from the Romani village.

'Alexander said no one in the Romani community objects. Permission is granted.'

My eyes welled up with tears, maybe because I was grateful to the Romani community or just plain happy for Alexander. Or perhaps because I was appreciating the unfathomable grace of God—a Romani man living in Siberia was to formally take up his spiritual journey.

When a person becomes a formal student of a Vaishnava teacher, he or she receives a Sanskrit name, often a name of the Lord or one of His devotees. This is to denote belonging to the greater family of Vaishnavas—much as a woman traditionally takes her husband's family name in marriage—and also to help the devotee and their friends remember the person's connection to the divine. On the way to the temple, I told Guru Vrata the name I wanted to give Alexander.

'I would like to call him Dina Bandhu das,' I said. 'It's a name of Krishna meaning friend of the fallen.'

Guru Vrata gulped. 'If I could make a suggestion,' he said, 'I don't think that's a great name for a Romani student. The Romani are sensitive to the fact that some people are prejudiced against them. They have certainly suffered a great deal historically in Europe. They won't appreciate that name.'

'What name would you suggest?' I asked.

'Perhaps a name with some nobility attached. This will make the Romani proud that one of their own is a devotee of Krishna.'

There were ten initiates that morning, ten new students who became my responsibility to guide. They each came forward and made vows: to follow the four regulations mentioned above and to engage in chanting meditation every day. Alexander was the last. It felt like a historic moment to me. I was thinking that possibly he was the first full-blooded Romani to become a formally initiated Vaishnava. I gave him the name Purusa Simha das: servant of God in His incarnation as Narsimhadeva, a half-man, half-lion incarnation who always protects His devotees.

'Be fearless, a lion among men,' I said, 'and teach your clan what you have learned about the benefits of chanting God's names.'

Russia

I have been visiting Russia regularly since the early 1990s, mainly to encourage my students, a large proportion of whom are Russian. When I arrived in Moscow in the spring of 2009, I could see that the country had been greatly affected by the global recession that was gripping the world at the time. A sharp decline in the price of oil, maturing debts, a nosedive in industrial output, and the loss of hundreds of thousands of jobs had made for a dramatic downturn in the country. In a desperate attempt to revive the economy, President Medvedev had injected the equivalent of 250 billion euros into the financial sector.

The next morning we drove to Vladimir, a city of 400,000 people, three hours to the east of Moscow. In the evening we had a hall programme with more than 400 devotees. They listened carefully to my lecture and danced blissfully in the kirtan. On the way back to our apartment I thought about how the Hare Krishna movement continues to grow with leaps and bounds in Russia. I saw something similar in America during the 1970s and '80s, but in Russia it just keeps on going. It may have something to do with the fact that life in Russia has often been difficult. Now, with the recession, things have become even harder. In my experience, this kind of situation can inspire people to turn to God, whichever faith or denomination one chooses to follow.

My schedule when visiting Russia tends to be overwhelming. I give classes to large groups every day and try to see as many of my students as I can. I rarely get an opportunity to go outdoors, but I asked Uttama-sloka one day whether he knew of any walks we could go on. It was still cold in Moscow that May, so we dressed warm and drove with several others to a forested area near a village. We walked together as a group and chanted softly on our beads. We had been walking for about forty-five minutes when I looked up and was surprised to see the ruins of a large castle sitting in what must have once been an opulent estate.

'In a lot of Western countries,' I said, 'something like this would have been restored and made into a heritage site.'

'Lucky it's still here,' said Uttama-sloka. 'During the revolution the communists destroyed many things connected to the aristocracy—the people Marxists call the bourgeoisie.'

Another of my students, Mahavan das, spoke up. 'It belonged to a Russian noble 200 years ago, and consisted of eighty rooms, with hot running water and central heating. There was even a private railway coming to the castle.'

'The whole area is rich in history,' Uttama-sloka said. 'The city of Vladimir was established in 990 AD by King Vladimir Svyatoslavich the Great, making it one of the oldest cities in Russia. Historians say he was a pagan king who later converted to Christianity and built the first church in the city. Some say the so-called pagan culture was the remnant of Vedic culture, which flourished in Russia for some time.

'In fact, there are a number of signs that Vedic culture existed here. We have several rivers in Russia with Vedic names, for example Indra, Kama and Moksa.'

'And in 2007,' Mahavan added, 'archaeologists unearthed a Vishnu deity in Staraya Maina, an ancient town in the Volga region. They say every square inch of the place is filled with antiques.'

'There's a group of Russian historians who support the idea of Vladimir's Vedic culture,' said Uttama-sloka. 'The historians say that after conquering the city of Kherson in southern Ukraine, Vladimir asked Emperor Basil II for his sister Anna's hand in marriage. But she was a devout Christian and said she would marry him only if he converted to Christianity. Madly in love, he agreed and was baptized in Kherson. After they were married, Anna convinced him to convert all in his kingdom to his new faith. Those who refused were beheaded.'

Uttama-sloka continued, 'Some historians say Vladimir ultimately destroyed all traces of Vedic culture, including a Vishnu temple on the site where he built a large church and to this day that church is revered as one of the most sacred places in the Russian Orthodoxy. Many scholars contest this view, but others point to the city of Arkaim as further evidence of Russia's embrace of the Vedas.'

'Where is Arkaim?' I asked.

'It was discovered in the Urals in 1987,' Uttama-sloka replied. 'Archaeologists call the site Swastika City or Mandala City and they say it is an ancient capital of the Aryan civilization, as described in the Vedas. They found many articles there related to Vedic culture. The name Swastika refers to the city's layout, which looks like a swastika, a symbol of auspiciousness in Vedic culture.'

'Srila Prabhupada writes in his books that Vedic culture once thrived all over the world,' I said. 'He mentions that Vedic culture once dominated the planet but gradually broke up because of religious and cultural divisions.'

'There's another piece of evidence that is even more compelling,' Uttama-sloka said. 'The Russian Veda.'

'Yes,' I said, 'I have heard of it. Several years ago, I met the chairman of the religious affairs committee of the Urals region, Professor Alexander Medvedev, who told me that many Russian scientists agree that Vedic culture once flourished in Russia, notably in the Volga River region. And he confirmed the existence of a Russian Veda. He said it is as old as Russia and the stories are exactly like those in the

Vedic scriptures. The central figure in the Russian Veda is a person called Krishen. He is the upholder of spiritual truths and the killer of many demons, such as a witch and a snake, which echo the stories in our scripture, the Srimad Bhagavatam, of the child Krishna's pastimes.'

'Gurudeva,' said Mahavan, 'one of your students, Jananivasa das, recently obtained a copy of the Russian Veda.'

'Wow!' I said, 'I'd love to hear something from that. Can we try to call him?'

Moments later, standing in the forest, I heard Jananivasa's voice through the phone. 'Gurudeva,' he said, 'Mahavan says you're interested in the Russian Veda.'

'I sure am,' I said. 'Can you just translate the first few sentences for me, so I can get an idea what it's like?'

'Sure,' he said.

I turned the cell phone speaker on so the other devotees could hear and Jananivasa began reading.

'This great knowledge, the Vedas, was imparted to the Russians, the grandsons of Dazhbog (the god of rain), by the Almighty Himself. The Russians carefully keep this knowledge that He gave to them. It is the essence of everything. It is the very blood of Russia and the revealer of our divine path.'

After the call to Jananivasa, Uttama-sloka turned to me. 'Gurudeva,' he said, 'the culture and philosophy put forward in the Vedas is so profound and beautiful. It would be nice if we could somehow revive Vedic culture here in Russia.'

'That's exactly what we are doing by teaching the philosophy of the Vedas and by practising the chanting of the Hare Krishna mantra,' I said. 'Each time a person takes up the chanting and the practice of bhakti yoga, the yoga of love of God, that is the knowledge of the Vedas in action.'

My visit to St. Petersburg in early June confirmed these words. It was one of the last stops on my 2009 Russian tour. Founded by Czar Peter I in 1703 and functioning as the capital of the Russian Empire for more than 200 years, St. Petersburg is one of my favourite places in the former Soviet Union. The Hare Krishna movement has a strong presence there, in that the devotees do regular street chanting, book distribution and hold a well-publicized ratha-yatra chariot festival each year through the city. Because of setbacks in the 1980s, the devotees lost a beautiful temple, but during the decade after the millennium they met each week in a hall near the centre of the city in the hope of someday buying a property of their own.

Driving through the city on the way to a programme, I couldn't help marvelling at the architecture and the serenity of the parks and waterways. But I knew that much of the beauty I was seeing was reconstruction. During World War II, St. Petersburg, then known as Leningrad, was blockaded by German forces for 900 days. More than a million people died, mainly from starvation and aerial bombardments. There are a great many memorials honouring the soldiers and citizens who perished protecting the city.

For me, these memorials are reminders of the urgent need to teach others about spirituality (and Krishna specifically), as history tends to repeat itself. Many of my initial students in Russia are from St. Petersburg and each time I visit I ask about their welfare. It had been many years since my last visit and I was going through the list with Uttama-sloka and the devotee who led the local community, Achyutatma das, when I came upon the name of Krishna-jivani dasi.

'I haven't heard from Krishna-jivani in six years,' I said to Achyutatma. 'She was my secretary in Russia in the early 1990s.

She and her mother, Dhara dasi, are both my disciples and in 2003 I took them to India for our parikrama in the month of Kartika. At that time Krishna-jivani could barely walk because she had caught a disease the previous year. Where is she now?'

'Sometimes her mother comes to the programmes,' said Achyutama, 'but we never see Krishna-jivani. She and her mother share a flat, but Krishna-jivani can't walk now so she never goes out. Sometimes devotees visit her, but mostly she lives a reclusive life. They're quite poor, living on a small government pension.'

When we arrived at the hall for the programme, I was surprised to see Dhara approaching.

'Welcome back to St. Petersburg, Gurudeva,' she said.

'Dhara! We were just talking about you,' I said. 'How are you?'

'I'm well,' she said, 'but I'm quite old now. Eighty-three, to be exact.'

'And how is Krishna-jivani? It's been so long since I've heard from her,' I said.

Dhara's expression became serious. 'She's fifty-four now and she hasn't left our flat in six years.'

'Six years!' I repeated somewhat shocked.

Dhara nodded, her eyes welling with tears. 'Yes,' she said, 'and she can't walk at all now.'

'I'm so sorry,' I said. 'What is your address? Can we visit you tomorrow afternoon?'

Dhara's face brightened. 'Yes, we would be honoured. Thank you so much,' she said.

The next afternoon, we were getting ready to visit Dhara and Krishna-jivani.

'Let's take that jar of honey,' I said to Uttama-sloka, 'and some of those sweet balls the devotees gave me yesterday. There's also a carton of milk in the fridge and some yogurt. And take that pen-and-pencil set I got yesterday.'

On the drive to their apartment, I prepared myself for a sobering experience. The first shock came when we pulled up in front of the building.

'Look at this place!' said Mahavan. 'It's so run down.'

'Now look, guys,' I said, 'I want you to be really positive when we're in there. Don't get caught up in their dejection. We're here to cheer them up.'

The elevator was broken so we walked up the five flights of dirty, smelly stairs and graffiti-covered walls. As we arrived at the door, I braced myself and knocked. Dhara answered with a sombre look on her face. 'Come in,' she said.

We took off our shoes and stood in the dimly-lit hallway.

'Where is Krishna-jivani?' I whispered.

'Come with me,' Dhara said. As we turned the corner into the one-room apartment, our eyes adjusted to the soft light from the window filtering through a white curtain. The room was sparsely decorated with only a few pieces of furniture, but it was immaculately clean. A large vase of flowers, looking opulent in the simple surroundings, stood to the side of a small altar that held only pictures of the Lord. Finally, my eyes came to rest on a lone figure sitting on the floor absorbed in chanting the holy names.

'Krishna-jivani,' I said softly. 'Is that you?'

She turned her face upward then opened her eyes and smiled radiantly. For a moment I was taken aback. It was not what I had expected. She seemed composed, sitting peacefully in a simple sari without make-up or jewellery. Her hair was cut short. She joined her palms and bowed her head as she offered me her respects.

'I'm so sorry to hear about your condition,' I said.

'There's nothing to be sorry about, Gurudeva,' she said with the same radiant smile. 'I'm fine.'

'But I can see that you're severely disabled,' I said.

'It's not a problem,' she said. 'It gives me more time to chant the holy names of God.'

'Well,' I said, looking for the right words to continue the conversation, 'how do you keep yourself engaged?'

'I chant,' she said.

'I mean after you've finished your daily two hours of chanting, what do you do?'

'Continue chanting,' she said.

'She chants day and night,' Dhara said, 'and sleeps only two or three hours a night. If she's not chanting, she's reading the scriptures.' I was struck by how Krishna-jivani had turned misfortune into fortune.

Krishna-jivani blushed a little. 'Mother,' she said, 'please don't say any more.'

'He's our spiritual master,' Dhara said, 'and he's entitled to know what you're doing.'

Krishna-jivani bowed her head.

'She's very austere. She eats only every two days or so and then not much more than a bowl of porridge. She's always been like that. When she was a little girl, I'd offer her and her sister cookies. Her sister would grab them, but Krishna-jivani just wanted porridge and with no sugar. Often, she'd just eat dry oats or buckwheat.

'She didn't want any toys and wouldn't wear anything but cast-offs. When she was three years old, she started singing songs in words we couldn't understand. One day a language professor from a local university visited us and was stunned to hear her singing. He told us she was chanting Sanskrit verses. She's always woken early, well before dawn, and taken cold baths. And she still takes cold baths,

even in winter. Whenever she's sick she fills the bathtub with freezing
water and lies there for hours at a time.

'She was an unusual girl. She never associated with boys and she
chose her friends carefully. When she grew up, she went to three
universities simultaneously and graduated with three different
degrees: medicine, Spanish and English. She never married and as
a qualified doctor she practised medicine for fourteen years. In 1991
she was out walking and met a devotee distributing books published
by the Hare Krishna movement. She wanted to buy one but had no
money on her. She came home, took some money and went back to
buy the books, but the boy had gone. She went out three days in a row
looking for him, but couldn't find him.

'One day her brother got some of the books from a friend. He
brought them home and she grabbed the books and immediately
began reading. The next morning, she started chanting. A week later
she moved out of our apartment and joined the temple, all the while
continuing her work. Six months later you came to St. Petersburg, and
you know the rest. She took initiation to formally become your student
and then in 1993 she gave up her medical career and became your
secretary in Russia, translating your letters to your Russian students.'

'That's amazing,' I said. 'I never knew those things about your life
before you became a devotee, Krishna-jivani.'

'She doesn't like to talk about herself,' Dhara said. 'And who would
she talk to anyway? She has just been sitting here and chanting twenty
hours a day, going on six years now. It's something we would all like to
do one day, but I worry about her. Her legs were bad when you took
us to India you know and the situation got much, much worse after
we returned.'

'I'm proud of you,' I said to Krishna-jivani. 'Others might have
been discouraged by the reversals you have faced. It's turned out to

be a mixed blessing. You use your time wisely, reading the scriptures and engaging in chanting meditation on the holy names. This will benefit you now and after your soul leaves this present body. One time Srila Prabhupada visited a sick disciple in a hospital in Mumbai. The young lady had a tropical disease and sat in bed chanting all day. When Srila Prabhupada arrived, she apologized and said that she couldn't do anything practical to help him in his fledgling movement. She was only able to chant. Srila Prabhupada said, "Actually, the goal is to chant continuously. It's the best glorification of God, but because you Western boys and girls are so restless, I have to create many other things for you to do'".

It was getting late and I had another programme to go to.

'I have to leave now,' I said with sadness, 'but I've been inspired by my visit here. Nothing encourages a spiritual teacher more than seeing their students making tangible advancement in Krishna consciousness. Krishna-jivani, you are setting a wonderful example for all of us. Is there anything I can do for you?'

'You are already doing everything for me,' she said. 'Please just bless me so I can chant the holy names purely. That's all I want.'

As we started to go, her hand was already back in her bead-bag, her eyes were closed and she was softly chanting the holy names with concentration. We stepped out of the apartment and into the stairwell and found ourselves back in the destitute world beyond their sanctuary.

'I don't know many people who could do what she's doing,' Uttama-sloka said. 'Where does she get the determination?'

I thought for a moment. 'Well,' I said, 'in the Bhagavad Gita Krishna reveals how an unsuccessful spiritual seeker takes another birth, but he or she revives the divine consciousness of their previous life and again tries to make further progress towards God. Her determination must be coming from a past birth; she has a strong desire not to return to the material world and to go back to the Lord's eternal spiritual abode.

'The fact that this is occurring here in Russia also shows that the philosophy of the Vedas is alive and well in this country. It may not be widespread as yet, but we have seen today that there are Russian people who have embraced the primary teachings of the Vedas—to dedicate oneself to the loving service of God—as the goal of their life. And in spite of Krishna-jivani's difficult life and her lack of material opulence, she is okay because she is in direct connection with the spiritual realm through the chanting of the holy name. Krishna-jivani has what everyone is looking for: happiness.'

One who falls from the path of yoga enjoys countless years in the heaves of the pious, and is then born on earth in a good and fortunate family. Or one is born in a family of transcendentalists full of wisdom. Such a birth is hard to find in this world. There one's former divine consciousness is reawakened and one strives further towards perfection.

—Lord Krishna in the Bhagavad Gita (6:41-43)

7

Sri Lanka

Feeding Survivors of the
Great 2004 Tsunami

Marco Polo described Sri Lanka as the finest island of its size in the world, and when I arrived in Colombo in January 2005, I could see why he had formed this opinion. Sri Lanka looked much like the exotic land described in the in-flight magazine I read on the flight from South Africa. The humidity, the endless array of rich green foliage, the luxuriant swirls of the Sinhalese alphabet, the multi-coloured Buddhist flags and the variety of fruits on sale all made for what seemed to be paradise.

However, I was arriving in Sri Lanka in one of the darkest months of its history. On the morning of 26 December 2004 just two weeks before I had arrived, a ten-metre-high wall of water created by an underwater earthquake, thousands of kilometres away in Indonesia, had ravaged much of the country's beautiful 1,340-kilometre-long coastline. The tsunami released energy that was equivalent to 40,000 Little Boy(s)—the atom bomb detonated over Hiroshima.

The undersea quake released power equal to a billion bolts of lightning. The explosion was so strong that studies show the earth might have wobbled on its axis by as much as two and a half centimetres and the length of the day altered by microseconds. So powerful was the earthquake that islands southwest of Sumatra (closest to the epicentre) moved by more than twenty metres. The quake created waves that fanned out and moved at speeds of up to 750 kilometres per hour across the ocean, eventually slamming into populated areas. The death toll of the deadly waves caused in the twelve countries around the Indian Ocean may never be known, but it is estimated that more than 200,000 people lost their lives and thousands of others were never found. Half a million were injured and millions left homeless.

Although Sri Lanka was indeed beautiful, I was not there to enjoy its beauty. I was there to assist the Sri Lankan chapter of ISKCON in its relief work. Like millions around the world, I had sat in disbelief as I read the news reports. The more the media revealed the suffering caused by the disaster, the more I began thinking of helping in the relief work. Although I am usually busy with various responsibilities, ironically at that moment I had the time.

I had planned to go to Durban, South Africa, just after the new year for a month-long break. The past twelve months had been particularly intense and I sorely needed time to recuperate my health. I also longed for time to engage in my personal spiritual practices, including reading the scriptures and chanting meditation. But when I had arrived in South Africa, I had received a call from Mahakarta das, the leader of the Colombo Hare Krishna community. He told me Hare Krishna devotees from around the world were willing to donate funds and to act as volunteers in relief work in Sri Lanka. And he offered me the opportunity to coordinate the relief effort.

Mahakarta briefed me on the situation as we drove to the temple from the airport. 'Since the tsunami hit, we have been distributing vegetarian food in several towns along the coast. But it's presently beyond our capacity to reach out effectively to the many victims of the catastrophe.'

'How many people have been affected here in Sri Lanka?' I asked.

'More than 33,000 have died,' he said. 'About 835,000 have been made homeless mainly in the southern and eastern coastal regions. The United Nations and numerous humanitarian organizations are working to give food, shelter and badly needed supplies in these districts, but aid distribution to some areas is being hampered by relations between the Sinhalese government and the Tamil Tiger rebels.'

I had an idea of the Sri Lankan political situation. By 2005, the country had been embroiled in a civil war for more than thirty years between the minority (18 per cent) Tamils in the north and the majority (74 per cent) Sinhalese in the south. More than 60,000 people had died until a ceasefire was agreed in 2002. The fragile truce had been threatened, however, due to Tamil dissatisfaction with alleged inaction over their demands for autonomy. The tension evaporated with the tsunami. Although bickering broke out when the government was accused of giving more foreign aid to the Sinhalese, both sides were preoccupied with burying their dead and caring for the survivors.

'We have to increase our food distribution,' Mahakarta said. 'Donors are sending a lot of funds and we're not yet making full use of them. And more importantly, people need that food!'

I agreed, but I was at a loss how to begin. Many relief organizations were already at work and the government had recently complained that some of the smaller groups were actually getting in the way. As destroyed roads were repaired and washed-out bridges rebuilt, tonnes of supplies were being shipped into the affected areas. Army personnel and doctors from around the world were setting up camps along the coast to help victims. Survivors were temporarily being moved into schools, sports stadiums, government buildings or tents. Plans were already underway for the reconstruction of villages; a law was quickly passed that no structures could be built within 500 metres of the shoreline—a precaution against future tsunamis.

It wouldn't be easy to just jump into such a professional, well-coordinated operation. The usual strategy used by the Hare Krishna food relief programme, Food for Life Global, was to drive to a downtown or other well-populated area and feed the homeless. But in Sri Lanka we would be working in a disaster zone. I phoned Food for Life Global director Priyavrata das to discuss a strategy. Together we came up with the idea of calling the Red Cross and offering our help. It seemed wise to join in already-successful efforts. But when I phoned, it became clear that we weren't the first to offer help.

'What particular contribution does your organization have to offer, sir?' asked the Red Cross secretary.

'We're prepared to cook and distribute hot meals, ma'am.'

'Give me your number and I'll call you back in an hour,' she said.

Forty-five minutes later my cell phone rang and the secretary said, 'I have made an appointment for you with the president's secretary at 4 p.m. today.'

'The presidential secretary of the Red Cross?' I asked.

'No sir, with the secretary of the President of Sri Lanka.'

'Oh yes, of course,' I replied, feigning nonchalance which I hoped hid my excitement and disbelief.

That afternoon, Mahakarta and I met the President's secretary, Mr Krishnan. Needless to say he was a little surprised when we entered his office in our robes.

'I am in charge of organizing the present relief work in our country,' he said, shaking my hand. 'I am dealing with the main disaster relief organizations, such as Oxfam, Care, Red Cross, Medecins Sans Frontieres, and UNICEF. Which organization do you represent?'

'Food for Life Global,' I replied, 'a food-relief charitable organization affiliated with the International Society for Krishna Consciousness. You can find out about us on our website.'

There was silence for a few minutes while the presidential secretary scanned the information on the website.

'This is quite impressive,' he said. 'So, you're saying your organization can distribute hot meals to the victims of the tsunami?'

'Yes sir. As you can see, we have a lot of experience doing this! It's vegetarian food—no meat, fish or eggs. Will people be inclined to eat that? I heard most of the tsunami victims were fishermen.'

'For now, that's not a problem,' he said. 'At the moment, the fishermen are not eating fish because they say the fish are eating the dead bodies of their relatives washed out to sea by the tsunami.'

'Oh, I see,' I said grimacing.

'How many can you feed daily?' he asked.

'Five thousand to begin with,' I replied. 'And more later.'

He picked up the phone and dialed a number. My eyebrows went up as he began to speak.

'Major-General Kulatuga? This is the presidential secretary. I understand you need help with food relief in the Matara district. I have a group of people here who can cook and distribute food for 5,000 people a day. They can increase that number as the weeks go by. Are you interested? Okay, I'll send them down immediately to discuss the details with you.'

The next day I set out by van with a few of the Hare Krishna volunteers who had arrived in Sri Lanka from around the world to help with our relief effort. We drove along the coastal road south towards the district of Matara, one of the worst affected areas. The mood in the car was upbeat. Within twenty-four hours of arriving in the country we had met the President's secretary, who had given us government authorization to distribute food in a designated area, and we were about to meet the military to discuss the logistics of distributing food to refugees. Forty-five minutes into our journey we rounded a bend on the winding coast road. Suddenly all of us became silent.

An entire village had been reduced to rubble. As our driver instinctively slowed down, we saw the destructive power of a tsunami. Not a house in the village was left standing, the entire place was a pile of broken concrete, twisted steel and splinters of glass and wood. The worst destruction I had ever seen was in Sarajevo, Bosnia, just after the end of the Balkan War. I thought I would never witness anything more terrible. But now my heart broke seeing people sitting dazed or crying in the ruins of what used to be their homes, twenty days after the tragedy.

We passed one home that was partially standing. The facade of the house had been ripped away revealing several bedrooms and in one, despite the force of the tsunami, children's clothes were neatly folded on shelves. We drove on through more villages and towns levelled by the tsunami and I realized we were witnessing something that was unprecedented in human history: an estimated 33,000 people had been killed in just under thirty seconds. There were fresh graves along the side of the road.

'There was no time to transport the bodies elsewhere,' said our driver. 'All of these roads were closed because of debris.'

Although Krishna says in Bhagavad Gita that devotees do not lament for the living or the dead because they understand that the soul is eternal, I felt genuine sadness for those people. Unable to offer any practical assistance at that moment I prayed they would have the opportunity for service to God, the panacea for all suffering in this material world.

After three hours of driving past crumbled homes, smashed cars, upturned boats and piles of rubble with untold pieces of household paraphernalia, I couldn't watch any longer. I took out my Bhagavad Gita to look for some words of comfort.

'From this day on,' I thought, 'if you entertain even the slightest desire to enjoy this world, you're simply a fool and the greatest hypocrite.'

'In this town 11,000 people died and 230 cars were washed out to sea,' our driver said as we drove through a village that to me was indistinguishable from the others we had already seen. I looked up and saw a little girl crying next to her mother on the steps of what must have been their home. I noticed that the traffic was moving slowly. There was none of the usual speeding and passing cars, the sound of engines roaring and the continuous honking that one generally experiences on Asian roads. Seemingly out of respect for the tsunami victims—living and dead—the traffic moved at a funereal pace.

A slight respite came sometime later, just before we turned off the road towards the army camp which was to be our base. Looking up from my reading, I saw a large black dog sitting in the ruins of a decimated house. I had noticed very few animals along the coast. Obviously, some had been swept away, while others, I was told, seemed to have anticipated the tsunami and run for shelter. Somehow this dog had survived and looked quite well. I asked the driver to slow down and I called out 'Hare Krishna!' to the animal. He heard me and ran excitedly towards the car. I waved as we passed him. A moment later I looked back and saw him sitting by the road wagging his tail, eyes still fixed on our car. Somehow our little exchange in the midst of all the sorrow had encouraged us both.

'In the worst of times,' I thought, 'a little love goes a long way. This dog is a spark of life in a landscape of death.'

A few minutes later we pulled into the army camp. The sergeant was waiting for us and quickly escorted us into a room with a large oval table surrounded by twelve chairs. Then Major-General Kulatuga entered, accompanied by six of his staff. Like Mr Krishnan the day before, he looked surprised to see our robes. The mood was formal as the major-general began his briefing. Standing with stick in hand, he pointed to the wall full of maps and charts.

'Here in Matara district there are 1,342 confirmed deaths, 8,288 people injured, 613 missing and 7,390 families without homes living in camps for displaced persons.'

Looking at me, he said in an emotional voice, 'We prefer not to call them refugee camps. They are our people, not refugees. Do you understand?'

With scenes of people sitting in their devastated homes still fresh in my mind, I replied, 'Yes sir. I do understand.' He nodded and continued.

'We are professional soldiers. We fought the Tamil Tigers for years. But now we are busy clearing the roads of debris, cleaning wells and repairing buildings. Our priorities are reopening the hospitals and schools, rebuilding the bridges and restoring communication. As of now 75 per cent of all telecommunication, 80 per cent of all contaminated water supplies, and 87 per cent of electricity have been restored.'

Looking at me again, he said, 'Your contribution will be to feed the people in camps for displaced persons. Mr Krishnan told me you can provide hot meals. Is that correct?'

'Affirmative sir,' I replied, automatically falling into the diction I used in the marines.

'You were a military man?' he asked.

'Yes sir,' I said with emphasis as a soldier does when addressing a superior officer.

Smiling, he nodded his head, obviously more comfortable with our cooperation.

'Now you will visit one of the camps so you can get an idea of what is happening. Major Janaka here,' he gestured to one of his staff, 'will take you to Rahula College about thirty minutes away. I believe we have over 1,000 displaced persons there. Everyone has lost one or more relatives and everyone has lost their home.'

When we walked into the camp, we were immediately the object of everyone's attention. Perhaps because of the humidity, only the children were active. Most adults sat about talking in small groups. I noticed a huge pile of clothes on the campus lawn, obviously donations, through which several people were rummaging. There was an improvised medical clinic in one classroom, where three members of the Red Cross were attending to a few infants. Five army soldiers obviously present at the camp for security, sat casually nearby.

It was a sober scene. Though the horror of the devastation was kilometres away on the beachfront, the reality was that these people had lost family members, homes and professions, and it showed in the look on their faces. When I smiled at one elderly couple sitting on the lawn, they stared back at me with no emotion. Others expressed their loss when I spoke with them.

'You can cook over here,' the major said, pointing to a nearby shed. Close to the site, I noticed a number of people cooking rice and vegetables on their own makeshift fires.

'Where are they getting their ingredients to cook?' I enquired from the major.

'We are providing them with ingredients,' he replied. 'All the camps in this area and around the country tend to provide basic provisions.'

I was taken aback. The media in the West had given the impression that victims of the tsunami were in desperate need of food.

'I thought people here were hungry, major.'

'They were in the initial stages of the disaster—for the first week,' he replied, 'but we have things under control now. The world has given us ample food, medicine and other supplies.'

'Then what part do we have to play?' I asked.

'You can help to lighten some of the burden. My men are overworked delivering supplies to the thirty-five camps in this region. We've been here for three weeks. All relief organizations have a part to play and every effort helps in serving the people who survived the tsunami. The government will be grateful for anything you can do, I assure you.'

'We'll play our part,' I said shaking his hand. 'We'll begin in three days.'

The day after returning to Colombo from our trip to Matara we quickly busied ourselves for the relief work ahead. We used funds donated from overseas to purchase the basics required for cooking: tonnes of rice, dal and vegetables, as well as spices, five huge new pots and various cooking utensils.

Ten devotees loaded everything on a government lorry, piled into a van themselves and returned to southern Sri Lanka, ready to begin serving daily meals to 5,000 displaced persons. Many people in the camp helped us gather wood for cooking, and they also helped us cut vegetables. The major arranged trucks for us to go out and distribute food to several camps in the area each day.

Once the cooking operation was up and running in the capable hands of our team, I and three others headed to the east coast of Sri Lanka to see if there was a need for food distribution there.

The thirteen-hour drive took us through a hilly area and across a 100-kilometre-long plain to the ocean. The horrors that I had witnessed in the southern coast seemed far away as we drove through the picturesque interior jungle. The winding road took us through some of the most beautiful scenery I have ever seen. The well-maintained road serviced the many tourists who flocked to Sri Lanka before and just after the war. An astonishing variety of colourful birds soared through the humid air, their beautiful colours clashing splendidly with the deep green jungle foliage. A tropical climate and diversity of habitats endow Sri Lanka with an abundance of bird life.

We passed nearby Kandy, which is the second biggest city on the island and the Sinhalese cultural and spiritual headquarters. In the centre of the city is a beautiful lake and on its northern shores sits Sri Dalada Maligawa, the Temple of the Tooth. This temple enshrines an original tooth of Lord Buddha, reputed to have been snatched from His funeral pyre in 543 BC and smuggled into Sri Lanka in the hair of a princess some 900 years later.

'How do we know when we're in Tamil Tiger territory?' I asked the driver.

'You'll know,' he said with a laugh.

Hours later, as twilight was settling in I drifted off to sleep but was rudely shaken awake by the jerking motion of our car bouncing up and down on the road.

'What's going on?' I asked the driver.

'We're now in Tamil Tiger territory,' he grinned.

Sticking my head outside the widow, I saw potholes in the road every few metres. The asphalt was cracking everywhere and there were few road signs giving proper directions.

'It's a different world from here on,' our driver said. 'Some parts of the area are patrolled by government forces … and others by Tamil Tigers.'

Sure enough, within minutes we came to a government army checkpoint barricaded with barbed wire. Soldiers came over to our van and shone their flashlights in. Not knowing exactly what to do, I simply smiled. To my surprise they all smiled back.

'They know you're here for relief work,' said the driver. 'Few tourists come this way anymore.'

'I can understand why,' I replied.

Just after midnight we arrived at our final destination: a small village near Batticaloa on the far-eastern shore of Sri Lanka. After being in the stuffy van all day, I wanted some fresh air. I was about to ask the driver if he could take me the short distance to the beach so I could take a walk. Then I remembered that it would be a terrible scene of devastation, like the other places along the coast.

We met a local Hindu priest with whom we had a prearranged meeting. He took us to a wedding hall across from a Ganesh temple where we were to rest that night. Inside there was a small light shining, and I was surprised to see many men sleeping on the floor.

'They're fishermen who lost their homes and families in the tsunami,' the priest said.

As I set up my mosquito net huge clashes of thunder pounded outside. Soon rain started pouring down. I quickly fell asleep, exhausted by the day's long journey. When I woke up the next morning, the fishermen were already up and cooking their breakfast in a corner of the hall. We bathed at the well outside.

The local priest acted as our translator when we visited the camps for displaced persons later in the day. I asked the priest if the people were getting enough food.

'Food is not the problem here,' he told us. 'Although the government has done little to help us, our people from the interior, unaffected by the tsunami, have been giving sufficient rice and dal. The Indian government has also sent several shiploads of the same. The real problem here is that most of the victims of the tsunami are suffering from trauma. People are still in shock. At least twice a week rumours circulate that another tsunami is coming, and people panic. They grab their children and belongings and run out of the camps screaming.

'Are you trained in dealing with trauma?' he asked me.

'No,' I replied, 'but perhaps we could go and sing with them.'

When we got out of the car at the first camp, I slung the mridang drum we were carrying in the car over my shoulder, just in case there was an opportunity to chant with the people. I noticed a distinct difference in this camp compared with those on the south coast. Some 700 people milled about. Things appeared much less orderly. There were no Red Cross representatives or army personnel. People seemed disoriented. A number had bandaged injuries. One woman's face was just beginning to heal from a bad burn. Sadness seemed to hover over the camp like a dark monsoon cloud.

Walking straight into the middle of the camp, I asked for a chair and sat down. The people started to gather around us. I began to sing Hare Krishna and played the drum as accompaniment. Within moments the whole camp was listening. As the tempo built up, I indicated that the people should clap along, which they began to do enthusiastically. After ten minutes I stopped.

'I can see they love the singing,' I said to the priest. 'They're clapping, but they're not chanting. Why is that?'

'They don't worship Krishna here,' he said. 'But they worship Ramachandra, the incarnation of God who appeared as a king. After all, this is Lanka, where the great demon Ravana lived and it is here that Rama defeated him.'

I began kirtan again, but this time I sang of Lord Rama: 'Raghupati Raghava Raja Ram, Patita Pavana Sita Ram.'

Sure enough, the people responded by smiling and chanting along. As the kirtan got faster some people started dancing. After twenty minutes I brought the kirtan to a close. The atmosphere was relaxed and joyful.

'Everyone looks so happy!' the priest exclaimed.

'Chanting the Lord's names provides relief from suffering,' I said. 'We have a famous phrase: chant and be happy. Today we have seen that in action!'

I stayed in Sri Lanka for several weeks, assisting people in whatever way I could. One thought kept coming back to me throughout my time there. It was a single line from a recording my spiritual master had made almost four decades earlier. I'd heard it a thousand times, but it had more relevance now: 'The whole show is only temporary.' It was true of both the good and bad aspects of the world.

Fortunately, Srila Prabhupada had also introduced me to the positive alternative: spiritual life. My experience in Sri Lanka gave my spiritual practices much more significance. By the time I left, I counted my blessings each day and found myself seeking more shelter in the daily spiritual activities that I had come to take for granted over years. In that sense, the tragedy of the tsunami started a renaissance in my spiritual life.

Those who understand the teaching of the soul, nature and the qualities of nature, regardless of their present state, will not be born again.

—Lord Krishna in the Bhagavad Gita (13:24)

8

International Airspace

Chanting in an In-Flight Emergency

I spend a lot of time in airports and on airplanes, places that are transient and almost seem to function as independent spaces between clearly defined nations. In early 2008, while waiting in transit in Atlanta en route to Chile from Los Angeles, I found myself at a boarding gate so crowded that I could find a seat only in front of a large television screen. I took the seat reluctantly because I don't like to engage myself in the media; I prefer wherever possible to try to absorb my consciousness in spiritual practice, especially when travelling, through chanting meditation or reading scripture. But the television was on loud, and sitting directly in front of it I could not escape the news it was broadcasting.

The news segment was about a woman who had become ill on a recent flight across the United States. When the woman asked a flight attendant for oxygen, she was apparently refused. When she asked again the flight attendant saw her desperation and tried to administer oxygen, but the oxygen bottle malfunctioned. Shortly afterwards the woman died. The broadcast continued to say that the airline was defending its actions, but it seemed obvious that there was negligence on the part of the cabin crew. The report concluded with advice on what to do if a passenger fell ill on a flight. 'Call the flight attendant, administer oxygen and try to keep the patient calm,' said a special guest on the show.

'How awful,' I thought. 'What a horrific thing to go through on a flight.'

I boarded the plane and took my seat, chanting quietly on my beads. I had been upgraded from economy to business class because of my frequent-flier points. The passengers seated around me all appeared affluent. Dressed in my renunciate's robes, I could sense that my presence made several of them uncomfortable. Nearby, a woman who was filing her nails looked at me suspiciously. The man seated next to her was reading *The Wall Street Journal*; he glanced up at me and shook his head disapprovingly. The lady next to me ignored me when I asked if this was her first flight to Santiago.

So as not to attract more attention than I already was getting, I put my beads aside and took out a book to read. As the last remaining passengers boarded the plane, the cabin crew went about their final duties before closing the cabin door. I smiled politely as the flight attendants from our cabin milled about making last-minute arrangements before take-off.

'Cabin crew, please be seated for take-off,' came the captain's voice over the loudspeaker.

Without warning, the man seated across the aisle from me next to his wife, started shaking uncontrollably. His eyes rolled back and he started foaming at the mouth. His wife shrieked in fear. My first thought was that he was having either a stroke or a heart attack. I quickly looked around to see if there were any flight attendants present, but they had all gone to the back of the aircraft. The passengers around me sat frozen in shock. The woman doing her nails held the file motionless above one finger. The man reading the newspaper stared in horror as the sick man started to fall out of his seat.

The scene was surreal. I had just watched a television report on in-flight medical emergencies, and now here was one happening before me. I jumped up and grabbed the man and carefully laid him down in the aisle.

'Sir,' I said to him in the calmest voice I could, 'can you hear me? Roll over onto your side.'

His eyes were closing. He appeared to be losing consciousness.

I glanced over my shoulder. Everyone was still immobile, their comfortable reality shaken by the ugly scene before them. The man's wife was crying.

'Somebody, call a flight attendant!' I shouted. The woman who had been sitting next to me closed her eyes. Others turned their heads away and looked out the windows, as if wishing they could remove themselves from what was unfolding in front of them if they simply didn't look.

'Is he epileptic?' I asked the man's wife.

'No, no,' she said frantically.

'Is he on some kind of medication?' I asked.

'No!' she said, shaking her head.

'Does he have a history of heart problems?' I asked, trying to breathe deeply.

'Please save him!' she screamed.

The man gasped for breath. I tried to position him so he could breathe easier. I also began to chant, softly at first but louder and louder as it appeared he might die. I looked up at the nearby passengers, who were still sitting frozen. I had to do something to get them to help.

'Oxygen!' I yelled. 'For Christ's sake! Somebody get a goddamn oxygen bottle or this man is going to die!'

Two men jumped up and ran towards the galley. Seconds later they returned with an oxygen bottle. All three of us struggled to get it working, and I put the mask on the man's face. All of this had unfolded in what must have been less than a minute or two.

Then, from the corner of my eye I saw several flight attendants racing down the aisle. They took control of the situation, administering the oxygen and calling for medical assistance. The captain arrived and called for a defibrillator (a device used in emergency treatment of heart attacks). Because of the cramped space, I was unable to move out of the way and sat pinned in the middle of the frantic scene. The man continued shaking, flailing his arms and grimacing in pain.

I couldn't offer any more practical help, but because I knew the man's life was in danger, I continued chanting clearly so that he could hear every syllable of God's names. It is said that if an embodied being, whether human or animal, hears the holy name of the Lord at the time of their death they will be taken to a better birth where they can continue their spiritual journey in their next life. And they even have a chance to escape the cycle of birth and death once and for all by returning to the spiritual realm through the power of the holy name.

At one point he briefly came to consciousness and our eyes met. I wanted to tell him that everything was going to be alright, but I sensed this wasn't the case. I leaned forward and chanted even louder hoping that, should he leave his body he would be fortunate enough to hear the names of the Lord. I kept wondering when a medical team would arrive.

When they finally did after what seemed like an eternity, I stood up and sat in the man's seat while the rescue team put him on a stretcher and quickly took him away. His wife followed. By that time, he was almost motionless.

'He may not make it,' I overheard one of the flight attendants say.

I returned to my seat and took out my beads to chant on. I no longer cared whether those around me found it disturbing or strange. My heart was still beating strongly and my adrenaline was surging. A flight attendant offered me a glass of water. I drank it and took some deep breaths. When I looked around the cabin, the woman who had been filing her nails smiled at me gently as if to indicate she was grateful for what I had done. The man with the newspaper nodded his head in approval. The lady sitting next to me leaned over and spoke softly.

'Thank you,' she said.

The plane took off and I soon fell asleep, exhausted from the ordeal. By the time I woke up most of the passengers around me were sleeping. I sat up in the dark and thought about the incident.

'We never know,' I thought. 'We never know when such a thing will happen to us. We see things like this on the news and we always assume it only happens to others. I pray that when my time comes, there will be somebody to chant the holy names for me as well.'

The more I thought about it, the more I realized that because I often travel alone, I may very well be by myself or with a group of strangers when I leave this world. The thought of dying from a heart attack in a plane 12,000 metres in the air or in bed at night alone in some far-flung country was unsettling. Even the most forewarned departure can be an embarrassing affair. Death is difficult for everyone.

'When that day comes,' I thought, 'I hope I'll be remembered for my service and not for the way I died.'

I thought about a story I had heard recently. A person was asked how his friend had passed away. 'Don't ask me how he died,' he answered. 'Ask me how he lived.'

Nine hours later our flight landed in Santiago. As the passengers disembarked, the head purser approached me in my seat and asked if I could remain behind for a few minutes. I sat patiently and when all the other passengers had left, she returned with several other flight attendants.

'We wanted to thank you for your quick action in helping that man,' she said. 'You may have saved his life.'

'I'm happy I could help,' I replied, 'although I didn't do that much. It was all of you who gave him the medical attention he needed.'

'What we really appreciated,' said one of the flight attendants, 'was the calming effect you had on everyone. When you were chanting, it felt like everything was going to be alright.'

'Yes,' said one of her colleagues. 'It was very special, so comforting.'

'What exactly were you singing?' asked the purser.

'I was singing the names of God,' I replied. 'I follow a faith from India where God is called Krishna. India's ancient scriptures say that wherever God's name is chanted there's nothing to fear.'

'We certainly have experienced that now, haven't we?' she said.

The group all nodded in agreement. 'Thank you,' one of them said.

'It wasn't me,' I replied. 'It was the Lord's holy name. So, the next time something terrible happens, remember to sing Hare Krishna.'

'Can you write the song down for us?' the purser asked. 'We want to be able to remember it.'

Always chanting My glories, endeavouring with great determination, bowing down before Me, great souls perpetually worship Me with devotion.

—Lord Krishna in the Bhagavad Gita (9:1)

9

Indonesia

The Vedic Roots of Bali's Mother Temple

When I looked out the airplane window as we circled in preparation for landing in Bali I was stunned by the beauty of the island from the air. It looked like a greenish-coloured pearl set in a shimmering blue oyster shell. The plane touched the ground and I was struck by the lushness of the tropical green foliage. I had read in an in-flight magazine that in Bali the temperature varies only a couple of degrees throughout the year, the flowers bloom without cessation and there are no wild beasts, poisonous snakes or spiders, or cyclones.

'Like heaven on earth,' I thought. It would be easy in such a pristine atmosphere to become distracted by the beauty of this world. I was to see in the days to come that the only real danger on the heavenly isle of Bali was that the idyllic nature of the place could make a spiritual seeker forget the transient nature of this world.

I had been to Bali only once before, fifteen years ago. At that time the Hare Krishna movement had been suppressed by the local Hindus, many of whom were demigod worshippers and saw our worship of Krishna as a threat. Fifteen years ago, public chanting and devotional gatherings had been banned and devotees had had to meet in secret. The situation had eventually been resolved through meetings and agreements for cooperation between our movement and the local Hindu community leaders.

Though Bali is 6,000 kilometres from present day India, Vedic culture has been there for thousands of years. Eighty-seven per cent of Balinese people practice a form of Hinduism that is a combination of local beliefs on the one hand, and influences of the Hinduism of India and other Southeast Asian cultures on the other. My intention while in Bali was to see what evidence I could find of India's ancient culture that had existed in Bali for centuries.

My guide during my stay in Bali was Padma Lochan das, one of the leaders of the Hare Krishna community there. He took me to various parts of the island throughout my stay, and everywhere I saw temples. Along some of the roads we took, the jungle was thick and often looked impenetrable. Once in a while I'd see crystal-clear waterfalls flowing into large pools. Monkeys played on the rocks, colourful birds flew in and out of the trees, and butterflies fluttered around. Many of the temples that I saw were constructed in the open Balinese style and all had fresh fruit offerings on the altars.

'There are more than 11,000 temples in Bali,' Padma Lochan told me.

'Are they very old?' I asked.

'Some of them are several hundred years old,' he replied.

'Not so old, then,' I said.

'The people here don't know very much about Krishna,' he said. 'At almost all the temples in Bali they worship demigods, ancestors and ghosts. They worship the ghosts so they won't disturb them. Do you see all these little offerings along the paths in front of the houses?

They're called yajna-sesus. They're for the ghosts.' I saw offerings of
fruits and flowers as well as cigarettes and wine in the leaf cups. The
latter were certainly not something I was used to seeing presented as
offerings!

In every village I noticed that in the centre of the traffic circles
were large dioramas depicting pastimes of the Lord from the Indian
epics the Ramayana and Mahabharata. In one place I saw Lord
Ramachandra, incarnation of Krishna and hero of the Ramayana,
engaged in battle with the demon king Ravana. In another, the saintly
princess Draupadi was depicted with her five Pandava husbands, the
great devotees of Lord Krishna in the Mahabharata. I realized that
although the dioramas were not ancient, they offered proof that these
scriptures were part of the culture of the island and that, therefore, the
roots of Vedic culture had existed in Bali for millennia. With this kind
of art all over the island, it would be easy to remember God, I thought.

One bridge that we passed over boasted ferocious carved figures
dressed in colourful, fresh cloth at each end.

'Who are they?' I asked.

'Minor deities who protect the traveller,' said Padma Lochan. 'The
people take good care of the deities, as you can see, and in turn they
believe the deities take good care of them.'

I was impressed that the Balinese recognized the forces of nature
as personal, and that they worshipped the controlling deities behind
every aspect of the natural world. However, I felt disappointed
that they didn't seem to understand there was a supreme God who
ultimately controlled everything and to whom everyone, including
those deities controlling the natural world, owed allegiance. However,
I concluded that there was no need to criticize the people's worship of
demigods. I didn't doubt that tourists to Bali could see such worship
as uncivilized, but in fact such worship showed a more advanced

understanding than that of modern science, which says everything is happening by chance.

'What I can offer to others here in Bali, as a devotee of Krishna,' I thought, 'is the understanding that if we simply worship Krishna, we please all the demigods, who are His devotees.'

The next day after Padma Lochan and I performed our japa chanting meditation on the beach, I sat and considered that if the Vedic culture actually flourished in Bali thousands of years ago there must be evidence of worship of Krishna or maybe Vishnu—for the worship of demigods and the worship of the Supreme Personality of Godhead have always existed simultaneously in Vedic culture.

'You mentioned there are thousands of temples in Bali,' I said to Padma Lochan, 'but all I've seen is worship of the demigods and ghosts. Is there a temple where Vishnu is worshipped?'

'Yes,' he replied. 'Pura Besakih. We call it the Mother Temple. It's the most sacred place in Bali. Brahma, Vishnu and Siva are all worshipped there.'

'Wow!' I said, 'that's what I've wanted to hear. Is it also several hundred years old, like the other temples we've seen?'

'No,' Padma Lochan said. 'It's 1,700 years old.'

I was speechless. 'That's the proof I need,' I finally said. 'It would support the Bhagavatam, which says Vedic culture was once spread worldwide.'

'It takes some time to get there,' Padma Lochan warned. 'It's on Mount Agung, a live volcano. But don't worry. The last time it erupted was in 1964. Many tourists go to see the temple, although there are some places they are not allowed. It's actually a large complex of many temples, like a small version of Angkor Wat in Cambodia.

'We should go tomorrow,' he added, 'because it's an auspicious day. There is a festival there every six months. Many Balinese make the pilgrimage on those days to pray. The people believe that God spared the temple during the eruption. The lava came within metres of the temple complex but caused no damage to any structures. Nearby, entire villages were wiped out. One thousand people perished.'

That evening there was a programme at ISKCON's Sandipani Muni temple in Denpasar. When I arrived, hundreds of devotees were waiting. In the lecture I discussed how all beauty in this world is temporary and ultimately has to be renounced. But I stressed that real renunciation was engaging everything in God's service and that the devotees could use the natural opulence of the island to glorify Krishna.

After the class a devotee approached me and said, 'We utilize the beauty of our beaches in the service of God by going to chant there every Saturday for the tourists.' When he showed me his photographs, I was surprised to see Australian and European tourists chanting Hare Krishna and dancing with the devotees on the beach. I congratulated him for bringing spiritual life to the attention of the sun seekers.

Early the next day we left for Pura Besakih. On the long drive through mountainous terrain covered by jungle on all sides, I marvelled that worship at the temple had been continuing for 1,700 years. I could hardly wait to take in the surroundings and the opportunity to find evidence of a Vedic connection in Bali's past. Eventually we arrived at a parking area just a kilometre from the temple.

'The tradition is to walk the last kilometre,' said Padma Lochan. 'Walking up the hill provides time to reflect on the greatness of God and how we are His humble servants.'

The climb was steep and it was hot and humid. I struggled on the last part until we crossed over a little rise. Suddenly the gigantic temple came into view, framed by the beauty of the jungle behind it.

'My God!' I exclaimed. 'I've never seen anything like this.'

We walked the final 200 metres and after catching our breath continued up a long flight of steps leading to the first assortment of temple structures. The antiquity of the site was overwhelming. I could hear priests making offerings in the temples. Like the other temples I had seen in Bali, they were not closed structures but open-sided and approachable from all angles.

As we walked around the large complex, I was awestruck by the unique architecture. Finally, we came to an opening that led into a vast courtyard where I could see many priests offering oblations.

'Tourists can't go in, only the faithful,' said Padma Lochan. 'And beyond here, where they worship the demigods, is the temple of Vishnu.'

'That's what I came to see,' I said eagerly. 'Will they let me through since I'm dressed in my robes?'

'We can try,' he said.

I put my hand in my bead-bag and started chanting loudly as we entered the compound. Padma Lochan put a traditional Balinese hat on my head. Several priests looked at me suspiciously. I chanted louder. Then, halfway across the compound, an elderly priest approached and said something in Balinese to Padma Lochan.

'Oh well,' I thought, 'it was a good try.'

But Padma Lochan smiled. 'If you want to pass through this complex,' he said, 'you must pray to the demigods. He wants you to offer these items.' The priest put out a mat with several items of worship including incense, a candle, fruit and spices.

'A strict Vaishnava doesn't worship demigods, but only worships God,' I thought. 'But if I don't offer some worship, I'll never make it to the temple of Lord Vishnu.'

The priest was becoming uncomfortable with my hesitation. Suddenly I had an idea. I had recently been reading the scripture

Srimad Bhagavatam in which the cowherd girls of Vrindavan offer prayers to a demigoddess, Katyayani Devi, so that she will bring them closer to Krishna. I had learned the Sanskrit prayer by heart, and so I now said that prayer aloud while offering the articles the priest presented to me.

The priest was impressed, and after giving us some holy water to drink, he happily sent us on our way to the temple of Vishnu. We walked through the courtyard and then up several flights of steps, finally reaching the top of the hill on which the entire temple complex was situated. From there we had a direct view of the volcano, Mount Agung.

'It must have been terrifying when it exploded,' I said.

'It's still very active,' said Padma Lochan. 'From time to time it belches thick smoke and ash. It's only a matter of time until it explodes again.'

When we finally entered the Vishnu temple, I was surprised to find we were the only pilgrims there.

'They mostly worship Shiva, the universal destroyer, and not Vishnu as supreme here in Pura Besakih,' said Padma Lochan.

'I'm sure it wasn't always like that,' I said. 'Just look at this magnificent temple, the intricacy of the stonework. At some point Vishnu must have been the principal deity here.'

Suddenly from around the back of the temple an elderly man, obviously the temple priest, appeared dressed in white. He offered a bowl of fruit on the altar to Vishnu and said some prayers. I waited patiently and when he was finished approached him.

'Sir,' I said with the help of Padma Lochan's translation, 'we are devotees of Lord Vishnu, or Krishna. We are touched to see you making an offering to Him with such devotion. How long have you been a priest at this temple?'

'Since I was a boy,' he replied. 'My father was a priest here, and his father and his father.'

'How old are you?' I asked.

'Eighty-three,' he replied.

'You don't look that old,' I said.

'A lady who lives in my village is 225 years old,' he said. 'She was born in 1783. In previous generations, many people here lived for well over 200 years.'

'How is that possible?' I asked.

'They worked hard in the fields,' he said. 'They drank water from the streams, they ate mainly rice and vegetables, and they visited this temple every day. They were happy, but none of us will live forever. What's important is where you'll go when you die.'

'Where do you hope to go when you die?' I asked, eager for the realization of one who had served the Lord his entire life.

'With Him, of course,' he said gesturing towards the altar.

'We have to go,' I said. 'Your darsan was worth the entire trip here. We're happy to have seen this ancient temple which stands as evidence that India's spiritual culture once reached far beyond its present borders and, most important, is still producing men of your calibre, full of faith in God.'

I am in everyone's heart as the Supersoul. As soon as one desires to worship some demigod, I make his faith steady so that he can devote himself to that particular deity. Endowed with such a faith, he seeks favours of a particular demigod and obtains his desires. But in actuality these benefits are bestowed by Me alone.

—Lord Krishna in the Bhagavad Gita (7:21-22)

10

Bhutan

Gross National Happiness in the Himalayas

Bhutan might appear an odd place for a Hare Krishna monk to visit, given that it's a Buddhist country. I take seriously my renunciate's vow to travel far and wide in the service of others and in my own spiritual quest. Proselytizing is forbidden in Bhutan, but I had no intention of proselytizing. I wanted to go for the sake of interfaith exchange and because I wanted to learn about something peculiar to Bhutan: gross national happiness.

Gross national happiness is a unique Bhutanese principle whereby development in society takes place when material and spiritual advancement complement and reinforce one another. Prior to booking my ticket, I had read that the government and the people of Bhutan were careful to maintain their ancient spiritual culture while slowly introducing material progress. The article I was reading reported that their king had said that gross national happiness was more important than gross domestic product (GDP), and that 45.2 per cent of

Bhutanese reported being very happy, 51.6 per cent happy, and only 3.2 per cent unhappy. That the ancient Bhutanese culture exists on such a large scale in modern times intrigued me, and I believed that the spiritual organization I served, ISKCON, could learn from that.

Exiting the terminal at Paro, the city that hosts Bhutan's only international airport, I was met by my friend and travelling companion Sri Prahlada das, as well as by Sakhi Rai das, one of my senior students from Australia, and by Tshering Sonam our Bhutanese tour guide. A guide was not optional. Bhutan had taken a cautious approach to the number of foreign tourists it allowed, understanding the effects mass tourism could have on its environment, culture and identity. All tourists were obliged to visit via a government-approved travel agency.

I had admired the mountains that stretched as far as the eye could see on my descent into Bhutan, but on the one-hour drive from Paro to Thimphu, the Bhutanese capital, I discovered that there is not a straight road to be found. The roads were narrow and winding along mountainsides with steep ravines. For the next ten days I never managed to conquer my fear of the vertical drops off the side of the roads.

Our first destination was the Thimphu Chorten, a large national memorial stupa, a mound-like monument housing relics associated with the Buddha and often used as a place of prayer and meditation. As we entered the grounds, I saw many people circumambulating the stupa, a practice followed by the faithful on auspicious days to gain spiritual merit. Fifty or sixty pilgrims dressed in traditional Bhutanese clothes were going around the stupa chanting the age-old Buddhist mantra: om mani padme hum (I offer my respects to the jewel within the lotus).

'Who do Buddhists understand to be the jewel within the lotus?'
I asked Tshering Sonam.

'We understand that it is Lord Buddha on the lotus,' he replied.

Both at the stupa and as we drove towards our hotel, I was
surprised to see that everyone wore traditional clothes.

'Is today a special day?' I asked. 'Everyone seems dressed up.'

Tshering Sonam laughed. 'No,' he said. 'We dress like this every
day. It's part of our culture. Bhutanese law requires all citizens to wear
traditional dress in public areas. Men wear a knee-length robe tied at
the waist called a gho, and women wear an ankle-length dress called
a keyra.'

'Look at all the buildings,' said Sakhi Rai. 'They're all so artistic
and beautiful.'

'This is another of Bhutan's cultural regulations,' Tshering Sonam
said. 'All new buildings, public and private, must follow the designs
and rules of traditional architecture. It's one of the ways we safeguard
our culture. You'll see throughout the country that the wooden
beams, the windows and the doors of the houses are painted with
floral, animal and religious motifs. In this way we are reminded of the
Buddha throughout our daily affairs.'

What he said was true. Every structure had a special charm to
it. What's more, I could see that religion was highly visible in every
aspect of life in Bhutan. On almost every mountain ridge I saw
a temple, and at every mountain pass I saw stupas and thousands
of colourful prayer flags. Prayer wheels, large enclosed wheels with
prayers written on rolled paper, seemed especially prevalent. It is said
that by turning the wheel one achieves the same spiritual piety as
reciting the prayers themselves. I saw many people turning the wheels
while at the same time praying on their beads.

'Double the benefit,' said Tshering Sonam with a smile.

That night I had great difficulty sleeping and when I finally did fall asleep, I found myself waking up and gasping for air. In the morning I had a pounding headache and felt nauseous, a feeling that only increased as we started out for our next destination, Phobjikha, which was 130 kilometres east. We were told that the journey would take five hours because of the mountainous terrain.

'We are a country of short distances with long journeys,' said Tshering Sonam. Then, seeing my suffering, he added, 'Bhutan is at a high altitude. We're at almost 3,000 metres. The altitude affects people in different ways. You will adjust, I promise.'

When we finally arrived in Phobjikha we walked up a mountain trail to Gangtey Goenpa, a Buddhist monastery built in the sixteenth century. The trail was steep and winding.

'How long will it take to get up to the monastery?' I asked Tshering Sonam. Already I was gasping for breath.

'It's a two-hour walk,' he said. 'It's the only way in. There are no roads to the monastery. That would defeat the purpose. The monks live there in isolation so they can focus on their rituals and prayers. They will be chanting mantras when we arrive. We should move faster.'

But Sri Prahlada, Sakhi Rai and I couldn't go more than a few steps without stopping to catch our breath. It took us three hours to complete the two-hour walk.

As we entered the sacred temple I was stunned by the scene before me. It looked much the same as it must have in the sixteenth century. Seventy or eighty monks of different ages, sitting in lotus positions, were chanting from memory hundreds, or perhaps thousands of verses from ancient palm-leaf scriptures at their feet. The only light came from small windows. The guru, a large man with a shaved head, sat on an elevated seat leading the rhythmic chanting. To keep the rhythm, several monks played on drums that looked like they had been there as long as the monastery. Other monks played large brass cymbals. Two young monks, around ten years old, blew on long brass trumpets.

The guru saw me and motioned for me to sit down among the monks. I took out my japa beads and began chanting the Hare Krishna mantra, while studying the monks around me. I was deeply impressed. They were all so focussed, intent on their spiritual practices and deeply absorbed in their faith. As the minutes turned into an hour, I felt a transformation coming over me, an awakening of the same determination they displayed. Amid the hum of the prayers, the beating of the gongs and cymbals, and the trumpeting of the horns, I found myself fixed on every syllable of the mantra I was chanting.

Then suddenly, without warning, everything stopped. The monks sat silently in meditation for several minutes, then opened their eyes as one of the younger monks came around with water and rice. He moved quickly from student to student, pouring a little water into each monk's cup and scooping a little rice into the monk's bowl. The guru motioned for him to bring me a cup of water and a bowl of rice as well. The monks finished their meal within sixty seconds and the mantras and prayers began again.

'Shall we go now?' Tshering Sonam whispered in my ear.

'I don't know,' I said. 'This is a very deep experience for me.'

'If you want to stay, you'll have to stay for six hours,' he said. 'They have two six-hour sessions a day. Once you sit down, you must finish the session. It would be very impolite if you left.'

Feeling a bit embarrassed, I prepared to leave. But just as I was going out, the guru signalled for me to come over. When I reached his sitting place, he took a thread from an old box and tied it around my right hand. Then he touched a palm-leaf scripture to my head.

When he saw my bead-bag he indicated he wanted see my beads. As I took them out his eyes opened wide and said something to me. Tshering Sonam rushed forward to translate.

'They are much used,' he said.

'Yes,' I replied. 'I have had them for many years.'

'And what is your faith?' he asked.

'I am a practising Vaishnava,' I said. 'And I chant names of God on these beads.'

'Which names?' he said.

'The names of Lord Krishna,' I said. 'Hare Krishna, Hare Krishna, Krishna Krishna, Hare Hare, Hare Rama, Hare Rama, Rama Rama, Hare Hare.'

He nodded. 'May the blessings of Buddha be upon you,' he said.

No one watched us go, so concentrated were the monks on their meditation.

On the long descent back down the mountain trail we had a discussion about the relationship between faiths.

'Vaishnavas offer their respects to all classes of transcendentalists,' I said. 'We don't embrace their teachings, but we understand that they are not ordinary souls. I was impressed with the focus the monks we saw today had in their spiritual practices. For twelve hours a day they chant and pray! I would like to have that determination in my own spiritual practices. We've come here to exchange: to learn and to teach. We need to remember that this spiritual culture has existed in Bhutan for hundreds of years. Let's get some impressions of how ISKCON can also survive the ravages of time!'

The next day, we drove ten hours higher into the mountains to Bumthang in the centre of the country. Along the way we encountered many people who were curious about us, because I always wear my renunciate robes. They asked me about my clothing and especially about the prayer beads we each carried. Many times, we showed our beads and explained the process of chanting Hare Krishna.

'Can you tell us more about how the Bhutanese blend modernization with their spiritual tradition?' I asked Tshering Sonam as we drove along another precipitous road through the mountains.

'We are not against material progress,' he said. 'It can also be used to serve our spiritual purposes. Bhutan used to be a kingdom with self-imposed isolation. It had its advantages and disadvantages. Take healthcare, for example: communicable diseases were widespread and more than half the children born in Bhutan died at birth or within the first few years of their lives. Malaria claimed hundreds of lives each year. But since Bhutan opened up to modernization in 1961, with far-reaching political, social and economic reforms, the health status of the population has improved. Now more than 90 per cent of the population benefits from full health coverage.

'Then in 2008 Bhutan became a democracy, after hundreds of years of monarchy. The king and the National Assembly work closely together. But while we incorporate modernization, we are careful not to do so at the expense of our spiritual culture. We feel strongly that the holistic development of the individual and society can be achieved through a balance of the economic, social, emotional, spiritual and cultural needs of the people.

'It's not always easy to find this balance, but we try our best. And once again, we judge our success by the happiness of our people. We have a saying: happiness is a place.'

After eight hours on the winding roads, I needed a break and asked the driver to pull over. We walked down an embankment and sat down to have lunch. I saw monkeys scampering through the thick foliage. Birds were chirping as the nearby river flowed by. It was an idyllic environment. I took out my japa beads and began to chant.

In such a natural, peaceful atmosphere it was easy to focus on the holy names.

'It's kind of sad,' I thought. 'I hardly ever get to be present in nature like this. This kind of environment is calming to the self. It's obvious why the yogis in days of yore chose such isolated places for their spiritual practices.' I imagined how rejuvenating it would be to spend a month in Bhutan just practising my japa meditation and reading the scriptures.

As I chanted, I happened to glance up at the mountain and saw a small monastery perched high on a ledge with many small cottages around it.

'What is that?' I asked Tshering Sonam.

'That's a special place of meditation for monks,' he said. 'After an initial nine years of training in a monastery, all monks are sent to that monastery to meditate in silence for three years, three months, three weeks and three days.'

My jaw dropped. So much for my one month. Once again, I was impressed by the seriousness the Buddhist monks express in their commitment to their spiritual practices. I also remembered those devotees in my own tradition, saints like Haridas Thakur and Raghunatha das Goswami in the sixteenth century, who chanted Hare Krishna twenty-two hours a day.

'Why don't we do that?' Sakhi Rai asked, when I mentioned them to my travelling companions.

'Well, Srila Prabhupada requested something different from us,' I said. 'A minimum of two hours chanting meditation per day. But as you progress in your spiritual journey, you naturally find yourself chanting more. Also, we do service to the holy names by telling others about the benefits of chanting. But while we're here, we can certainly pray for the determination these monks have in their daily rituals of spiritual life.'

'We have come here to learn, as well as to teach,' repeated Sakhi Rai with a smile.

'Yes, and we are accomplishing both,' I said.

Day after day we drove through the mountainous countryside, visiting monasteries, astrology schools and administrative buildings called dzongs, which serve also as small refuges for monks. Everywhere we were greeted with friendliness and respect.

'I haven't seen one person get angry since I've been here,' said Sri Prahlada one afternoon. 'I'm sure it happens, but in most countries, you often see people get upset or angry in public.'

'The way of life here bears sweet fruit,' I said.

After almost two weeks we reached the furthermost point of our journey, Mongar in eastern Bhutan.

'We'll be visiting a special monastery today,' said Tshering Sonam. 'It's called Drametse Lhakhang. It was founded in 1511 by Ani Choeten Zangmo, the granddaughter of the Bhutanese saint Pema Lingpa.'

Although the names didn't mean much to me, I could see that they did to him, and I respectfully thanked him for the opportunity to visit there.

That afternoon we entered the sanctified atmosphere of the monastery and again found monks chanting in the main hall with the guru seated nearby overseeing everything. We walked in slowly, sat down among the monks and took out our beads again in an attempt to imbibe the mood of concentration. Afterwards we were taken on a tour of the monastery. As we took in the age-old surroundings, I noticed the guru standing nearby observing us.

'Let's go speak to him,' I said to the others.

'No, no,' said Tshering Sonam. 'We cannot approach such men of wisdom.'

'But that's what they're here for,' I said as I pulled him along to translate for me. 'Sir,' I said to the guru, 'may I have the honour of speaking with you?'

'Yes, of course,' he said smiling.

'I would like to understand the goal of your practices,' I said. 'What is it you hope to achieve through a lifetime dedicated to prayer, meditation and ritual? My understanding of Buddhism is that by eventually ceasing all material desire, one achieves a state of non-existence.'

'We follow the path of Vajrayana Buddhism,' the guru said, 'which teaches that the consequence of deeds in previous lives, or karma, forces all beings to reincarnate. All human effort should be to attain enlightenment through which the gate to Nirvana is opened. When one reaches the state of Nirvana, he does not take birth again.'

'Thank you for your explanation,' I said. 'I would like to know if according to your teachings the soul remains an individual when attaining enlightenment. In our philosophy the liberated soul goes to a spiritual abode to associate eternally with the Supreme Soul, God.'

'In Vajrayana Buddhism,' he said, 'we also believe in a heavenly abode: the land of Buddha.'

'But what exactly is it like there?' I asked.

'That, no one knows,' he said.

'Thank you,' I said. 'We will take our leave now.'

'It's interesting,' I said as we walked back to the car, 'that Buddha advocated an atheistic philosophy, not one that focusses on a personal God as our tradition does. But he did so because people at that time were using the Vedas to condone the killing of animals. Therefore, Buddha said, "Don't follow the Vedas. Follow me." Thus, he tricked them into following the Supreme Personality of Godhead. By doing so they would gradually become purified and eventually be able to once again understand the soul as the eternal servant of God. Because the guru we just spoke to is on that path, we must respect him.'

As we drove, I looked up ISKCON'S Interfaith Statement:

In ISKCON we view all communities and philosophies advocating love for God and founded on revealed scripture as representative of the ultimate religious expression. We also respect the spiritual worth of paths of genuine self-realization and search for the Absolute Truth in which the concept of a personal deity is not explicit.

I was struck by my good fortune to have come to Bhutan, an entire country devoted both in principle and practice to its faith. I prayed that ISCKON would continue to maintain its founding principles. I felt enriched and wiser from my journey into the heart of Bhutan, but I hankered to be back in the transcendental abode of Vrindavan again, where the Supreme Lord performs eternal pastimes as a person with His loving devotees. With renewed determination I looked forward to chanting, praying and studying the scriptures, just as I saw the monks do in Bhutan.

I am the basis of the immortal and imperishable Brahman, the abode of everlasting truth and ultimate happiness.

—Lord Krishna in the Bhagavad Gita (14:27)

11

Australia

The Parliament of World Religions

In late 2009, Hare Krishna devotees in Melbourne were invited to speak at the Parliament of World Religions, which is held every five years and strives to foster understanding and cooperation between spiritual cultures. The parliament dates back to 1893 when representatives from Eastern and Western spiritual traditions met in Chicago for inter-religious dialogue.

I had been contacted by the devotees in Melbourne who asked whether I would consider putting together a short stage show drawn from the performances that make up the summer festival programme I oversee in Poland. I had jumped at the chance and had arranged for twenty-eight of the best performers from the Polish festival to journey to Australia to entertain some of the 10,000 visitors expected at the parliament. We were scheduled to perform on the second day of the parliament at prime time in one of the main auditoriums. Alongside this exciting engagement, we would tour to the major cities of Australia and New Zealand to hold festivals over the next three months.

I felt that the parliament was a great opportunity to network and connect with other spiritual traditions and to engage in interfaith dialogue. Interfaith dialogue is supported by the Governing Body Commission, the main managerial body of the Hare Krishna movement. Several years ago, Saunaka Rishi das set up the ISKCON Interfaith Commission in Oxford, England, so people of different faiths could work together for the benefit of society.

Flying in from Hong Kong, I was nervous because Australian customs is never easy. The officers are serious about protecting the country from incoming diseases. Passengers arriving by plane are not allowed to bring in any foods, minerals or seeds. Wood in any form is closely inspected. Often a wooden article is impounded and fumigated before being returned. Everything must be declared in writing, and if customs officers find something not declared a large fine is likely. A few years ago, an Australian customs officer had grilled me extensively, gone through every item of luggage and confiscated a few things.

This year I was nervous because I was carrying a number of wooden articles, mostly beads made from the holy tulasi plant. Hare Krishna devotees wear tulasi beads around their necks, just as Christians wear crosses, and their meditation beads are generally also made of tulasi wood. I was also carrying items that I use in the worship of my personal deities, items that could potentially be considered exotic and questionable like sandalwood (a soft wood that can be ground into a paste and is considered holy), aguru oil (a fragrant oil drawn from the agarwood tree), blocks of camphor, 200-year-old rudraksha prayer beads given to me by a Lord Shiva devotee in south India, boxes of saffron, and my salagrama-silas (holy stones which come from the Kali Gandhaki River in the Himalayas).

I joined a long line of weary passengers. A woman was directing them to different inspectors. The customs officers were checking everyone's luggage, and a number of people looked frustrated at the way they were being searched. Finally, I came to the front of the line.

'Next!' shouted the woman. 'Stall four!'

As I rounded the corner into the stall, the officer had his head down and his back to me. Then he lifted his head and revealed himself to be a burly Sikh wearing a blue turban.

'Hare Krishna, Swamiji,' he said. 'Are you coming to visit the Hare Krishna temple in North Sydney?'

'What!' I exclaimed. 'Oh yes ... yes I am.'

'Have you been to the Hare Krishna temple at Juhu Beach in Mumbai?' he asked conversationally.

'Yes, I have,' I replied. 'I've been there a number of times ... Would you like to see my declaration?'

'Did you eat in the restaurant at Juhu temple? Very good food. I recommend it.' I noticed one or two of the other customs officers glancing in our direction. 'I've also been to the North Sydney temple with my wife. Very nice singing.'

'I'm really glad you enjoyed it,' I said and put the declaration form on the table in front of him. 'Here's my form.' He picked it up but didn't look at it.

'Have you anything to declare?' he asked. I had a long list ready and decided to start with my japa beads. I took a deep breath.

'Here,' I said, 'we can start with these meditation beads.'

'Oh, they're sacred wood aren't they, Swamiji?'

I cleared my throat. 'Uh ... yes, they are.'

'That's fine then,' he said as he stamped the form and put it in the drawer in front of him. 'You can go now.'

'I can go?' I asked.

'Yes Swamiji,' he said with a big smile, 'and all the best!'

On the opening day of the parliament, I went with one of my students to the convention centre where the event was being held to see what was taking place. In the foyer were thousands of people dressed in all sorts of spiritual attire going here and there, to lectures, seminars and workshops. In an exhibition hall, the different participating religions each had a booth where visitors could meet representatives and get books on the teachings. Crowds milled about amongst what seemed to be hundreds of booths.

In the midst of it all I saw our own booth with a sign: International Society for Krishna Consciousness. The booth was full of people browsing through the books on display and talking to the devotees in attendance. I was headed in that direction when a gentleman in Arab robes intercepted me.

'Swami,' he said, 'I am Sheikh Abdul from Jerusalem. I am giving a seminar on Religion, Conflict and Peace Building in the Middle East. I was speaking to some of your members here and I find your philosophy very interesting.'

'It's wonderful to meet you,' I said shaking his hand.

'I notice you are wearing a ring with Arabic script on it,' he said looking at my hand. 'But you are a Hindu. Why are you wearing an Islamic ring?'

'It was given to me by a Muslim holy man,' I said. 'I defended his faith in an argument with another man and in appreciation he gave me his ring. He said the script on the stone is 300 years old.' I took the ring off my finger and handed it to him. 'Do you think you could translate the inscription for me?'

He studied the ring then read the inscription: 'Allah, the merciful one, bestows longevity and a healthy life to the bearer of this ring.' He handed the ring back to me and smiled.

'Swami,' he said, 'what are your views on the many conflicts we have in our world, particularly in the Middle East?'

'Such conflicts are due to our being in the bodily conception of life,' I said. 'Because we think we are our bodies, we identify with the nation we were born in or live in. But we are not these bodies. We are spirit souls. In reality, we are children of one God. People are fighting over their differences, but peace will come only when we focus on what we have in common. On the spiritual platform we are all brothers and sisters.'

'Yes,' said the sheikh. 'The Koran advocates peace, even when one is wronged. Chapter three, verse 172 says: "For those who responded to the call of Allah and the messenger after the wound had befallen them—those among them who do good to others and guard against evil shall have a great reward." This is the message I am trying to preach in Jerusalem. Swami, why don't you visit my centre sometime? You could share your beliefs with our people and I could enlighten you about Islam.'

'Thank you for the invitation,' I said. 'If I am able, I would like to take you up on it.' We exchanged business cards and he promised to attend our show the following day.

At the ISKCON booth I took the time to speak to several visitors and then went to the area where the seminars were being held. Many people were standing around discussing what they had heard in the various lectures. In the distance I saw an elderly Buddhist monk of Eastern origin dressed in flowing robes sitting with a number of his followers, also in robes. They were worshipping him with incense, flowers and a yak-tail fan. As I came closer, the master saw me and immediately rose to greet me.

'Welcome,' he said. 'We are honoured that you have come.'

'Honoured that I have come, Your Holiness?' I enquired. 'I am only an aspiring transcendentalist. Seeing the faith your followers have in you, I can ascertain that you are a realized soul.'

In response, he smiled and began telling me a story.

'A student once asked the Buddha, "Are you a God?"

'"No, my son," said the Blessed One.

'"Are you a saint?" the student asked.

'"No, my son," said the Blessed One.

'"Are you a magician?" the student said.

'"No, my dear one," said the Blessed One.

'"What are you then?" the student asked.

'"I am awake," said the Buddha.'

'Words of wisdom,' I said. 'Most of us are asleep, unaware of the true purpose of life.'

'Yes,' he said, 'but your eyes show that you are not asleep.'

I laughed. 'It's your kindness that you can see the potential for something that has not yet come.' I reached forward to embrace him and his students reacted with alarm. One moved forward to stop me.

'No!' said the master to his student. He put his arms around me and we embraced for a long time. 'I have enjoyed meeting you, my brother,' he said. 'I would like you to visit our monastery in Thailand. You will be my guest for three months. I will teach you about Buddhism and you will enlighten me about your faith.'

We exchanged cards and I promised to try to find an opportunity to visit his ashram. I thought about how I could benefit by learning about the teachings of the Buddha.

'Buddha is an incarnation of Krishna,' I thought. 'And there is surely something to be learned. Just look how controlled these young monks are. See how they are sitting so composed and serene. Surely that is favourable for the practice of bhakti yoga.'

The next day we held our two-hour festival programme in a hall with 400 seats. The place filled up well before the programme started and we were turning people away when I saw Sheikh Abdul walking towards the entrance. I ran from the side of the stage and reached the sheikh before the devotees could block his path.

'Come with me,' I said out of breath. 'I've reserved a seat for you.'

As we passed by the sound desk, I grabbed the engineer's chair and carried it with me to the front-row aisle. Apologizing to the guests seated there, I squeezed in the chair and asked the sheikh to sit down. The programme began immediately and as I surveyed the audience, I understood that many important religious leaders like the sheikh were there to see our show.

Twenty minutes into the programme I saw a woman making a call on her cell phone. I quietly asked her to please put her phone away during the performance so she didn't disturb others. She looked up. 'This show is so amazing I'm calling one of the directors of the parliament to come down from his office and see it,' she said.

I asked the devotee at the door to make sure that when the director arrived, he would be given a seat.

The crowd roared in approval after each performance. During my twenty-minute talk I spoke from the Bhagavad Gita. I knew that these profound truths would impress many in the audience. After the show we sold twenty Gitas from the book table. The sheikh loved the show and afterwards he shook my hand repeatedly while glorifying all the performers.

'May I have the honour to invite you to my seminar tomorrow in room 104?' he asked. 'I am coordinating a session in which representatives of Jewish, Christian, Druze and Muslim faiths will share stories of peacemaking and hope in Jerusalem.'

'It would be a privilege to attend,' I said.

Just as we were about to leave the hall a director of the parliament came up to me.

'I would like your group to perform at the closing ceremonies in four days,' he said. 'Your show is astounding, like a spiritual Cirque du Soleil.'

'Thank you,' I said. 'Your comment means a lot to us.'

'There are going to be several four-minute performances,' he said. 'There will be 4,000 people attending. I'll slot you into the second spot right after the invocation.'

The next day, I returned to the Parliament of World Religions to hear the sheikh's lecture. The seminars I had seen so far had been attended by between thirty and fifty people, so I expected this session to be similar. But when I arrived, I was surprised to see more than 300 people crammed into the seminar room. There wasn't a seat free and people were standing alongside the walls. Spectators four deep lined the back of the room. Sheikh Abdul was already speaking to the audience, but he noticed me standing awkwardly at the entrance.

'My spiritual brother has come,' he said into the microphone with a big smile. 'He is thinking of visiting me in Jerusalem. Please make way for him and give him a seat in the front row.'

Two or three people immediately stood up in the front. As I made my way forward the crowd respectfully parted for me. I felt humbled and honoured to be in the sheikh's presence.

The sheikh gave a moving appeal for peace in the Middle East.

'People are fighting over their differences. But peace will come to our region only when we focus on what we have in common. On the spiritual platform we are all brothers and sisters,' he concluded, glancing at me with a twinkle in his eye.

'Isn't that exactly what I said the other day?' I thought. I was touched, sensing the power of our newfound pledge to work together to help people. I made a vow then and there to visit the sheikh's centre in the Middle East, recalling a poem I had read that morning in one of the parliament brochures:

Your friends are very special things,
Their love is like the rarest gem.
But friends are hard to find and keep
Unless you are a friend to them.

—Anne Cragg

When the lecture ended, I filed out with the other guests and looked at the brochure to see if there were any other interesting seminars taking place. A panel discussion on the 'Goal of Religion' caught my eye. There would be speakers from Christian, Muslim, Hindu, Sikh and Buddhist faiths. I quickly made my way to the room and found it almost as well attended as the sheikh's seminar. This time I myself managed to find a seat close to the front. Everything went smoothly as the speakers shared their perspectives on the goal of religion.

Then the floor was opened for questions. Someone asked why women were not allowed to play more significant roles in world religion. Most of the panel said their faiths were open to women taking leadership roles, but when a Roman Catholic cardinal said that women had no role in the priesthood because it was not the Church's tradition, he was booed.

After the seminar, people surged forward to meet the various religious leaders, but no one approached the cardinal. Seeing he was alone I went up to him.

'The gender issue is a difficult territory for religions,' I said. 'In our tradition, women have historically been excluded from the priesthood too, but my spiritual master made adjustments to this principle when he came to the West.'

'What group are you from?' he said.

'The Hare Krishna movement,' I said. 'Our tradition is based on the Bhagavad Gita spoken 5,000 years ago by Lord Krishna in India. Practising ancient religion in a contemporary setting is a delicate balance. We can't compromise the word of scripture and yet there's always room for adjusting things according to time, place and circumstance.'

His face had darkened. 'The Hare Krishnas believe in many gods,' he said.

'That's not true,' I said. 'Our philosophy is monotheistic. We believe in one God, just like you.'

'Really?' he said. 'That's not what I was told.'

'Ultimately we follow the same commandment as you,' I said. 'To love and honour the Father with all our hearts and souls.'

'That's in your scriptures?' he said.

'Yes,' I said, 'but expressed in a different way.'

'How?' he asked.

I quoted a verse from the Bhagavad Gita:

Man-mana bhava mad-bhakto
Mad-yaji mam namaskuru
Mam evaisyasi satyam te
Pratijane priyo si me

(Always think of Me, become My devotee, worship Me and offer your homage unto Me. Thus you will come to Me without fail. I promise you this because you are My very dear friend. Bhagavad Gita [18.65])

He looked at me. 'Please bless me,' he said.

'Father,' I said, 'how can I presume to bless you? You are my senior, much older than I am. It is you who are in a position to bless someone like me.'

'No,' he said. 'You came to comfort me. Now please bless me.'

'No Father,' I said. 'I can't do that.' But suddenly I thought of Poland, where I spend a lot of my time. There, a priest—what to speak of a cardinal—would never think of such a thing. An idea came to me.

'Father, I will bless you if you bless me.' We took each other's hands and sat alone in that empty room, our eyes closed, blessing each other.

When I went back to the Melbourne temple later that day, the performers were practising our presentation for the closing ceremony. We devised a performance that included all parts of our normal two-hour show: classical Indian dance, yoga, artistic martial arts, and kirtan. Although the presentation would be only four minutes long, it took a couple of hours to put it together. I thought of the famous quote by the writer Blaise Pascal: 'I have made this letter longer because I have not had the time to make it shorter.'

When our troupe of twenty-eight devotees arrived at the parliament three days later, we were whisked backstage. I looked out from behind the curtain and was amazed to see the huge crowd. When the lights dimmed the master of ceremonies welcomed everyone, especially the spiritual leaders from different traditions around the world. As he stepped back behind the curtain, Buddhist monks came onstage and beat a huge gong while playing large brass horns as other monks chanted spiritual incantations. It was beautiful and mystical and lasted for ten minutes. When they came offstage, the stage manager pointed to us.

'You're on,' he said. 'Good luck.'

The Hare Krishna mantra filled the auditorium. I could hear the audience gasp at our group's beautiful clothes and costumes and as we went through our routine, I saw that everyone was enthralled. When we came forward dancing in a straight line and threw large bunches of flowers into the audience, everyone cheered. Then it was over almost as soon as it had begun. The crowd kept cheering as we left the stage. Backstage, the stage manager complimented us.

'That was wonderful!' he said. 'Listen to that applause. They can't stop.'

After the dignitaries' speeches and other performances, our troupe went to the foyer where people were exiting. A large crowd formed and people took their photos with us. But after an hour, I had to stop it.

'Let's move on,' I told the team. 'We have another show starting in an hour. The organizers phoned me ten minutes ago and said 800 people are already seated in the hall. We can't be late!'

We may not have had time to relish our success, but that didn't matter. We bundled into our vans and headed off to our next festival, tired but happy that we had met so many spiritual leaders and spiritual practitioners. The parliament had shown that we were all children of God, and it had been an honour to have met my new spiritual brothers.

A person of faith is not lost in this world or the next. One who does good, My friend, is never overcome by evil. The spiritual seeker, carried effortlessly onwards by the influence of former practice, passes beyond the conventions of religion.

—Lord Krishna in the Bhagavad Gita (6:40 and 6:44)

12

USA and Canada

Lessons from the Road

B oarding my flight to the US I felt exhaustion descend upon me, but I forced myself to stay awake as a flight attendant demonstrated the safety procedures. I had just completed a vigourous festival circuit in Australia and was about to embark upon another in the US.

When the flight attendant had finished, I drifted off to sleep offering a prayer to my spiritual master: 'Srila Prabhupada, please accept the results of our service. Our troupe of thirty devotees did forty-eight festivals, practically without a break. Twenty-seven thousand people came to the two-hour cultural programmes. We sold 3,500 books and 21,000 plates of prasad.'

Having arrived in Los Angeles fifteen hours later I gathered my hand baggage and walked towards passport control and customs. I handed my passport to the immigration officer.

'Where are you coming from?' he asked.

I was groggy from the long flight and I had to think for a moment. 'Oh ... uh ... Sydney,' I said.

He chuckled. 'Don't worry,' he said. 'Long-haul flights affect everyone.'

I slung my hand baggage over my shoulder and walked towards the luggage carousel. 'This tour of the US will not be easy,' I thought. 'This year I'll be doing it by myself without help. But not to complain: it's the duty of a renunciate to travel alone and learn to depend on God.'

Three days later in San Diego, barely recovered from jet lag, I prepared to board a flight for Vancouver with a transit in Seattle. As always, I wore my sannyasi robes. I was going to attend the wedding of one of my students. Usually, sannyasis don't go to weddings, since renunciates strive to focus upon the spiritual reality rather than family life, but I wanted to be there for my student to encourage her.

Approaching the check-in counter, my mind went blank and I had to think hard to remember where I was going. No doubt it was due to my being tired. As I handed my ticket to the woman behind the counter, I asked her to check my bags through to Seattle; I was transiting through there to Vancouver, but would return there in the evening after the wedding.

'I have a two-hour layover,' I said. 'I'll give the bags to a friend. I'll just be in Vancouver for the day and I'll get a ride back to Seattle in the evening. I won't need the bags in Vancouver.'

As her face darkened I immediately realized I'd made a mistake. Some time back it was a terrorist tactic to have a bag of explosives off-loaded from a flight through one city while continuing to another.

'Why is that?' she asked. 'Why only to Seattle?'

'Well, I was thinking to have my bags dropped off in Seattle, but now I realize—'

Before I could finish the sentence, she picked up the phone and called a security officer. A big man appeared out of nowhere and asked me to follow him. People stared at me as we walked away.

Soon I was seated in a room as he leafed through my passport.

'You have a lot of visas for Muslim countries,' he said. 'Kazakhstan, Azerbaijan, Uzbekistan, Bahrain and Oman, to name a few. What business do you have in those countries, sir?'

I was starting to feel nervous. 'I'm a missionary,' I said. 'I travel around the world.'

'What sort of missionary are you?' he said.

'I'm from the Hare Krishna movement,' I replied.

'That's Hindu, isn't it?'

'Well … yes.'

'I see,' he said. 'A Hindu missionary in Muslim countries.'

'I know it sounds odd …' I started to say.

He looked me straight in the eye. 'If you're on an international flight, why check your bags to a city you're transiting through?'

'I'm only spending the day in Vancouver going to a wedding and won't need the bags there,' I explained.

'That doesn't sound quite right,' he said.

Then a call came through. They had checked my bags and found no explosives.

'You can go,' he said coldly.

I felt foolish and slightly shaken as I walked back to the counter and finished checking in. As the flight to Vancouver took off, I thought about the incident.

'That was a stupid mistake,' I said to myself. 'Being exhausted doesn't help anything.'

Because of the delay checking in, I'd been given a middle seat in a row of three between two men. They both looked surprised to see me in my saffron robes. A few minutes into the flight the man on my left turned to me.

'Isn't it great how well America is doing in the Winter Olympics?' he said. I knew the 2010 Games were taking place in Vancouver, but I knew nothing of the results.

'Yeah, it is great,' I said.

'What did you think of the performance of Bode Miller?' asked the man on my right.

'Bode Miller?' I asked.

They both stared at me in disbelief.

'Yes, Bode Miller,' the man on my left said, 'the skier Bode Miller.'

'Are you American?' said the man on my right.

'Yes, I am,' I replied.

'And you don't know Bode Miller?' he said. I was silent.

'What about Shaun White?' he continued. 'America's best bet for a gold in the half pipe.'

'The half pipe?' Again, they stared at me.

'How about Lindsey Vonn?' said the man on my left. 'She injured her shin recently, but she's still going to ski. You know her, right?'

'Uh … Can't say that I do,' I said.

'Man, what planet are you from?' he said. I didn't answer. 'If you're American you'd better get your act together. America's gonna kick butt up there in Vancouver. We'll cream those commies from Russia.'

'What!' I responded. 'Commies? Russia's been a democracy for years. Why do you call them communists?'

'Whatever they are, they ain't Americans and we'll pulverize 'em,' he said.

'Yeah,' said the other man, 'along with those Chinese wimps.'

'Wait a minute,' I said. 'That's not the spirit of the Olympics. Tell me, do you guys travel much? I mean, have you ever been out of the United States?'

'Nope,' said the man on my left. 'This is my first trip.'

'Me too,' said the other man. 'I'm going to the Olympics.'

'Well,' I said, 'if you'd travelled more widely, you'd see that people are pretty much the same everywhere. We're all spirit souls struggling in this material world.'

They looked at me blankly and fell silent. I settled back in my seat.

'As difficult as it is to be a travelling monk,' I thought, 'it has its advantages, one of which is seeing the spiritual equality of all living beings.'

Before I drifted off to sleep, I remembered the words of the writer Mark Twain: 'Travel is fatal to prejudice, bigotry and narrow-mindedness, and many of our people need it sorely on these accounts. Broad, wholesome, charitable views of men and things cannot be acquired by vegetating in one little corner of the earth all one's lifetime.'[3]

In Seattle I caught my connecting flight and upon landing in Vancouver I grabbed my hand baggage and raced to immigration. The wedding was scheduled to start in just ninety minutes.

I came to the immigration counter and handed my passport to an officer. He typed my name and passport information into his computer, and then looked up with a quizzical look on his face.

'Please step to the side for a moment,' he said.

'Is something wrong?' I asked, but he didn't answer.

Another immigration officer said, 'Follow me.' People were staring at me as they'd done in San Diego. Two minutes later I was sitting in yet another office, this time in front of three immigration officers. I sensed the officers in San Diego had contacted them.

'Why have you come to Canada?' the first officer asked.

'I'm here to attend a wedding,' I said. 'I'll be leaving for Seattle soon afterwards.'

'What are the names of the bride and groom?' he asked.

I froze. I didn't know their legal names.

'I'm sorry officer,' I said. 'I don't know. I only know their baptized names.' He shook his head.

'What is the address of the venue where the wedding will take place?' he asked. Again, I hesitated. I had no idea of the address. All I knew was that someone was meeting me at the airport and taking me directly to the wedding.

'I'm not sure,' I said. 'I'll look it up on my phone.'

He leafed through my passport. 'I see you spend a lot of time in Russia,' he said. 'Why?'

'I'm a travelling monk in the Hare Krishna movement,' I said. 'I was in Russia before the fall of communism and I've been helping to take care of our congregation ever since.'

'Have you ever worked for the US Government?'

'The US Government? No!'

'Have you ever served in the armed forces?'

'Yes, I did. I was in the Marine Corps in the 1960s,' I said. 'But what does that have to do with anything? I'm here for a wedding and I'm leaving tonight.'

'And yet you don't know the names of the couple or the address of the ceremony!'

'Usually, I just get picked up and driven—' I started to say.

'We'll need to send him back,' the officer said to his colleague as if I wasn't there.

'What! You're going to send me back to San Diego?'

The third officer took my arm firmly and started leading me to the door. Suddenly I had an idea. 'Wait a minute, officer,' I said. 'Let me give you a number you can call. It's my secretary. She can vouch for me. She's at the wedding.'

My student, Rasika-siromani dasi, who arranges my travel in the US, had driven to Vancouver with several other devotees from Seattle. The officer called Rasika and had a hushed conversation with her for fifteen minutes.

'All right,' he said after hanging up. 'Looks like you are going to officiate at that wedding.'

He picked up his pen to sign the paper in front of him, but first he looked at me.

'Is there anything else you're planning to do while you're here?' he said.

Another idea came to me. 'If there's time,' I said, 'I might catch some of the Olympics. I mean Bode Miller, Shaun White and Lindsey Vonn are all favourites for gold medals.'

When I finally walked through to the terminal, the devotee who was there to pick me up ran over to me looking worried.

'What happened?' he asked. 'Did you lose your luggage?'

'No,' I said, 'I didn't lose my luggage. I just made a mistake. It happens sometimes. But I learned a lesson, a good lesson from the road.'

These experiences at the San Diego and Vancouver airports got me thinking about the merits of travelling in plain clothes in America, rather than in my robes. Airport security measures had been heightened throughout the country because of terrorist threats, and any passenger who looked unusual was more likely to be subjected to searches and questioning. There was concern that people of various racial, ethnic, religious or national groups were being singled out, but that didn't stop it from happening on the ground. And no doubt, my flowing saffron robes drew attention.

In the end I decided against changing my dress.

'Experience has shown that the advantages of wearing my robes far outweigh those of pants and a shirt,' I thought, 'if only because of the number of people who approach me to ask about spiritual life.'

Two weeks into my US tour, I checked in for a flight from Boise to Salt Lake City. Sure enough, I was pulled aside while going through security.

'Stand with your legs spread and your arms out to the side while I do a body search,' said the officer.

I smiled. 'No problem,' I said. 'I'm used to it.'

Starting from my arms his hands slid down to my waist. 'Is this sheet tied on tight?' he asked.

'It's called a dhoti, sir,' I said. 'And yes, it's tied tight.'

'Just thought I'd ask,' he said. 'The last time I patted down one of you guys the sheet fell off.'

I chuckled. After the pat-down he led me to a table to search my hand luggage.

'Actually, I'd like to ask you a question if I could,' he said as he opened my briefcase.

'No problem, officer,' I said. 'That's what you guys are supposed to do. I appreciate these security measures. They keep us safe.'

'No, I mean another kind of question,' he said. He glanced around as if to make sure no one was taking notice. 'You're a spiritual person and you look happy to me. Can you tell me why I'm suffering so much in life?'

'Suffering will always be there in this world,' I said. 'You can alter it somewhat, but you can't change the fact that we all get sick, grow old and die. You have to go within and discover your spiritual self, which is eternal and full of knowledge and bliss.'

'What does the spiritual self look like?' he asked, as he made a show of looking through my suitcase.

'We're spiritual beings,' I said, 'with a spiritual body and spiritual senses and emotions. That body is eternal. It never grows old.'

He looked up. 'Does God really exist?' he said.

Another security officer called out, 'Hey Bill, is there a problem? What's taking so long?'

'There's no problem,' Bill yelled back. 'Just double checking.' He then looked at me for the answer to his question.

'Of course God exists,' I said, 'and you can see Him. But you need the necessary qualifications.'

'Which are?' he asked.

'Bill,' the other officer shouted, 'move that person on! The line is backing up here!'

'What is the qualification for seeing God?' he said.

'Love,' I replied.

'But how do I—' he started to say as the other security officer walked over.

'Bill,' he said, 'does this gentleman pose a security threat?'

'No,' Bill replied.

'Then move things on,' said the officer.

'I wanted to ask him one more question,' said Bill.

'Then ask,' said the officer.

'I mean about life,' Bill said.

The officer shook his head. 'Bill, this is not the place.' He looked at me and said, 'You can go now, sir.'

'But I need to know—' Bill started to say.

'Back to work,' the officer said sternly.

'Can I give him my card at least?' I said to the officer as I started to walk away.

'No,' the officer said. 'He's on duty.'

I looked back and saw Bill was getting a scolding. I headed to the departure gate still thinking about him when a young woman came up to me.

'Are you a Hare Krishna?' she said.

'Yes, I am,' I replied.

'Do you have any literature?' she asked. 'I've always wanted to know something about your faith.'

'I'm sorry,' I said, 'I don't have any on me, but if you send me your address, I'll mail some books to you.'

The card I had wanted to give Bill was still in my hand and I gave it to her.

'Great!' she said. 'Don't forget.'

I smiled. 'I won't forget,' I said.

By dint of my frequent flyer points, I was travelling business class. Twenty minutes into the flight a woman walked up the aisle next to my seat.

'Are you a Buddhist?' she said.

'No,' I said. 'I'm a monk in the Hare Krishna movement.'

'I'm a Buddhist,' she said. 'Can you tell me the difference between Hare Krishna and Buddhism?'

The man seated next to me put down his *Wall Street Journal* to see what was happening.

'The basic difference is that Hare Krishna accepts God as a person,' I replied. 'Buddhism states that ultimately everything is void.' The man went back to reading his newspaper.

'Yes,' she said, 'that's true. So, what do we have in common?'

'A number of things,' I said, 'beginning with our belief in reincarnation.'

'Just a minute,' she said and turned to the man next to me. 'Sir, do you think you could change seats with me? I'd really love to talk to this monk.'

The man lowered his newspaper. 'Are you in business class?' he said.

'I'm not,' she said. 'I'm in economy. But I have an aisle seat.' He looked at her incredulously. 'It would mean a lot to me. Please. I really need this.'

'All right,' he said to my surprise, 'if it means so much to you.' He gathered his things and taking her boarding pass walked to her seat in economy. She sat down next to me.

'So,' she said, 'you were saying something about reincarnation?' We then discussed the differences between Vaishnavism and Buddhism throughout the ninety-minute flight.

At Salt Lake City I was walking through the airport to the baggage carousels when a woman stopped me.

'Excuse me,' she said, 'may I ask what faith you are practising?'

'I'm from the Hare Krishna movement,' I replied. 'I follow an ancient spiritual tradition from India.'

'I see,' she said. 'And is there a special significance to the clothes you're wearing?'

I smiled and said, 'Yes, there is. We dress like this so people will ask us questions.' She laughed.

'Seriously,' I said. 'A person's outer appearance reflects their inner nature. Before becoming a monk, I led a degraded life. My dirty and unkempt clothes were an indication of my unclean heart. Now I'm striving to understand God and these clothes are a sign of my pure intentions.'

'Beautifully put,' she said. 'Are you going to visit the Mormon temple in Salt Lake City?'

'Sure, if I have time,' I said.

'Visit Brigham Young University too,' she said. 'Most of the students are nice young Mormons.'

'I'll certainly try,' I assured her.

We shook hands. 'Safe travels,' she said.

I was struggling to pull my hand-trolley up some steps to another level when a young man behind me put his hand on my lower back and gently pushed me up.

'Thanks a lot,' I said.

He laughed. 'Figured it'd get me some kudos from above,' he said.

While I was waiting for my bags at the carousel a woman in her fifties approached me.

'You're American, right?' she asked. 'But you're following an Eastern path. Why is that?'

'This tradition answered all my spiritual questions,' I said.

'And how many years have you been practising?' she said.

I had to think for a moment. 'Forty years,' I said.

'Forty years!' she exclaimed. She lowered her voice and leaned closer. 'And have you been faithful all those years?' she said. 'Are you keeping your vows?'

I nodded my head. 'Yes,' I said. 'I've been faithful and I've kept my vows.'

'George!' she called out to her husband waiting at the baggage carousel. 'Bring me twenty bucks.' Her husband reached into his pocket, walked over and handed her a twenty-dollar bill. The wife put the money in my hand. 'Keep up the good work,' she said.

The night before I left Salt Lake City, I received an e-mail from the US State Department. It must have been sent as a result of the number of times I'd been taken aside for screening in airports.

Dear Sir,

We are reaching out to your organization on behalf of the US Department of Homeland Security to obtain information about issues or concerns regarding religious expression or exercise during airport security screening. For example, do individuals of your faith who wear religious dress believe they are treated differently in the airport screening process because of the clothing they are wearing or religious symbols they possess? Your assistance in helping us address religious exercise and expression issues at airport security is welcomed.'

I replied:

'Dear Sirs, I am sometimes singled out for screening because of my religious dress. But I have no complaints. Considering the apparent threat of terrorism in our country, such security measures are acceptable. What's more, it gives me an opportunity to share my faith with all of you. With best wishes, Indradyumna Swami.'

The next morning, I took a flight to Dallas. I was seated next to a man who was absorbed in reading what appeared to be the Bible. When he put it in the pocket of the seat in front of him, I asked if I might borrow it to read for a while.

He smiled. 'It's the Book of Mormon,' he said.

'Fine,' I said. 'I'm always interested in learning about other faiths.'

'Me too,' he said. 'Do you have a copy of the Bhagavad Gita?'

'Do you know the Gita?' I asked.

'Well ... no, I don't,' he said. 'But I know it's the scripture of the Hare Krishnas, and from your dress I can see you're a Hare Krishna.'

With that exchange began an in-depth discussion about religion that lasted the entire two-and-a-half-hour flight.

'You can keep the book,' the man said when we landed. It was large and ornate, obviously a special edition.

'Thank you,' I said. 'I consider it a very special gift. If you give me your business card, I'll send you a Bhagavad Gita.'

'I'd be honoured,' he said and handed me his card.

That evening, I remembered some words from the Prophet Mohammed: 'Don't tell me how educated you are. Tell me how much you've travelled.'

For those who worship Me with devotion, meditating on Me alone, I bring what they need and preserve what they have.

—Lord Krishna in the Bhagavad Gita (9:22)

13

South Africa

Food That Brings People Closer to God

The Hare Krishna movement's vegetarian food is so famous that the movement is sometimes called 'the kitchen religion' by members and non-members alike. As well as hosting a global network of vegetarian restaurants, cafes and mobile food stalls, we also distribute food for free en masse to those in need. The Hare Krishna Food for Life programme was established in 1974 in Mayapur, West Bengal, when my spiritual master Srila Prabhupada saw a group of hungry village children fighting dogs for food scraps. That day he made the statement that remains one of Food for Life's guiding maxims: 'No one within a ten-mile radius of a Hare Krishna temple should go hungry.'

Hare Krishna Food for Life became Food for Life Global in 1995, and Food for Life became an independent not-for-profit entity based in the US in 1995. It is the largest vegetarian food distribution programme in the world: spread across sixty countries, its volunteers distribute up to two million free meals a day.

One of the most active Food for Life projects in the world is centered in Durban. Its slogan is Creating a Hunger-Free South Africa. I had taken part in food distribution activities there in the 1990s, and in 2010 I had the chance to go back to be a part of it again.

South Africa is well-known for its high levels of crime and violence, but things seemed worse than I remembered when I returned there in 2010. I was picked up from the airport by Swarup Damodar das, the president of the Durban Hare Krishna temple. Driving towards the temple, he told me about a devotee family who had been attacked in their home two days earlier.

'So many of us here have experienced what are classified as minor crimes—burglary, carjacking and like,' he said. 'But this family experienced something much more traumatic. A sophisticated, well-coordinated gang of criminals posing as police officers pulled over a member of our congregation on his way home from work. They were brandishing high-calibre firearms and said he was being investigated for fraud and that they needed to search his home. They handcuffed him, put him in their vehicle and drove him to his home.

'When they got there, other criminals also posing as police officers were waiting outside. They took him into his house and tied up his mother and his sister. His sister's six-month-old baby was also in the house and she began crying as they ransacked the house looking for cash, jewellery and firearms. When they found nothing they threatened to kill the whole family if they didn't say where they kept their valuables.

'The devotees said they didn't store valuables in the house and pleaded for their lives. The crooks pointed their guns at the family and put a plastic bag over the baby's head. Then the man who seemed to be the leader of the operation came across the family altar with pictures of Srila Prabhupada and Krishna. He shouted to the others, "Don't harm them. They're Hare Krishna devotees. They feed people in the townships."

'One of the men took the plastic bag off the baby's head and slapped her back to get her breathing again. The leader then ordered the others to leave and told them to put back whatever they had taken. The gang dumped a few watches, several appliances and some coins on the floor. As the leader stepped through the front door, he apologized to the family, saying he didn't realize they were associated with Food for Life.'

'That poor family,' I said. 'It sounds like the Food for Life programme is very much appreciated by the poor in this country. It will be an honour and a pleasure to be able to go out with them while I'm here.'

'You'll have a police escort,' Swarup said.

'Is that necessary? I asked. 'If the poor like Food for Life—'

'Most of them do,' he said, 'but we always have to take the criminal element into account here and be prepared for it. The people you meet out there may not always be as accommodating as those who tried to rob that devotee's house. Two of our congregation members were murdered in similar burglaries.'

Three days later as the Food for Life team loaded big pots of freshly cooked vegetarian food into a van, a police constable picked me up in his squad car.

'Paul's my name,' he said putting out his hand. I shook it. I could see I had nothing to fear with Paul by my side. He was a tall African man in his forties, and he looked as strong as an ox. Hanging from his belt were a handgun, two cans of mace and a pair of handcuffs. He had a wide, 15 centimetre scar across his forearm.

'Thanks for coming along,' I said.

'It's a pleasure,' he said as he looked at the large Canon EOS camera hanging around my neck. 'You'll need me. If only for that fancy camera you're carrying.'

We headed out in a convoy to rural Kwazulu-Natal, home to almost nine million Zulus. On the panel behind Paul's head in the car there was a locked and loaded shotgun. I couldn't take my eyes off the little armoury that surrounded him.

'Do you ever use that stuff?' I enquired.

'All the time,' he said without taking his eyes off the road.

An hour later, we turned off the highway onto a winding road into the Valley of a Thousand Hills. The scenery was picturesque, but villages looked dilapidated.

'There's a lot of criminal activity out here,' Paul said as we arrived at our destination village. 'They'll use an AK-47 assault rifle to rob a store for a few packs of cigarettes.'

The radio in his car crackled and a voice gave notification of a robbery taking place.

'That's just 300 metres ahead,' Paul said.

I felt my throat tighten. 'Do you have to go there?'

'No,' he said calmly. 'We never go in alone. There has to be at least three of us in a squad car. Even then we have to assess the situation. If they have superior firepower, which they often do, we hold off.'

We drove another 200 metres and Paul turned down a side street where there were a small group of houses and a few people milling around. A devotee jumped out of the van in front of us and picked up a megaphone.

'Prasad! Prasad! Prasad!' he called out, using the Sanskrit word that literally means 'mercy', but which is also used to refer to food that has been offered to God.

People began pouring out of the houses carrying cups, bowls, plates and even pots. Some of them, including children, were running towards the van. The kids smiled and laughed as they pushed and shoved their way into a long line waiting for the distribution to start. They had definitely done this before! The Food for Life crew opened up vats of steaming hot stew made from rice, beans and vegetables. I saw a number of children get their bowls filled and then immediately return to the back of the line. I smiled as I watched them eat all the way up to the front and then present their empty bowls for more. Some came three or four times.

Those devotees who were not serving the food got out drums and brass cymbals called kartals and began to sing the Hare Krishna mantra. All the Zulu children started dancing and singing along.

'They even know the words!' I said.

Paul was looking over the crowd and the surrounding area, surveying for any sign of trouble. 'And why not?' he asked, not diverting his attention from his task. 'Hare Krishnas were passing out this food and singing this song to their parents when they themselves were youngsters.'

A group of young men started walking towards me.

'Watch your camera,' Paul said. 'We do what we can out here, but these people are very poor, so crime is always on the rise. Not many take the risk to come here and help them like you do. This is an especially bad area. A few months ago, I chased a criminal into the bush in the next village. He suddenly jumped out just two metres in front of me and fired off four rounds at point-blank range.'

'What happened?' I said.

Paul chuckled. 'He missed, but it wasn't luck. It was the Lord above watching over me.'

'So, you're a religious man,' I said.

'Yes, I sure am,' he said. 'Every time I go into action, I look up at the sky and say to the Lord, "Cover me". It's the only explanation for why I'm still here today.'

'Even though it might seem not related to what you experience on a daily basis in your job, what we eat can actually have an influence on crime and violence,' I said.

'How so?' Paul looked skeptical.

'Well,' I said, 'in our main scripture it says that the kind of food we eat has an effect on the way we think and behave. Foods that are obtained by killing will affect the consciousness of the eater in a negative way. We only eat and distribute food that can be obtained without violence, and we offer everything we cook to God with love so that the food becomes blessed. By eating prasad—God's mercy—the eater comes closer to God.'

'That makes sense,' said Paul. 'I haven't ever thought about food in that way.'

'The other thing is that it makes economic sense to be vegetarian,' I said. 'There's such a high cost to producing meat—both economically and environmentally. I read an article on my flight here that said that the additional food that would be produced as a result of a shift to a vegan diet in the US alone could feed an extra 350 million people. A vegetarian diet means more money, less poverty, and as a result, less crime.'

Two hours later the devotees packed the empty containers into the van and jumped in with their musical instruments. Only when everyone was inside did Paul indicate that we could get back in the squad car. Soon we were winding our way down the hill to the main highway.

'They love you guys out here,' Paul said. 'One day it will all pay off.'

'It already has,' I said, thinking of the gang who had spared the devotee family.

'Do you mind if I ask you something?' he continued. 'What is the meaning of that song you all sing out there? You know, the Hare Krishna one.'

I thought for a moment. 'It means "cover me",' I said.

Paul smiled from ear to ear. 'Anytime you guys need my services just give me a call,' he said. 'I'm always happy to do my part.'

If you offer Me with love and devotion a leaf, a flower, fruit or water, I will accept it.
> —Lord Krishna in the Bhagavad Gita (9:26)

Another important building block for new democracy is the love and goodwill we show to each other. That is the spirit of masakhane, of bringing one another together. It is also the spirit of today's festival organized by Hare Krishna Food for Life.
> —Nelson Mandela

14

Macedonia

Encounters with Significant Macedonians

In the autumn of 2012 when my flight landed in Skopje, Macedonia, I couldn't hold back a smile. The airport was named after one of my childhood heroes Alexander the Great. I had been fascinated by the adventures of the young Alexander as he conquered much of Asia, even part of India. But most important, Alexander was one of the first figures to awaken my curiosity about spiritual life, a curiosity that my spiritual master, Srila A.C. Bhaktivedanta Swami Prabhupada, eventually turned into a full-fledged pursuit of the Absolute Truth.

My mind drifted back to when I was eleven. We were given a school assignment to write about one of our heroes from the past. I chose Alexander the Great. That afternoon I enthusiastically went to the public library to read up on him. What I found that day changed my life.

I learned that he was born in 356 BC, but how did he die?

'Did his final moment come in the midst of a furious battle?' I wondered as I flipped to the end of the book. 'Was he alone, surrounded by enemy soldiers? Did he cry out the name of his country with his last breath?'

I was surprised to learn that nothing of the sort had happened. Alexander, who had fought passionately for many years, conquering and pillaging entire nations, died of an unknown disease on his way home to Macedonia. And instead of glorifying his country at the end of his life, he shared with the world the deep wisdom he had acquired. As Alexander lay on his deathbed, he called his generals.

'I will depart from this world soon,' he said with half-closed eyes, 'but I have three desires. Please fulfil them without fail.' His generals immediately agreed.

'My first desire,' Alexander said, 'is that my physicians alone will carry my coffin to my grave.' The generals nodded in consent. 'My second desire is that the path to my grave be strewn with the gold, silver and precious stones in my treasury.' The generals looked at each other, perplexed, but again nodded their consent. 'And my last wish is that my hands be kept dangling out of the coffin.' The generals recoiled but consented.

Then Alexander's top general stepped forward. He kissed his king's hands and placed them on his own chest.

'Dear King,' he said, 'we assure you that your final desires will be fulfilled. But please tell us why you have given us such strange orders?'

Alexander opened his eyes. 'I would like the world to know three lessons I have learned in life,' he said. 'I want my physicians to carry my coffin because people should realize that no one can protect us from inevitable death. Life should never be taken for granted.

'Having my treasury strewn on the path to my grave will show that we cannot take anything with us at death. People should realize that chasing after wealth is futile.

'And having my hands dangling from the coffin will show that we come into this world empty handed and leave empty handed.'

When I got home that afternoon, I went through my dresser drawers and closet and started throwing my belongings out on the porch.

'What on earth are you doing!' my mother exclaimed. 'What's got into you?'

'We can't take anything with us at death,' I said.

Once I had disembarked the plane and arrived at the Hare Krishna temple in Skopje, I had a chance to talk to some of the local devotees about Alexander the Great.

'Interesting, isn't it,' I said, 'that the airport here is named after him?'

'Macedonians are proud that he was born here,' a devotee said. 'Unfortunately, there's an ongoing debate with our Greek neighbours, who say he was born in Greece in a region they also call Macedonia.'

'Anyway, it's not so important,' said another devotee. 'After all, he wasn't a very enlightened or spiritual person. He just plundered other people's property.'

'No,' I interjected. 'He had some wisdom. He changed some hearts. He changed my—' I stopped before finishing the sentence because I had just met these devotees.

'Anyway Maharaja,' the devotee said, 'the programme will be downtown in the main square. There's a huge statue of Alexander the Great right in the middle of it.'

'I'd like to pay my respects,' I said.

Two hours later I left for the square in the city centre with a group of twenty devotees. The square had been renovated recently and was a popular place for the people of Skopje to spend warm summer

evenings sitting, talking and eating in nearby restaurants. The statue
of Alexander towered over the square.

'That statue is quite impressive,' I said to one of the local devotees.

'Yes,' he replied. 'Alexander the Great left Macedonia to conquer
the world. He built a huge empire, but it was too much to manage and
he never returned home.'

The devotee pointed to the other side of the square. 'There's also
another important landmark over there,' he said. 'It's the home of
Mother Teresa, who was born here in 1910 and left at seventeen to
go to India as a missionary. The house is now a national memorial.
Macedonians are honouring the anniversary of her departure today.
Let's take a look at it while devotees are setting up the festival.'

As we entered the memorial, I noticed a few pamphlets and
brochures about the life of Mother Teresa. I picked up one and began
reading a poem she had written on the boat as she left Europe in
1928. I was so touched by the poem that I had to sit down. It was true
to the spirit of a missionary's life, a life I had also chosen by taking
sanyasa, the life of a renunciate:

Farewell
I'm leaving my dear house
And my beloved land
To steamy Bengal go I
To a distant shore.
I'm leaving my old friends
Forsaking family and home
My heart draws me onward
To serve my Christ.
Goodbye, O mother dear

May God be with you all
A Higher Power compels me
Towards torrid India.
The ship moves slowly ahead
Cleaving the ocean waves,
As my eyes take one last look
At Europe's dear shores.
Bravely standing on the deck
Joyful, peaceful of mien,
Christ's happy little one,
His new bride-to-be.
In her hand a cross of iron
On which the Saviour hangs,
While her eager soul offers there
It's painful sacrifice.
Oh God, accept this sacrifice
Help, please, Thy creature
To glorify Thy Name!
In return, I only ask of Thee,
O most kind Father of us all:
Let me save at least one soul
One you already know.
Fine and pure as summer dew
Her soft warm tears begin to flow,
Sealing and sanctifying now
Her painful sacrifice.

—Gonxhe Bojaxhiu

'Maharaja,' the devotee said, rousing me from my absorption, 'we should get going. The devotees are already doing kirtan in the square.'

The sound of the kirtan carried across the square. There was a large crowd of onlookers surrounding the singing devotees. I was overwhelmed by the beauty of the music and the singing. I stood quietly for several minutes listening, then I went up to a devotee giving out sweets from a basket.

'Would you mind giving me the basket and letting me distribute the sweets to the people?' I asked her.

Making my way to the other side of the square with the basket, I was surprised that not a single person refused to take a sweet. I walked so far that the sound of the kirtan faded into the distance. Small groups of elderly women chatted on benches while their husbands played cards on rustic wooden tables. A number of young couples walked past me, obviously surprised by my bright saffron robes, but everyone was courteous and respectful. In fact, several times after a short discussion people invited me home for dinner. One elderly couple even asked if I needed a place to stay that night.

'This is where I want to be,' I thought. 'It's where I am happiest: talking to people about God on the street.'

I laughed to myself, thinking that even the fumes from passing cars were exhilarating as they reminded me of the years spent doing kirtan on city streets around the world.

The next morning, everyone started preparing for a second evening programme that was to be held in an outdoor amphitheatre which was part of Mother Teresa's memorial. The programme had been advertised all over town: An Evening with Indradyumna Swami. The devotees told me they were expecting about 150 people to attend.

'Will there be security at the amphitheatre?' I asked. Macedonia used to be part of Yugoslavia, and I remembered the incidents of violence I'd encountered years earlier in Croatia and Bosnia.

'No need,' a devotee said. 'We generally don't have problems.'

By 8 p.m., the outdoor theatre was filled with guests. I took my seat in front of the crowd and as I was adjusting my microphone and speaking to my translator, I suddenly noticed five heavy-set, well-dressed men enter the amphitheatre and take up strategic positions around the festival site. They all wore small microphones and wires sticking out from behind their ears, so I thought they must be a security team. At the entrance, I noticed a smaller man standing with two guards on either side of him.

'I guess it is actually a little dangerous down here,' I thought, 'but the devotees probably didn't want to alarm me. They must have hired these guys just in case something does happen.'

My mind peaceful, knowing that any disturbances would be easily dealt with, I picked up a Bhagavad Gita and began my lecture. The audience was attentive and appreciative of my talk, so I went deeper into the philosophy, even explaining who Krishna was: His name, fame, form and pastimes. Then I stressed that the philosophy of Krishna consciousness was practical in our contemporary world. I quoted Srila Prabhupada, who said that we had spiritual solutions to material problems. People were nodding in agreement and I noticed the small man flanked by the security guards nodding too. I felt embarrassed by the rousing applause when the lecture concluded.

'I only did my duty as a sanyasi,' I said to my translator, 'and that is to repeat the teachings of my spiritual master.'

As I made my way to the book table, I noticed the security team moving quickly to the exit.

'Why aren't they staying until the end of the programme?' I wondered, but I quickly became absorbed in talking to the people at the table. Pen in hand, I set about signing the books, as well as writing a few words of encouragement.

Then a devotee tapped me on the shoulder.

'Maharaja!' he said. 'Wasn't that amazing! It's just incredible! I can't believe it.'

'What happened?' I asked.

'Didn't you see?' he said. 'The prime minister of our country attended your lecture. He arrived just as you began and stood at the entrance with guards on either side of him. He stayed to the very end of your talk.'

'I saw the security,' I said, 'but I didn't know the prime minister was here. That certainly is the icing on the cake of a wonderful visit to Macedonia.'

'There's also the cherry on top of the icing,' said the devotee with a big smile. 'The prime minister sent a message through his secretary saying that he loved your talk.'

I shook my head in wonder. 'It is simply the wisdom of Bhagavad Gita and the mercy of my spiritual master.'

Knowledge about Krishna is the summit of education, the innermost secret, the supreme purifier and the perfection of religion. It can be learned by direct experience, is easily and joyfully practised and lasts forever.

—Lord Krishna in the Bhagavad Gita (9:2)

15

India

A Saint in Surat

In December of 1970 my spiritual master Srila Prabhupada spent fourteen days in Surat, in Gujarat, India, with twenty-five of his Western disciples. This journey to India occurred only five years after he had travelled to the West on the order of his spiritual master Srila Bhaktisiddhanta Saraswati, to teach the chanting of the Hare Krishna mantra as the swiftest path to spiritual realization.

The India of the 1970s was a place in which spiritual culture was in rapid decline. At the behest of its political leaders, the country was following the path of capitalism forged by Western powers. India's first Prime Minister, Jawaharlal Nehru, once said: 'We have achieved political freedom but our revolution is not yet complete and is still in progress, for political freedom without the assurance of the right to live and to pursue happiness, which economic progress alone can bring, can never satisfy a people.'4

Srila Prabhupada wanted to remind the people of India that the country's real glory was in its spiritual culture and that this alone could give lasting satisfaction and happiness. The way that he did this was very interesting: he returned with his Western disciples to show his Indian compatriots how Vedic culture was capturing the imagination of the entire world. He proudly called his Western disciples 'dancing white elephants', a phrase that draws on India's reverence of white elephants as a symbol of royalty.

Nothing could have prepared Srila Prabhupada and his disciples for the reception the people of Surat in Gujarat gave them. Gujaratis are famous for being devotees of Krishna, but their enthusiasm in welcoming Prabhupada was unprecedented. The whole city closed down, throngs of people headed by the mayor greeted the party at the railway station, thousands attended the lectures and kirtans that Prabhupada gave during his visit and hundreds of people followed the daily chanting parades (Harinams). During those famous kirtans, shop owners would offer devotees various goods and wares and people would garland them, anoint them with sandalwood paste and shower them with flower petals.

For eight of their days in Surat, Srila Prabhupada and his disciples stayed at the home of Mr Bhagubhai Jariwala, a wealthy businessman. Each morning Prabhupada would take a morning walk through the neighbourhood and would then give a lecture on the first floor of Mr Jariwala's house. Neighbours would often attend.

Forty-four years after Srila Prabhupada's visit, I found myself in Surat with forty other devotees. We were on a seven-week festival tour of the main cities in Gujarat. I asked the local devotees about Prabhupada's time in Surat and they surprised me by saying that our first programme would be in a hall that he had held a programme. That night thousands of people came to our four-hour show which included classical Indian dance, theatre, martial arts, puppet shows, and a big kirtan. I gave my lecture on Bhagavad Gita that night from the very spot in which Srila Prabhupada had spoken. I distinctly felt his presence and empowerment.

The next day, the local devotees offered to take our group to Mr Jariwala's house, the house where Prabhupada stayed. It turned out the house was a small four-storey apartment building. The windows and doors were all heavily bolted with locks and chains. Standing in front of the building, I noticed many people coming out of their homes, curious to see so many foreigners in their neighbourhood.

I tried to envision Srila Prabhupada at this heavily barricaded place.

'Do you think they would let us go inside?' I asked the man who had brought us.

'Not very likely,' he said. 'Mr Jariwala passed away years ago. His grandson sold the building to a man that the locals say is a drug dealer. They say he stores all his contraband in the house. You can see he has made it into a small fortress.'

'We should still try,' I said.

One of the neighbours came forward. 'The problem is that no one has ever seen the new owner. Apparently, he lives a few streets away, but no one will dare go to see him personally.'

'I'll go,' said a tall, stout teenager. 'I don't believe the rumours anyway.'

'We would appreciate that,' I said. 'It would mean a lot to us to have the chance to see where our spiritual master stayed while he was here.'

More and more neighbours gathered and more people started speaking up.

'I saw your spiritual master,' said one man. 'I was seven years old when he came and stayed in our neighbourhood. I used to see him going for a walk in the morning with his disciples. All the local children would follow him. He was always talking about Lord Krishna. He made such an impression on us. We would watch him as he paced back and forth on the balcony up there. He would often wave to us, and we felt privileged because we understood he was a great saintly person.'

'When he came back to the house, he would lecture from the Srimad Bhagavatam,' said another man. 'I remember how he used to effortlessly quote so many verses from the scriptures. I too was just a boy at the time, but I didn't miss a single class.'

'Then every day after the class, he would send his disciples to sing Harinam around the neighbourhood for one hour,' said an older man. 'Everyone loved it and huge crowds would join them. I was twenty years old at the time. Once I approached him and asked how he knew so much about Krishna. He smiled and gave me a copy of the Bhagavad Gita. In fact, he even signed it. I still have it and I read it.'

'I remember my parents preparing fruits and sweets for him and his disciples,' a woman said. 'They would take everything on silver plates to Swamiji and his disciples in the evenings. I remember my mother polishing the silver plates every afternoon. She told me: "Everything has to be perfect for the guru."'

'Nobody knew of the Hare Krishna movement before he came,' another woman said. 'We were mesmerized when he suddenly arrived with his white-skinned disciples. His disciples were very serious about their devotional activities. Some of us became more serious about our own devotion to Lord Krishna as a result of seeing their sincerity. In fact, after all these years, people in this neighbourhood still talk about his visit.'

'My parents used to talk about his visit,' someone else said, 'but I never met him. Are you his disciple?'

'Yes, I am,' I said. The people looked impressed.

'You are very fortunate,' one of them said.

'Yes, I am,' I repeated, trying to contain a wave of emotion that overcame me.

'Are you going to sing like your friends did when they were here all those years ago?' asked one of the children. 'That would be wonderful!'

'Yes, we are going to sing,' I replied. 'But I was hoping to be able to get inside the building to—'

I didn't complete my sentence because I saw the people become suddenly anxious. The crowd parted and a large man, obviously the owner of the house, walked towards me. He was dressed like a perfect gentleman. He didn't look like a drug dealer to me, but from the corner of my eye I saw some of the children run into their homes and close the doors.

'I understand you want to go inside my house,' the man said in a deep voice. I couldn't tell whether what he said was a challenge or a simple enquiry.

'Sir, my spiritual master, Srila A.C. Bhaktivedanta Swami, stayed in your home with his disciples when he visited Surat forty-four years ago. We would be most honoured if we could see the rooms in which he stayed.'

He broke into a big smile. All my apprehensions melted away.

'You are most welcome to visit my house,' he said. 'I would be honoured. I have heard of your spiritual teacher. He was a great saintly person. Great sinners need the mercy of saints.' He winked at the crowd, obviously aware of the rumours circulating about him.

'Follow me,' he said as he led us across the street. He unlocked several padlocks and beckoned us. 'I will show you where he gave his classes.'

We passed row after row of large open burlap sacks full of various textiles. On the first floor he led us into an airy and empty room.

'This is where the classes happened,' he said. 'He would sit there against that wall on a cushion and his students and people from the neighbourhood would sit around the room.'

He led us into another room. 'And this was his bedroom,' he said pointing to a corner of the room. 'His bed was just over there.'

'You seem to know a lot about his visit, sir,' I said.

'He is well known in this neighbourhood,' he said.

'Can we have kirtan in memory of our teacher?' I asked.

'Yes, of course,' he replied. 'Sing as long as you want.'

Closing my eyes, I began chanting prayers to my spiritual master. When I opened my eyes, I saw deep loving emotion on the devotees' faces as they responded. I started chanting Hare Krishna and the devotees raised their arms and swayed back and forth. The owner of the house also raised his arms and began chanting and dancing along with us. The local people broke out in big smiles seeing him.

'That looks like the end of the rumours,' I thought, laughing to myself as the kirtan ended. 'We were all perfect strangers one hour ago. Srila Prabhupada, your potency continues to purify the world.' Aloud I said, 'Now we must follow in our master's footsteps and take the chanting to the streets.'

We thanked the owner of the house and he smiled at us as he put the big locks back on the door. 'You are welcome any time,' he said.

'We will return,' I said. 'Your home is a holy place.'

As we gathered our instruments for Harinam, one of the local men who had been in the kirtan came up to me.

'I want to caution you that a lot of Muslim families now live in this area,' he said. 'In fact, most of the vendors in the market across the street are Muslims. Gujarat has a history of Muslim-Hindu tension.'

I decided to assess the situation before beginning the Harinam. I walked thirty metres to the corner and surveyed the large open-air market. There were hundreds of people shopping at stalls that appeared to sell a seemingly endless variety of goods, including fruits, vegetables, textiles and furniture. A tall bearded Muslim man in the midst of the throng made eye contact with me and held my gaze. He was surrounded by ten or fifteen other similar-looking men.

'Wait here,' I said to the other devotees. Taking a couple of male devotees with me, I crossed the street and walked towards the Muslim men.

'Assalamu alaikum,' I said, extending my hand to the man.

'Wa alaikum as-salam,' he replied. He took my hand and broke into a big smile.

'We are devotees of Lord Krishna from Western countries,' I said. 'We are here to honour our spiritual teacher who stayed in a building across the street many years ago.'

'It is the duty of the spiritual practitioner to honour he who shows the path to Allah,' said the man. 'As you honour your teacher, we honour Mohammed. Praise be upon him.'

He was so friendly and open that I decided to take another step. 'We would like to celebrate the glory of God by singing His names throughout the marketplace. We would like to know if you or anyone else would object to us doing this.'

Some unfavourable looks crossed the faces of some of the men. A few of them began whispering to each other. But the tall man, who obviously was prominent among them, shook his head.

'Nobody will object. Allahu Akbar, God is great. You may sing His names in this market.' Some of the men looked surprised, but he continued. 'We have no differences here in our neighbourhood between Muslim and Hindus. But just in case, I will send my two brothers to accompany you. Should any trouble arise from any Muslim in the market they will take care of it.'

He gestured for two men to step forward. 'This is Abdul Qawi and Ahmed. Ahmed is the karate champion of Gujarat.'

I shook both their hands. 'Gentlemen,' I said, 'let's proceed.'

As the devotees chanted and danced in ecstasy through the market, I thought of how Srila Prabhupada had sent his disciples out to chant on the very same street so many years ago. A number of fruit vendors offered us bananas, apples and grapes. People smiled and waved at us as we passed, and when we stopped people rushed forward to dance with us. But I also noticed Abdul Qawi and Ahmed exchanging strong words with a group of young Muslim men. When Ahmed saw me watching he smiled and waved as if to say, 'We have it under control.'

A huge crowd gathered and I saw Hindus, Muslims and Farsis all with big smiles on their faces.

These are the qualities that belong to those born to the divine nature: fearlessness, purification of one's existence, generosity, self-control, willingness to serve, study of the sacred books, austerity, simplicity, nonviolence, truthfulness, freedom from anger, renunciation, tranquility, aversion to faultfinding, compassion for all beings, freedom from craving, gentleness, modesty, steady determination, energy, forgiveness, fortitude, cleanliness, and freedom from malice and pride.

—Lord Krishna in the Bhagavad Gita (16:1-3)

16

India

The Singing Janitor

In early 2016 I visited a hospital in Mumbai to have a PET scan to check for any recurrence of the cancerous skin cells I'd had surgically removed the previous year. My student, Narottam Das Thakur das, accompanied me to the appointment.

'I'm doubly nervous,' I said to Narottam as we sat in the waiting room. 'Nervous that the cancer has come back and that I'll have to go through another operation. And nervous about the scan.'

'Why?' asked Narottam. 'Scans don't hurt.'

'I know,' I said. 'But it gives me the creeps when they lay me out on the table and roll me into that machine. It's as if they were feeding me into the mouth of some big monster.'

I looked across the room and saw a janitor in a khaki-coloured uniform pushing a broom across the floor. He was talking loudly to himself and laughing at his own jokes. His voice was high-pitched and reedy.

'That man is making everything worse,' I said, aware that my annoyance was stemming from my nerves.

'Maybe he's a little unwell, I mean mentally,' said Narottam.

'He's not unwell,' said the man next to us. 'I come here often and always see him. He's just eccentric.'

The janitor strode past us. He had a thin frame and his brown eyes darted here and there. He was pushing his broom in wild motions, seemingly unaware of the patients in the room. I could see that others were disturbed by him too, especially when he began singing.

'He's very off-key,' I said to Narottam.

The man next to us heard what I said and he laughed. 'He keeps the place pretty clean, though,' he said. 'And he means well.'

The receptionist behind the desk called out to the sweeper. 'Mahesh! Deliver this package to Doctor Agarwal. He's in room sixteen on the fourth floor.'

Mahesh's broom made a loud clattering sound as he dropped it on the floor and hurried over to the desk. He took the parcel and as he walked to the elevator he said something loudly in Hindi which I didn't catch.

'He sounds oddly official,' Narottam said. 'He said, "Doctor Agarwal, room sixteen, fourth floor," as if he were announcing it over a loudspeaker.'

The elevator doors closed, obscuring his grinning face. I breathed a sigh of relief. 'Eccentric is an understatement,' I said to Narottam. 'Anyway, it's quiet at last.'

But just ten minutes later the elevator door opened and he was back.

'Done!' he announced to the full waiting room. He hurried to pick up his broom and began sweeping again in the same big strokes, all the while singing in his shrill voice. The noise was oppressive, but I managed to doze off for a few minutes until I heard my name being called over the loudspeaker.

'Welcome sir, please take a seat,' said one of several nurses in the room. And there, busily organizing a medicine cabinet at the far end of the room, was Mahesh.

'Oh no,' I thought. 'What's he doing here?'

'Mahesh,' said one of the nurses over her shoulder, 'could you kindly take this bag to Doctor Reynolds in room 404?'

Mahesh didn't say a word. He danced across the room to collect the bag, then he opened the door with a theatrical flourish and disappeared down the hallway.

'While we are preparing the solution for your scan,' the nurse said to me, 'please put on this hospital gown and then come and sit in this chair.' When I returned, she set about putting a needle into a vein in my wrist.

'Ouch!' Something didn't feel right with what she was doing. Out of the corner of my eye, I saw that Mahesh had come back into the room. My chair suddenly began to slip under the pressure of my weight and knocked against the table where the nurse had all her equipment. A glass bottle teetered on the edge and as she reached out to grab it, she accidentally yanked the needle out of my wrist.

'Mahesh!' she called. 'Quick! Help!'

Mahesh dashed across the room, caught the bottle and put it back on the table. The nurse picked up the syringe which was now in my lap. 'Mahesh,' she said, 'could you please hold this gentleman's chair while I inject him.'

'Ha,' he said in Hindi, giving his assent. He gripped the chair with both hands, a serious look on his face.

'Ouch!'

The nurse had found another vein.

Mahesh leaned over and, to my surprise, began to speak in fluent English.

He said, 'Sir this is a most auspicious day for me. Somehow by dint of my past pious activities, I have the good fortune to serve a sadhu. Such opportunities are rare.'

Then he quoted a verse that I immediately recognized as being from the Padma Purana:

Aradhananam sarvesham
Vishnor aradhanam param
Tasmat parataram devi
Tadiyanam samarchanam

(My dear goddess, of all types of worship, the worship of Lord Vishnu is the best, and even better than the worship of Lord Vishnu is the worship of His devotee, the Vaishnava.)

I said, 'How do you know that verse?'

'I study sastra,' he replied still gripping the chair.

'Are you a devotee of Krishna?' I asked.

'One day I hope to become a devotee of the Lord,' he said humbly.

'Are you from a family of Vaishnavas?'

'No,' he said. 'I'm an orphan. The devotees of the Lord are my family.'

Then he quoted a verse from the Bhagavad Gita:

Machchitta mad-gata-prana
Bodhayantah parasparam
Kathayantash cha mam nityam
Tushyanti cha ramanti cha

(The thoughts of My pure devotees dwell in Me, their lives are fully devoted to My service, and they derive great satisfaction and bliss from always enlightening one another and conversing about Me. Bhagavad Gita [10:9])

I suddenly realized that I had been so busy criticizing him that I hadn't noticed his peaceful face and his moist, sparkling eyes.

'Sir,' Mahesh said, smiling slightly, 'when I saw you in the reception room earlier, I knew in my heart that the Lord had sent you to give hope to all the unlucky people suffering in this place. Your presence alone brings joy.'

The nurse's voice brought me back to the present. 'All done, Mahesh, thank you. Sir, the injection is done. Please go to the next room to wait for your scan.'

'Sure,' I said. 'But first let me ask Mahesh if—' I turned back to him, but he had gone.

'Where did he go?' I asked the nurse.

'To sweep, probably,' she said.

As I waited for my scan, I felt a wave of remorse wash over me. 'I misjudged that man,' I thought. 'I was ridiculing him in my mind, but he is more of a devotee than I am. I've committed a serious offence. I'll have to beg him to forgive me.'

A sign flashed my name. It was my turn for the PET scan. A nurse welcomed me and helped me lie down on the scanning machine. 'Stretch your arms over your head,' she said. 'You need to lie completely still for a full ten minutes.'

Although I had been nervous about the monster, I relaxed and slowly drifted off to sleep. I woke up when I felt someone touch my feet. I heard a voice singing softly: 'Hare Krishna, Hare Krishna, Krishna Krishna, Hare Hare, Hare Rama, Hare Rama, Rama Rama, Hare Hare.'

I opened my eyes. 'Mahesh,' I whispered, 'I need to talk to you.'

But again, he vanished as quickly as he had appeared. The scan ended and the sense of remorse came over me again. 'I'm just an offender,' I thought as I changed into my clothes. I followed the exit signs until I came to the reception room, now twice as crowded as before. I was signing some papers at the reception desk when I heard the high-pitched voice of Mahesh singing. I looked up and saw him dancing across the back of the room pushing his broom.

I rushed across the room. 'Mahesh! Mahesh!' I called out. 'I need to speak to you!' But before I could reach him, he had disappeared through a glass door. As he danced down the hallway to another part of the hospital, I fell on my knees and offered a prayer for forgiveness:

Vancha-kalpa-tarubhyas cha kripa-sindhubhya eva cha
Patitanam pavanebhyo Vaishnavebhyo namo namah

(I offer my respectful obeisances unto all the Vaishnava devotees of the Lord. They are just like desire trees who can fulfil the desires of everyone, and they are full of compassion for the fallen conditioned souls. [Sri Vaishnava-pranati])

When I stood up, I suddenly remembered that I was in a crowded waiting room. Everyone was staring at me.

'Let them stare,' I thought. 'At the worst they'll think I'm crazy and at best they'll think I'm eccentric. But I'll know I am paying my respects to the wonderful Vaishnava I unexpectedly met today.'

After many lifetimes, one in knowledge surrenders to Me, saying 'Krishna is all.' Such a great soul is very rare.
—Lord Krishna in the Bhagavad Gita (7:19)

17

USA

Memorial Day with the Mob

'Hey man, what's with the dress?'

I was alone in Newark airport enroute to a large kirtan festival in North Carolina. Experience has taught me to ignore such remarks about my traditional saffron robes. Especially when I'm alone.

It was Memorial Day weekend, but most people seemed more interested in enjoying a weekend in the warm spring weather than remembering America's fallen soldiers.

'Hey! I'm talking to you! You with the bald head and the ponytail.'

The person taunting me was obviously not going to give up easily. I glanced over my shoulder and saw a group of eight well-dressed young men plus one older man.

'So?' said one of them. 'I said what's with the dress?'

'I'm a monk,' I said. 'I follow a spiritual tradition from India.'

'Frankie,' said one of the other young men to my interlocutor, 'he must just be one of those Hare Krishnas who sing on the streets in New York.'

'The ones who beg for money,' said another.

'You don't work?' the man named Frankie asked. 'Pay some taxes. Do something for your country!'

I considered whether or not to engage with his defiance. It was Memorial Day weekend, so I said, 'I served my country. I was in the Marine Corps during the Vietnam War.'

'So, you were in 'Nam?' he asked. He looked surprised.

'No. I didn't fight in 'Nam in the end,' I replied. 'I trained to go, but circumstances ended up stopping me from going. What about you?'

'Me, well I—'

'Leave him alone.' The older man spoke up in a thick Italian accent. 'He was a soldier. He did his time in the military.'

He gestured casually with his head to the corner. 'Come over here,' he said to me. 'Listen, I appreciate what you did in the military. You've got the right to choose the religion you want.'

'Thank you, sir,' I said.

'You're on your way to board your flight?' he said.

'Correct,' I replied. 'My flight's in two hours.'

'Then come with us,' said the man. 'There's an Admirals Club lounge just around the corner. You can sit with us there for a while.'

At the club desk, the receptionist asked each of us for our membership cards. 'I'm sorry,' I said. 'I don't have one.'

'Then you can't come in,' she said.

The older man spoke up. 'What do you mean he can't come in? This is Memorial Day weekend. He did time in the military. How's that respecting our soldiers?'

'I was only in for about a year,' I said.

'You wore the uniform, right?' the older man said. 'That's more than can be said for these lazy boys with me.'

Turning to the receptionist he said, 'Let him in.'

'I'm really sorry sir,' she said, 'It's company policy that I can't let anyone in without a membership card unless a member pays for the person to enter.'

'How much?'

'One hundred dollars,' she said.

Without missing a beat, he handed her a hundred-dollar bill. We were in.

'You want some coffee?' the older man asked me.

'No thank you,' I said. As a strict practitioner in the Hare Krishna tradition, I avoid all stimulants, including caffeine. At the same time, I didn't want to seem rude.

'Some bagels?' he asked.

I hesitated.

'Frankie, run over there and get him some bagels.'

When Frankie jumped up and ran over to the buffet, I got the sense my host was someone important.

'May I ask who you are,' I said. 'What do you do?'

The group of young men looked over at the older man, who gave a little smile.

'You don't wanna know,' he said.

I thought maybe he was being humble, so I said, 'No, I really would like to know.'

'The boss said you don't wanna know!' said one of the young men a little too loudly.

'Boys, boys,' the older man said. 'You go over there. I want to have a talk with this gentleman. 'Now,' he said turning to me, 'what do I call you?'

'I'm sorry,' I said. 'I didn't introduce myself. You can just call me Swami.'

'Swami?' he said. 'That's your name?'

'It's my spiritual name. It indicates that I'm a monk.'

'So, it's a Hare Krishna name?' When I nodded, he said, 'I know the Krishnas. When I was young, they used to come to the market in their robes to collect fruits and vegetables. My father took a liking to them and told all the sellers to give them whatever was left over at the end of the day. It went on for years. When I was ten years old, we saw them singing on the streets downtown. Curious, I started walking over but my father grabbed me and said, "That's not for you. You have your family." But now we're here and I've got some questions I need to ask.'

'Sure, go ahead,' I said.

'I've lost a lot of friends through the years,' he said. 'Some of them good, most of them bad. I wanna know where they went. You know, like reincarnation.'

'You believe in reincarnation?' I was taken aback.

'Yes,' he said. 'As a matter of fact, I do.'

'Okay,' I said. 'Well, it all starts by understanding we're not our bodies. We're the soul in the body, like a passenger in a car. When the body dies the soul moves on. Depending on our actions during our life and our desires at the moment of death, we take birth in another body within another family.'

'What about the bad souls?' he asked.

'They take birth in unfortunate circumstances,' I said.

'What kind of unfortunate circumstances?' he said.

'Like in impoverished conditions,' I said. 'Or with little or no chance for education. Or they may be subject to disease or traumatic situations throughout life.'

He sat silently as if mulling this over.

'It's called karma,' I said. 'Reaction to our actions. But such reactions can be dissipated by chanting God's name. We can be free from the cycle of reincarnation through chanting God's names.'

'You can remove bad karma through God's name?'

'Yeah, you can, but it does more than that. By chanting God's name, you can end the cycle of reincarnation permanently. No more dying and being reborn.'

'Hmmm,' he said. 'That sounds like a good deal. What is God's name?'

'One of God's names is Krishna,' I answered.

'That's what you people sing outside the subway,' he said. 'But why do you all sit on the ground?'

'Excuse me,' I said.

'Why do you sit on the ground? The ground is so dirty. It forces everyone to look down on you. I see you guys sitting down on the ground and singing your song. If you gotta message, you gotta look people straight in the eye. Tell whoever's in charge that I said that.'

'Sure,' I said.

'Excuse me for a minute,' he said. 'I gotta go to the men's room.'

In his absence, the young men drifted back towards me.

'Frankie here wants to know if you got any proof that you were in the military,' said one of the boys. 'We just wanna be sure you're not spoofing the boss.'

'Why would I do that?'

'Just show us some proof.'

'Like what can I show you?'

'A card,' he said.

'A card?' I had to smile, although the young man looked serious. 'It was forty-eight years ago!'

'This isn't a joke,' he said.

Then I remembered something.

'Hold on,' I said. I opened my computer and searched through my email until I found what I was looking for.

'Look at this. It's a message from the Marine Corps for my birthday. They get in touch every year on May 20 without fail.'

I read aloud: 'Hello Swami. We at Marine Corps, USMC Community, would like to wish you a very happy birthday today! Semper Fi!'

Frankie looked impressed. 'What does Semper Fi mean?' he asked.

'It means faithful to God, country, family and your fighting unit,' I said. 'I like to think I'm still faithful too. I've just traded my gun for my Bible, so to speak.'

'Hang on, but you weren't a monk then. So why do they address you as Swami?'

'I guess they follow my life,' I said with a smile. 'We're family. You know what I mean?'

'Yeah, I do,' he said. 'I know what you mean. We say omerta. It means that we are bound by the code of silence and secrecy. A code of honour.'

The hair on my arms stood on end and a chill ran up my spine because I knew that term. It was from the Cosa Nostra, the Sicilian Mob.

Frankie came closer and looked at the email. 'It's the real thing,' he confirmed to the others.

When the boss came back, all the young men except Frankie scuttled away again. While he hovered on the edges of our conversation, the boss and I talked until it was time for me to leave.

'I have to catch my flight,' I said.

'Okay,' he said. 'Before you go, I want to apologize for the way my boys spoke to you.'

'Don't worry,' I said. 'It happens sometimes.'

'Look, if you ever need help just call me.' He held out a piece of paper.

I hesitated.

'I mean it,' he said. 'If anyone causes you trouble, I'll help you out.'

'We don't really work that way,' I said.

'Take it!' said Frankie. 'You don't argue with the boss!' He shook his head in disbelief as I accepted the piece of paper.

'Memorize the number,' the boss said, 'and then throw it away.'

'Sure,' I said. 'It was nice meeting you.'

'The pleasure was ours,' said the boss.

Walking out of the Admirals Club, I made a note of the number and threw the piece of paper in the trash. When I reached my gate, an announcement was made that the flight was delayed by half an hour.

I was chanting softly on my beads when I noticed Frankie watching me from thirty metres away. I motioned for him to come over.

'What's up, Frankie?'

'Boss told me to watch over you until you board your flight, Swami. He's got your back.'

As the one within the body moves from childhood to youth to old age, so it passes into another body at death. The wise are not confused by this change. [But] one who understands the divine nature of My birth and actions is not reborn after leaving this body, but comes to Me.

—Lord Krishna in the Bhagavad Gita (2:13 and 4:9)

18

India

A Meeting of Monks

'Welcome home!' Mahavan das greeted me as I came out of New Delhi's slick new airport terminal, tired after my flight from Bengaluru. Mahavan, originally from Russia, was my secretary when I was travelling in India. He wore saffron and shaved his head because he was a brahmachari, a Hare Krishna student. His bag was always stuffed with gadgets—cell phones, iPads, earbuds, chargers.

'We're not home yet,' I said. 'I wish we were, but Vrindavan is still a good three hours away.'

'Well, let's get there quickly,' he said. 'The car is just over here.'

We began working our way through the crowd of people that were going into and coming out of the terminal. Mahavan pointed to an elderly man in soiled burgundy-coloured robes in the midst of the throng.

'Gurudeva,' he said, 'look at that Tibetan Buddhist monk. It looks like he's asking people for help.'

'It's part of his tradition to approach others for alms,' I said. 'Buddhists believe it helps the monks develop humility.'

Generally, in India those begging alms—whether beggars or renunciates—are tolerated and seen as a part of the tapestry of Indian society. It is common for people to give their loose change to those less fortunate than themselves; a monk, especially, would usually be a recipient of charity because people believe that they will be blessed by donating to a monk. Therefore, I was surprised that he was ignored by the affluent people walking past him. I was even more surprised when I saw a teenage boy shove him aside. I felt like I wanted to intervene so that the monk was not subjected to such disrespect.

The monk noticed me watching him and walked towards me.

'Please let me stay with you for a while,' he said in English. 'I need the shelter of spiritual people.'

'Sure,' I said. 'Why don't we sit down?'

'Do you have the time?' he asked.

'For someone like you I have all the time in the world,' I said. We sat down on the bench and he continued to hold on to my sleeve.

'Are you hungry?' I asked. 'Can I get something for you to eat?'

'Thank you, no,' he replied. 'I am not hungry.'

'Have you lost your way?' I asked. 'Maybe I can help you get to your next destination.'

'Just a minute,' he said. He straightened his back and closed his eyes, assuming a meditative pose. As he slowly inhaled and exhaled his face became serene and composed.

'How in the world did he manage to find such peace right after being mistreated like that?' I wondered. The minutes passed, and I felt a wave of tranquility wash over me as well. Finally, he opened his eyes. He didn't look directly at me, but stared into the distance as he told me his story.

'My name is Tsering Lama,' he said. 'I come from the Sera monastery in Lhasa, Tibet. I lived there from the age of five.'

I had been fascinated with Tibet when I was young, with its philosophy and its monks and its ways of life which I regarded as unconventional as a teenager. I had pored over a well-loved copy of *The Tibetan Book of the Dead* which I found in the Eastern spirituality section of an alternative bookstore in San Francisco. That was until I found Srila Prabhupada's *Bhagavad-Gītā As It Is*, which answered my questions in a way *The Tibetan Book of the Dead* hadn't.[5]

'Tibet is a long way from Delhi,' I said. 'How old are you now?'

'I am seventy years old,' he replied.

'And what service do you do in the monastery?' I asked.

'I study the scriptures,' he said. 'Since my childhood I have studied the teachings of Master Lama Tsongkhapa who lived in the fourteenth century. He was the founder of the Gelug-pa School, which I belong to, and a highly respected teacher of the Buddhist scriptures. My main service is to debate with others about the scriptures. It is an integral part of our tradition.'

'I am honoured to meet such a learned scholar,' I said. 'And I am sorry to see how people treated you today.'

He shook his head as if to suggest the mistreatment was of no concern, or perhaps to dismiss my praise. 'It has been my lifelong dream to visit Bodh Gaya,' he said. 'It is the place where Buddha attained enlightenment. That holy site is here in India in the state of Bihar. Several months ago, I said goodbye to my beloved disciples and set out on foot alone for Bodh Gaya.'

I wondered how many hundreds or even thousands of disciples such a man could have.

'When I arrived here in Delhi,' he continued, 'two men invited me to spend the night at their home. I was exhausted from months of travelling, so I accepted their invitation. That night they fed me and gave me some tea to drink. The next thing I knew I was waking up on the sidewalk in a Delhi slum. It seems that the tea they gave me was laced with some drug that caused me to fall unconscious. I discovered that they had stolen everything I possessed: my clothes, my passport, my money of course, and even my sacred chanting beads. I had been saving that money since my childhood for this pilgrimage, and suddenly it seemed impossible that I would make it to Bodh Gaya.

'Now I have nothing. I have been here at the airport for three days begging for money to complete my journey. Nobody has given me a single rupee, most likely because I look so dirty and dishevelled.'

I took his hand. 'I will help you,' I said.

'No, no,' he said. 'I will not take money from a holy man like you.'

'It's okay,' I said. 'I am not holy yet. I'm trying, but I'm just a beginner really. I have a long way to go. Believe me, you can safely accept some money from me.'

'What you say in humility is not true,' he said soberly. 'I studied your face. I can see your true self through your eyes.'

'What do you mean, you can see me through my eyes?' I asked.

'I have learned this from our Tibetan masters.' He looked straight into my eyes with a steady stare. Feeling uncomfortable I looked away, but he caught my chin with his hand and turned my head towards him so he could study my face. His small hand had a powerful grip.

I also looked at his face. His dark brown eyes peered out from slanted eyelids that curved upward at the outer corners, reminding me of Tibetan art. He had a small, flattish nose and his thin lips that, though fixed in a determined line, seemed to be slightly, almost imperceptibly smiling. He obviously had not shaved for some days. His golden skin bore a few small scars. He seemed to glow with a radiance that I could feel more than see, and the softly pungent fragrance of Tibetan incense still hovered about his stained, travel-weary clothes. Though his head barely came up to my nose, I had the feeling that I was standing in front of someone large and powerful, someone who could knock me over with the flick of a finger.

After some minutes he spoke. 'You have served your master well in this life.'

'I have done some service. Like I said, I'm trying but—'

'You have spread his glories through the written word, through discourses and through festivals that you hold in distant lands.'

'Festivals?' I thought. 'How could a Tibetan monk know that I hold festivals, especially in distant lands?'

'But your service was interrupted last year by disease,' he said.

'Well ... yes. I had a bout with cancer and—'

'In March.'

I caught my breath. 'Yes. You are exactly right. It was in March of last year.'

'And there is more disease to come.'

'Oh really?' I said, hearing the disappointment in my own voice.

'But don't worry,' he said. 'I will help you.'

He got off the bench and sat down on the ground in a full yoga asana. He closed his eyes once more and quickly seemed to be transported to another plane. After a few minutes his eyebrows furrowed in the intensity of his meditation and his lips moved as he chanted mantras in the Tibetan language.

People stopped to stare at the unusual sight: a sanyasi sitting on a bench and a Buddhist monk meditating on the ground next to him. They looked at me as if asking for an explanation, but I had none. I could only sit silently while he offered prayers on my behalf.

Twenty minutes later he opened his eyes and turned to me. 'I have removed the obstacles,' he said. 'You will live a long life in service to your master.'

'Gosh,' I said. 'Thanks so much.' I got up and helped him back onto the bench.

'Compassion is central to the teachings of Buddha,' he said.

'I know that,' I said. 'But why are you being so kind to a stranger like me?'

'We are not strangers,' he said. 'I am returning a favour you offered me several lifetimes ago.'

I felt the hair on my arms stand up.

'You mean ... How did we know each other in a previous life?'

'Some things are better left unsaid,' he replied. 'And I must go. I must try to fulfil my dream.'

'Wait,' I said. 'Wait a minute. I want to help you.'

'No,' he said. 'As I already told you, I would not accept money from you. You are using it to help people less fortunate than yourself.'

'How do you know how I use money?' I asked. 'We've only just met.'

'As I told you, the eyes show the light of the soul,' he said.

He turned and started walking back towards his begging spot near the terminal.

'No!' I said running after him. 'I won't let you be mistreated by those people again. Please take this donation. It's enough to get you to Bodh Gaya and back to Tibet by train.' I pushed some bills into his hand.

He looked at the money and when he looked up his eyes were moist.

'I will accept your kindness,' he said slowly. 'And I will not forget you.'

He started walking away again, but then stopped and turned back.

'We won't meet again in this lifetime,' he said. 'But I will leave you a special gift in the monastery in Lhasa. When you arrive, mention my name. The monks will direct you.' He took a small piece of paper from the sleeve of his robe and wrote down the address of the monastery.

'Please make sure you go there,' he said. 'What I am leaving for you will be a great asset in service to your master.'

'Do you mean money?' I asked.

'Oh no,' he said. 'Nothing like that. It is something more wonderful than anything money could ever buy. You will not be disappointed.' And he turned and walked away without looking back.

I turned to Mahavan. 'What just happened? Was that a dream?'

'No,' he said looking as astounded as I felt. 'I saw it with my own eyes. Will you actually go to Lhasa?'

'Yes,' I replied. 'Well, I'll try. I've always wanted to go to Tibet. And now I have the best reason ever to go: to increase my service to my spiritual master, Srila Prabhupada.'

One who is not disturbed in spite of the threefold miseries, who is not elated when there is happiness, and who is free from attachment, fear and anger, is called a sage of steady mind.
 —Lord Krishna in the Bhagavad Gita (2:56)

19

Tibet

Pilgrimage to Kailash, the Mountain of Lord Shiva

The promise by Tsering Lama of a spiritually significant gift was a prompt for me to renew my attempt to visit Tibet. My teenage fascination with Tibet had taken a backseat in my life after I had embraced the faith and spiritual practices of the Hare Krishna movement. But three years before I met the monk in New Delhi airport, an opportunity to visit Tibet arose when several devotees invited me to join them on a pilgrimage to Mount Kailash, the sacred abode of Lord Shiva situated 6,705 metres above sea level. However, our plans ended abruptly when the Chinese government refused our visa applications.

Then, a few months after I met the monk, I received a call from the group which had planned the original journey to Tibet. The Chinese government was again issuing visas for Mount Kailash. Would I be interested in going? Oh, would I ever! Thirteen of us were granted visas through an official Tibetan travel agency.

Why would I, a devotee of Lord Krishna, be interested in going on pilgrimage to a site associated with Lord Shiva? Lord Shiva is part of a universal trinity: Lord Brahma creates the universe, Lord Vishnu maintains it, and Lord Shiva ultimately destroys it. Some Hindus worship Lord Brahma and Lord Shiva as God, but within the Vaishnava tradition they are understood as extremely powerful and significant demigods, or deputies, of Lord Vishnu who is an incarnation of Krishna, the original form of God. Vaishnavas worship Lord Shiva as the greatest devotee of Krishna. My objective in visiting Mount Kailash was to obtain the blessings of Lord Shiva who is said to reside with his consort, Parvati, atop Mount Kailash. In Vaishnava teachings we learn not to approach God directly, but through His pure devotees.

Mount Kailash is revered by followers of multiple faiths. In my faith, Shiva is said to meditate upon Lord Krishna there. It was at Mount Kailash that the Ganges descended with great force from the spiritual world to the material world and was caught by Lord Shiva in his matted locks. Kailash is also known as Mount Meru, the centre of the universe. Throughout the ages it has been called by various names including Jewel Peak, Lotus Mountain and Silver Mountain. The city of Kuvera, the treasurer of the demigods, is said to be near Mount Kailash.

Local Buddhists recognize the spiritual significance of the mountain and consider it one of their holiest places of pilgrimage. It is also fervently worshipped by followers of the Bon religion, the religion of Tibet prior to the arrival of Buddhism in the seventh century. Tibetans say that there is an invisible ladder connecting Kailash to heaven, and the rulers of ancient Tibet were said by their citizens to have descended to Kailash from heaven attached to ropes of light.

Because of the mountain's sanctity in the eyes of several of the world's great religions, no one has ever attempted to climb it. Reinhold Messner, the famous Austrian mountaineer who had scaled all fourteen of the 8,000-metre-high mountains of the world, was offered a license to climb Mount Kailash by the Chinese government in the 1980s. 'Of course, I declined,' he writes. 'It would not have been intelligent to do otherwise. One should not trample on gods.' A Buddhist saint once said: 'Only a man entirely free of sin can climb Kailash. And he wouldn't have to actually scale the sheer walls of ice to do it. He'd just turn himself into a bird and fly to the summit.'

Through the centuries Westerners have been attracted to visit Kailash, not necessarily for spiritual reasons but out of curiosity. The first recorded Westerner to visit Kailash was an Italian Jesuit missionary, Ippolito Desideri, in 1715. He wrote:

> Kailash is a mountain of excessive height and great circumference, always enveloped in clouds, covered in snow and ice, and most horrible, barren, steep and cold. The Tibetans walk devoutly around the base of this mountain which takes several days, and they believe this will bring them great indulgences. Owing to the snow on the mountain my eyes became so inflamed that I well-nigh lost my sight.

Instead of climbing the mountain, the faithful walk around it with their right sides to the mountain. The purpose of our visit to Kailash would be to walk around the mountain, a journey of some fifty-two kilometres that we estimated would take us over two days (approximately fifty-five hours) on foot to complete.

In Tibetan this is called 'kora', literally 'pilgrimage'. Vaishnavas call the circumambulation of a sacred object or site 'parikrama'.

Sometimes pilgrims undertake a kora or parikrama on foot, simply walking around the worshipful site. Others do a more arduous pilgrimage—they conduct their circumambulation by prostrating themselves, offering a prayer or number of prayers, then rising and prostrating themselves again. It takes them three weeks to complete their journey one body length at a time.

And so, following more in the footsteps of the pilgrims and less in those of the curious, our group left Kathmandu, Nepal, on 15 September 2016 and headed for Lhasa, the capital of Tibet. Our short flight over the beautiful Himalayan mountains was meant to take only one hour. Unfortunately, as we were to experience repeatedly in the coming two weeks, we encountered an obstacle. Forty-five minutes into the flight, the captain announced that we would not be able to land in Lhasa due to inclement weather and that the flight was being diverted to Chengdu in southwestern China, two hours away. I knew something wasn't right. The weather in Lhasa was fine and was forecast to be fine for several days. I had checked it on the internet just before we took off. Later we learned that the flight had been diverted to Chengdu to pick up more passengers for Lhasa.

The airline accommodated us in a hotel in Chengdu for the night and we flew to Lhasa the next day. The austerities in the detour were bearable, but little known to us there would be serious flow-on effects from the delay.

Lhasa is one of the highest cities in the world, situated 3,490 metres above sea level. I had acclimatized myself somewhat before the trip by spending twelve days in the mountains of Kashmir, but within hours of our arrival most of the other members of our team began struggling with altitude sickness which is caused by reduced air pressure and lowered oxygen levels. Altitude sickness can be life-threatening, causing pulmonary oedema or cerebral oedema (fluid

accumulation in the lungs or brain), both of which require the sufferer
to be evacuated to a lower altitude. In most cases though, symptoms
are mild: difficulty in sleeping, dizziness, fatigue, headache, loss of
appetite, nausea and vomiting.

While everyone else rested, I decided to take a look around the
old city of Lhasa that I had heard about during my youth. It was
harder to find than I expected. Much of the city had been rebuilt with
endless modern structures like apartment buildings, office buildings
and shopping complexes. I visited the famous Potala, formerly the
residence of the Dalai Lama. Built at various stages beginning from
1645, it is rich in Tibetan history. The palace was visually stunning,
a reminder of the mysterious enchantment of old Tibet. I also
visited the sacred Jokhang temple (built starting from 1652), the
most important site of pilgrimage in Tibet. Thousands of Buddhist
devotees were bowing down repeatedly while others walked around
the temple fingering their wooden prayer beads as they chanted 'Om
mani padme hum' (I worship He who sits on the divine lotus).

I joined the surging crowd circumambulating the temple and
then sat among the pilgrims. Being white and dressed in my monks'
robes, I immediately became an object of discussion. I was pleasantly
surprised that everyone without exception welcomed me and several
even came over to congratulate me on my good fortune to be there.
When I took out my japa beads to chant, swarms of curious people
surrounded me and listened attentively to my chanting of the Hare
Krishna mantra.

I had been chanting for a couple of hours when two young women
approached me.

'Are you a Lama?' one asked.

'Do you mean a priest?' I asked. She nodded. 'Well, I am trying
my best,' I said.

'We are honoured to meet you,' said the other woman. 'My name is Nima.'

'And I am Zaya,' said the first woman.

'You speak English very well,' I said.

'Yes,' said Nima. 'Here in Tibet, we learn three languages in school: Chinese, Tibetan and English.'

'Why is English mandatory?' I asked.

'It's the international language, of course,' Nima said.

'Ours is a beautiful country,' she continued, 'and the most important thing for Tibetans is our spiritual tradition. That's why every morning more than 15,000 people circumambulate Jokhang temple.'

'I very much appreciate the pilgrims' devotion,' I said.

'My grandma tells me that you Western people have very strange habits,' said Zaya, abruptly changing the reflective tone of the conversation.

'Like what?' I asked.

'She said most of you take a bath every day.' They both giggled.

'Yes,' I said. 'Don't you do that in Tibet?'

'No!' exclaimed Zaya, looking horrified. My grandmother bathes once a year. She says if she were to bathe every day, the blessings she received by prostrating herself before the temple 300 times a day would be washed away.'

'We all bathe during a special festival called Karma Dunba,' said Nima. 'Everyone, even Zaya's grandmother, goes down to a river and takes a full bath. Strict followers wash their clothes just once a year on that day.'

'But times are changing now,' said Nima. 'I bathe once a month.'

'And I bathe once a week,' said Zaya. 'Some of my friends even bathe every day like you Westerners!'

I laughed and then realized that as locals, these girls might be able to help me with information about how to find the Sera monastery. The monk I had met in Delhi had told me he would leave me a gift there. Our time in Lhasa was short and I knew I needed to find the monastery soon.

'Sera means wild rose,' Zaya said. 'It is one of our most important monasteries. You can find it in the northern suburbs of Lhasa.'

'Is it a big building like Potala?' I asked.

'Oh no!' she said. 'The monastery consists of thirty-six buildings scattered over twenty-eight acres of land.'

'Thank you,' I said, suddenly feeling despondent. It would be impossible to find the priceless gift in a complex so huge.

I returned to the hotel late in the evening and quickly fell asleep. I dreamed that our group was visiting an old Buddhist monastery. Guests were being given headphones that guided them through various parts of the monastery. Everyone in our group except me was given brown headphones. I was handed a silver set that glowed brightly in the dark. When I put the headset on, I heard the familiar voice of Tsering Lama.

'I told you we would not meet again in this life,' he said, 'but I will speak words regarding the gift I promised you. I cannot give you anything greater than that which your spiritual master has already given you. Be content with his boundless mercy alone and with it attain the highest perfection.'

I woke suddenly and raced around the room to find paper and pen before I forgot the monk's words. My spiritual master, Srila Prabhupada, said that dreams are usually not to be taken seriously, being concoctions of the mind. However, when the spiritual master or a great devotee appears in a dream, their words can carry significant instruction. I felt that to be the case now. Part of me wanted to knock on the other devotees' doors to tell them about the amazing dream, but I also felt shy. Afterwards, it took me hours to fall asleep.

The next morning, we were meant to fly to Ngari, a city just 100 kilometres from Mount Kailash, but we were informed at breakfast that the flight had been cancelled. China's security was on red alert because of North Korea's recent test-firing of missiles. It was another setback in our pilgrimage. The only other way to reach Mount Kailash was a four-day drive across 1,300 kilometres of mountainous roads.

Our government travel agency provided two SUVs with drivers, a small truck for our luggage and cooking equipment, and two official guides who were required to be with us every minute of our stay in Tibet. Ultimately, their presence worked to our advantage because wherever we went, we were subjected to security checks.

Upon departing Lhasa, we learned that a cold front was about to descend on western Tibet. We had to get to Mount Kailash as fast as possible. By driving seventeen hours one day and eleven hours the next, we managed to cut the journey time in half. The long hours in the car were austere, but gave me time to reflect again on the purpose of our journey to Mount Kailash—to obtain the blessings of Lord Shiva that we might become better devotees of Lord Krishna and His representative, my beloved spiritual master, Srila Prabhupada.

After two days of driving, we arrived at a lake called Manasarovar (Mapham Tso in Tibetan). Every pilgrim must visit Manasarovar before commencing their pilgrimage. It is famous for three things: its changing colours, its infinite variations of reflection, and its fearsome storms. The lake is said to have been created from the mind of Lord Brahma. On the top of Mount Kailash, Lord Shiva and Parvati once sat in deep meditation on Lord Krishna for twelve years by the calculation of the demigods. No rain fell in the area during that period, so Lord Shiva called Lord Brahma to create a sacred lake where he and his consort could bathe. After their bath, a self-manifested golden Shiva lingam appeared in the centre of the lake.

Later the same day we reached Darchen, a small village situated at an altitude of 4,575 metres just a few kilometres from Mount Kailash. Darchen serves as the starting point for every pilgrim's journey around the sacred mountain.

We rested in a simple hotel there for two days to prepare ourselves for the arduous journey ahead. Despite our best efforts to be in good physical shape and to avoid altitude sickness by acclimatizing ourselves, we all felt that faith in Krishna and His devotee Lord Shiva were the most important qualifications for completing the kora.

Two days later, at long last all thirteen of us set out on our kora around Mount Kailash. We would do it at a pace that would take us three days. The first day is called the day of purification, the second the day of departure (from one's illusory self or the false ego), and the third the day of renewal. Many Tibetans do the pilgrimage in a single day.

Most of our gear and kitchen paraphernalia had gone ahead on yaks to meet us where we would stay the first night, twenty-two kilometres further up the winding road. We were carrying just basic necessities in our backpacks as we started across the barren moonscape terrain towards Mount Kailash. Eager to get the journey underway after so many days of waiting, everyone started out at a fast pace.

'Slow down!' I called out. 'At this height you have to pace yourselves. And remember to drink three litres of water as we walk along today. It's easy to get dehydrated up here.'

After we had been walking for a couple of hours, I noticed that Alexey, a strong, healthy, well-built Russian man in his early thirties, was missing from our group. He had come on the trip to help Ananta

Vrindavan das film the expedition. I retraced my steps along the path and found him trailing far behind us. His steps were slow and heavy.

Saradiya-rasa dasi came up behind me with our Tibetan guide. 'He doesn't look good,' she said. The guide nodded in agreement.

'Maybe he's just exhausted from travelling here. Do you think he should stay back this morning?' I asked the guide. 'Maybe one of the other guides can stay with him.'

'Yes,' he said. 'I can get one of them to take him back to the hotel and I'll ask him to keep in touch by phone to let you know how he is doing. Your phones should certainly work on the first day of your pilgrimage before we travel out of range. If he feels better this afternoon, they can catch up by horse.'

As the road gradually got steeper, I didn't have to remind the others to slow down. The altitude accomplished that on its own. Soon we were walking only ten paces at a time before having to stop and catch our breath. To our left the huge treeless Barkha plain was dotted with white nomadic tents and herds of sheep and goats. After four hours we arrived at a 'chaktsel gang', one of four places on the kora where pilgrims offer prostrated obeisances to the mountain. At these sites there are images on rocks which are said to be places where Lord Buddha left his footprints when he visited Kailash in the fifth century BC.

While resting at the chaktsel gang we had a clear and direct view of Mount Kailash's beautiful awe-inspiring southern face. Everyone in our party lay down on the ground for a few minutes of rest. It was only the first day and I was already exhausted by the high altitude. I began to wonder if I could carry on, especially when I saw the trail ahead. It entered the glacial Lha Chu valley, a flat rocky wasteland that wound along vast scraggly mountain slopes.

The silence of the party was broken by the ringing of Saradiya-rasa's cell phone. When she hung up, her face was pale.

'Alexey is in critical condition,' she said. 'He has pulmonary oedema, the worst-case scenario in high-altitude sickness. Our guide has taken him to the hospital.'

'We need to act quickly,' I said. 'Pulmonary oedema can be fatal in a matter of hours. The golden rule is to get the patient to a lower altitude as quickly as possible.'

'But that's the problem,' said Saradiya-rasa. 'We're on the Tibetan plateau and there are no lower altitudes easily accessible. Our guide says the doctors are trying to stabilize him with oxygen and some medication, but he's not responding. He is unconscious, his extremities are cold and he's shaking like a leaf.'

Everyone was dazed by the news. I stood up quickly.

'Okay,' I said. 'We're aborting the pilgrimage. We have to turn around and go back to Darchen to assess Alexey's situation. Let's move now.'

'It's serious, but surely not all of us have to go,' Saradiya-rasa said. 'Maybe one or two of us can go to be close by and wait for news. We can break into two groups and meet along the trail tomorrow. We don't all have to break the kora.'

'Forget the kora!' I said loudly. 'No kora is as important as a person's life. We need to go back to Darchen as a team. We'll have kirtan together and pray that Krishna protects Alexey.'

Everyone stood up and we began following our tracks back to Darchen. We passed many pilgrims who looked at us quizzically as if to say, 'You're going the wrong way.'

All the way back Saradiya-rasa was on the phone with our main guide, who suggested that we put Alexey in a car and drive him several hundred kilometres south where the altitude was slightly less.

'It's not enough!' Saradiya-rasa shouted. 'We have to get a helicopter in to take him to Kathmandu.'

I felt her demands wouldn't be possible. The only helicopters in Tibet were used by the military. The officials would never give permission for a helicopter to fly in from another country to rescue someone who, for them, was just a tourist. I had read extensively about the region before our journey began and knew there were risks attached to the Kailash kora because the place was so remote. Our guide had privately told me that more than thirty pilgrims, mostly Indians, had already died on the kora this year, almost all from high-altitude sickness. The situation looked bleak at best.

But by the time we reached Darchen three hours later, Saradiya-rasa was making things happen. She had contacted both the Russian Embassy and the Chinese Ministry of Foreign Affairs in Beijing to ask for assistance. She had also contacted a private helicopter service in Kathmandu.

'The Russian Embassy called the Chinese Ministry of Foreign Affairs and told them to get into action,' she said. 'The ministry has called the local Darchen police station and told them they have one hour to get Alexey into an ambulance and start driving him to Kodari, a small village on the border with Nepal about 200 kilometres south of here. Once we make it to Nepal, there will be a helicopter from Kathmandu to collect Alexey and fly him straight to the hospital. It's a five-hour flight with one stop for refuelling.' She was a miracle worker.

The only ambulance in Darchen was broken down, so Saradiya-rasa arranged a private car. In the meantime, the rest of us visited Alexey in the hospital, which was nothing more than a few rooms with some beds and oxygen canisters. The nurses and doctors all seemed capable, despite the lack of facilities.

Alexey opened his eyes when he heard us enter his room. He spoke a few faint words of greeting.

'Much of the water has receded from his lungs,' his doctor said. 'It could return without warning though. His condition is very, very serious.'

A few minutes later, the hospital staff helped us move Alexey into the car. Saradiya-rasa and her husband Sukanta das were to travel with him as far as the border, and another member of our party, Rasika Mohan das, would accompany him all the way to Kathmandu.

The next morning at 6:15, I received a call from an exhausted Saradiya-rasa. I had been up most of the night chanting and waiting for news.

'The mafia was waiting for us at the border,' she said. 'They demanded a $50,000 cash payment to allow Alexey to cross into Nepal. They had weapons with them but I got out of the car and was arguing with the leader when my phone rang. It was the Russian Embassy following up on our progress. I told them where we were and handed the phone over to the mafia leader. Within moments he and his gang were gone. A representative of the helicopter company was waiting halfway across a rope bridge over a river between Nepal and Tibet. We helped Alexey and Rasika Mohan to the halfway point on the bridge and left them in the care of the man from the helicopter company. They all disappeared into the night. As soon as it was light, the helicopter took off for Kathmandu. The doctor on board called me to say we had gotten Alexey out just in time and with proper medical care he should be okay in a week or so. We're on our way back now.'

After Saradiya-rasa's call I collapsed in bed, but a few short hours later I was awoken by my friend, Chaturatma das, knocking on my door.

'Maharaja, let's go,' he called. 'Back on the kora. We have to walk fourteen kilometres today.'

The weather was changing for the worse and we didn't want to lose time, so we rode in jeeps to where we had stopped the day before. After walking for an hour, I realized how physically and emotionally exhausted I was from the events of the previous day. I asked one of our guides if he could arrange a horse for me and a couple of the others. The guide found horses to rent farther down the valley for three of us.

We rode and the others walked at different paces, braving the high altitude. We all chanted and absorbed ourselves in the remarkable beauty of the scenery. The mountains were beyond description.

As we moved through the valley a strange sight caught my eye, a flat area a little above the plains was draped with Tibetan flags flying majestically in the wind, with many large vultures sitting or flying about.

'What is that?' I asked the guide. 'A special temple?'

'No,' he replied, 'it's a sky burial site. In the Buddhist tradition we don't bury or burn the dead. We lay their bodies out in the open for vultures to eat. That might sound repugnant to you, but you Westerners bury your dead in the ground and worms eat the body. Worms or vultures, it's the same principle. The only difference is that in a sky burial, family members watch the vultures feast on their loved ones while priests chant mantras.'

'Wow!' I answered.

'Yes,' he said. 'It allows us to confront death and understand the impermanence of earthly life, and it helps us appreciate the importance of searching for the eternal life of the spirit.'

By late afternoon we reached Diraphuk, our campsite for the night. The yaks carrying our luggage were waiting for us. Situated around

5,000 metres, the site allowed us a view of the soaring, resplendent north face of icy Mount Kailash. It was the closest we would come to the mountain itself.

'Could we walk a bit closer?' I asked the guide. 'I would like to take a small stone from the face of the sacred mountain. I want to worship it as "tadiya", something connected to a holy place.'

'Not possible,' he said, without a moment's hesitation. 'The government no longer allows pilgrims to come closer to the mountain than we are now. They used to issue permits for the inner kora along a path that runs close to the mountain, but too many pilgrims were killed by landslides. Plus, the area immediately surrounding Kailash has high velocity winds. Many times pilgrims just disappeared from there without a trace.'

Exhausted from the day's walk, we all settled down for a good night's rest. But sleep was difficult because of the altitude, and temperatures plunged well below freezing during the night. The accommodations were austere. We slept on wooden beds in huts made of concrete without insulation or heating. The toilet was a hole in the ground outside with a bucket of icy water. There was no facility for bathing.

At 2 a.m. I crawled out of my sleeping bag to answer the call of nature. I couldn't find my flashlight, so I stumbled outside and made my way along by the light of a full moon. I looked up at Mount Kailash and was amazed at the sacred mountain's beauty in the moonlight. The moon's rays gave the snow a shimmering, luminous effect and made the whole mountain glow silver in the darkness. I stood there dumbfounded as if seeing a mystical vision, unable to take my eyes away from the mountain.

Then one of the yaks appeared from around the corner of a small building and began to charge towards me. Its aggression broke my meditation and I ran for the shelter of our room. I made it inside just in time. So ended our first day of the kora, our day of purification.

We began our second day—the day of departure from the false sense of self—after a breakfast of hot porridge. Nobody ate much, as digestion is difficult at high altitudes and dampens the appetite. The guide warned us that the second day posed the greatest challenge of the kora. We had to walk (or ride) around ten kilometres upwards to the highest point of elevation on the kora, a pass called Drolma-la, at 5,630 metres. It would take approximately seven hours.

Again, we made our way in small groups at different paces. Clouds moved in by mid-morning and rain began to fall. The storm we had feared was upon us. Several hours later, cold winds picked up and the rain turned to sleet and snow. Everyone, including our guides and horses, moved at an agonizingly slow and painful pace, our faces whipped by little drops of ice and freezing cold droplets of water. Each step took an immense amount of strength and I could see everyone in our party gasping for oxygen in the rarefied atmosphere. Numerous Tibetan pilgrims walked past us at a steady pace singly or in groups, eventually disappearing in the distance.

I was wearing many layers of clothes, but was chilled to the bone. As I was contemplating the severity of the cold, a jeep with an open cab and several somber-faced policemen inside rumbled over the rough terrain towards us. When it passed by, I gasped at the sight of a dead man lying face up in the back of the cab, his ankles and wrists tied with rope. He was dressed like the other Tibetan pilgrims doing the kora. Had he died while doing it? I glanced over at one of our guides. He shrugged his shoulders as if to say, 'No big deal, it happens every day.' My lamentation about the cold melted away in my gratitude to be alive.

The three of us on horseback moved faster than the others and ended up far ahead of them. My horse took me so far ahead that I could see no one behind me or ahead of me. The track began to ascend so steeply that I had to hold on to my horse to keep from sliding off backwards.

I reached a small plateau. A passing pilgrim told me it was the famous Shiwa-tsal charnel ground, named after a place of cremation at Bodh Gaya in India. Pilgrims undergo a symbolic death at Shiwa-tsal. It is traditional to leave an item of clothing or a bodily part such as hair, teeth or blood to represent the renunciation of life. In fact, what is being renounced is the false ego, the false sense of self—the erroneous identification with the material body—in favour of a true spiritual identity. For followers of the Vedic tradition, such renunciation means giving up all temporary bodily designations such as race, nationality, family, name, fame, beauty and all material attachments, and realizing oneself as a pure spirit soul, a servant of God. I left a favourite hat as a sign of renunciation and prayed to Lord Shiva to help me realize that I am an eternal servant of Krishna.

We continued on for another two intense hours—I, my horse and my guide. At one point, the guide and the horse both stopped abruptly, exhausted from the steep climb.

'White Lama,' my guide said to me after he caught his breath, 'if you are fortunate, you will see a yeti. Sometimes a Lama will see them, but your people have little faith in such things. Your countrymen live in mundane lands devoid of the mystics, sages and rishis we have here in our sacred mountains. Nothing out of the ordinary happens in lands where your people dwell.'

I gazed at the mountains.

'Have you ever seen a yeti?' I asked.

'No,' he replied. 'But my father and uncle have seen them many times, much higher up in the mountains. They are very large. Edmund Hillary and his Sherpa guide Tenzing Norgay reported seeing large human-like footprints at 22,000 feet as they ascended Mount Everest for the first time. The footprints are several inches shorter but at least four inches wider than a human. Other mountaineers in the Himalayas have photographed such footprints.

'It is said that hundreds of years ago there was an entire village of yetis near here, but they became intoxicated during a feast and practically killed each other off. Only a few families remain, hidden in the vast mountains and valleys of our Himalayas. They live a very long time because of the medicinal herbs that are found in the fertile valleys of these mountains.'

'It's all very interesting,' I said, 'but I have not come here looking for yetis. I've come to receive the mercy of Lord Shiva, who can help to destroy my false ego and become a pure devotee of Krishna.'

'I understand,' said my guide with a smile. 'And if you are fortunate, you may even see Lord Shiva. But if you are more fortunate, he will see you.'

We finally reached Drolma-la pass which was festooned in prayer flags. My horse had put in hours of strenuous effort. I marvelled at his strength and agility on the rough surfaces, which were steep and strewn with boulders. My guide told me that Genghis Khan used the same species of horse (more a large pony than a horse) to conquer the known world.

Though I had ridden and not walked up the steep path, I was exhausted from the harsh atmosphere, the altitude and the cold. A posted sign read 5,630 metres. Because of the altitude, pilgrims are warned not to stay there longer than ten minutes. I could see the way down the mountain was precariously steep.

'Thank goodness I have my horse,' I thought.

'You have to get off the horse and walk for five kilometres now,' my guide advised as if reading my mind. 'The incline down is too steep for the horse to carry you. I will lead the horse down and meet you at the bottom of the mountain.'

My heart was racing as I stood alone on top of Drolma-la. I felt nauseated and increasingly disoriented. A snow flurry descended on the pass and it occurred to me that I might die at Mount Kailash. My friend, Bada Haridas, arrived at Drolma-la and relinquished his horse too. We picked our way down the steep slope, but I was unsure where I was going. I fell behind and lost Bada Haridas. I was completely alone.

I managed to walk fifty metres further before resting on a boulder. I thought about lying down for a short sleep, but something inside me resisted the idea. Chaturatma later told me that when he had reached the summit of the pass a few hours after me, he actually did lie down and felt himself drifting off. A passing Tibetan pilgrim shook him violently to wake him. 'Don't do this!' he shouted. 'You will never wake up again!'

Navigating my way down the steep ridge, I saw to my right a beautiful turquoise-green lake that I had seen in photos. It was the beautiful, sacred Gauri kund, the lake of compassion. The lake is the bathing place of Parvati, Lord Shiva's consort. It was here that Parvati performed austerities to win Lord Shiva as her husband. Devout followers of the Vedic tradition bathe in the frigid waters to become free from sin.

I contemplated bathing for a minute as I watched two pilgrims struggle to get down the jagged hill to bathe in the kund. Instead, I paid my respects to the lake and took several serious vratas (vows) which I had been planning to take while on the kora. Generally, a Vaishnava does not reveal his vratas, but for the benefit of my disciples I will share one of the vows I took on that day: for the rest of my life I would not watch, read or listen to any mundane media— no internet news sites, no newspapers, no magazines, no movies. I imagined the demigods calling out 'Bhisma! Bhisma!' (How horrible! How horrible! What a horrible vow!) but I realized that I, as a person in the order of renunciates, should have had the determination to give up mundane news long ago. As Lord Chaitanya said to Raghunatha das Goswami:

Gramya-katha na sunibe, gramya-varta na kahibe
Bhala na khaibe ara bhala na paribe
Amani manada hana Krishna-nama sada la'be
Vraje Radha-Krishna-seva manase karibe

(Do not talk like people in general or hear what they say. You should not eat very palatable food, nor should you dress very nicely. Do not expect honour, but offer all respect to others. Always chant the holy name of Lord Krishna, and within your mind render service to Radha and Krishna in Vrindavan. [Sri Chaitanya-charitamrta Antya-lila 6:236-237])

One reason for going on pilgrimage to holy places is that in the sanctity of the dhama one gets the inspiration and strength to take courageous steps forward in spiritual life.

The trail became increasingly treacherous beyond Gauri kund. Even the Tibetan pilgrims were slipping. Some of them slid part way down the dangerous slope. After several hours, Bada Haridas and I finally reached the valley at the bottom of the mountain where our horses were waiting for us. I felt I couldn't go another step, but our guide told us we still had another ten kilometres to go. We rested for half an hour and then mounted our horses for the final leg of our second day on the kora. We now found ourselves in the midst of a terrible storm. Our walking team members caught up with us and we all trudged along shivering through sheets of cold, driving rain.

When we reached our campsite, we found the same rudimentary facilities as those of the previous night. Once our packs were brought off the yaks, I changed into dry clothes and jumped into my sleeping bag to try to warm up. Later that evening as I was dozing off in the freezing cabin, I wondered if the second day on the kora—the day of departure—had had any tangible effect on me. I once again prayed to Lord Shiva to help destroy my material attachments and grant me eternal residence in Krishna's abode.

We awoke to a sunny morning on the last day of the kora, the day of renewal. Renewal means that having gone through so much austerity on the kora, the pilgrim would be purified of sin so that his or her spiritual nature would shine forth. When I looked in the mirror that morning all I saw was an unclean, bearded, dishevelled person. But in my heart, I had the feeling I had become purified. That morning I chanted my japa with extra attention and relish.

However, the kora was not over by any stretch of the imagination. We still had twelve kilometres to trek until we reached our original starting point, the village of Darchen. The path wound up and down several gorges that run along the Indus River (in ancient times called the Sindu). The gorges were so steep that they were unsuitable for the horses. When we were one hour into the trek that morning, the Tibetan family that had rented the horses to us appeared from nowhere to reclaim them. All that kept us going from that point on was the thought that by evening we could take our first shower in days.

Clouds once again darkened the sky. I looked for a sign that we had achieved the mercy of the Lord's greatest devotee, that Lord Shiva had noticed our endeavour. On a hillside, I saw an interesting formation of rocks that bore distinct impressions.

'What is this?' I asked our guide.

'This is where Shiva and his bull, Nandi, come down to congratulate pilgrims on the completion of the kora,' he said. 'These marks are the impressions of Nandi's hooves and Shiva's feet.' As I reached out to touch the impressions, the sky cleared briefly and the sun burst through, giving the atmosphere a golden hue for just a moment. When I finished touching the stones, the clouds covered the sky again.

Perhaps it was just the beauty of nature shining forth. But maybe, just maybe, it was a sign from above that we had received the mercy of Lord Shiva. Certainly, such signs are not unusual in a sacred place that, as my guide had said with such confidence, is inhabited by mystics, sages and rishis.

It was late afternoon when we walked out onto the open plain and into Darchen. Our kora was officially finished. We all prostrated ourselves on the ground in the direction of Mount Kailash and paid our final respects. I stayed on the ground for a long time, reflecting on the journey and all that I had undergone. It had been an adventure, but having completed the Kailash kora I concluded that the risks had been too great for us. Things could have gone terribly wrong. But I indeed felt I had become a different person, reborn, purified and cleansed. While walking the path of the kora, I felt I had also journeyed farther along on the path of bhakti.

I got up and took a last glance back at the arduous path we had traversed. Then, without looking back again, I walked forward towards my next service. But wherever that service takes me, part of my heart will always remain in the mountains and valleys of Mount Kailash.

Of the great sages I am Bhrigu; of vibrations I am the transcendental Om. Of sacrifices I am the chanting of the holy names (japa), and of immovable things I am the Himalayas.

      —Lord Krishna in the Bhagavad Gita (10:25)

20

India

Lost and Found at the Kumbh Mela

Ever since becoming a devotee of Lord Krishna in 1970 I have been fascinated with the Kumbh Mela festival. In 2019 I made the decision to journey to the Ardha Kumbh Mela where, from 15 January to 4 March, ISKCON devotees were to follow in Srila Prabhupada's footsteps by bringing his books, the holy names and prasad to the festival.

Kumbh Mela is the largest religious gathering in the world. Estimates anticipated that 120 million pilgrims—nearly double the population of England and France combined—would visit the mela over seven weeks. The mela takes place four times within a twelve-year period on the banks of four of India's most holy rivers: the Godavari River in Nashik, the Shipra River in Ujjain, the Ganges River in Haridwar, and the confluence of the Ganges, Yamuna and Saraswati rivers in Prayagraj (formerly known as Allahabad). In contrast with the West where rivers are treated merely as resources, in the ancient spiritual culture of India these rivers are regarded as goddesses with the power to purify and bless human beings.

The 2019 Mela was held at the confluence site at Prayagraj. The point of convergence is called Triveni Sangam. Bathing in any of the sacred rivers has a purifying effect, but it is said that the purification is increased a hundred times at the sangam and a thousand times at the sangam during Kumbh Mela.

My spiritual master, Srila Prabhupada, wrote:

Bathing during the month of Magha at the Magha Mela [Kumbh Mela] still takes place. This is a very old mela (assembly), dating from time immemorial. It is said that ever since the Lord in the form of Mohini took a bucket of nectar and kept it at Prayag, holy men have gathered there every year and observed the Magha Mela. Every twelfth year there is a Kumbh Mela, a great festival, and all the holy men from all over India assemble there. Bathing at the confluence of the Ganges and Yamuna, near the fort at Allahabad (Prayag), is mentioned in the revealed scriptures: 'If one goes to Prayag and bathes at the confluence of the Ganges and Yamuna in the month of Magha, he attains the result of giving hundreds and thousands of cows in charity. Simply by bathing for three days there, he attains the results of such a pious activity.'⁶

I had a special desire to attend Kumbh Mela this year as the main bathing day, 4 February, was on Mauni Amavasya, which creates a special auspicious segment of time that appears only once every 200 years. However, my main motivation to go was to meet with the holy men Srila Prabhupada described above, and to share with them in chanting the holy names of God.

The origin of Kumbh Mela is described in the Vedic scriptures. It is stated that in bygone ages, the demigods and demons assembled together to churn the ocean of milk to produce the nectar of immortality. Mandara Mountain was used as a churning rod and Vasuki, the king of serpents, became the rope for churning. The demigods took Vasuki's tail and the demons his head, and they churned the milk ocean for a thousand celestial years. Among many other amazing things, a pot of immortal nectar was produced. The demigods were fearful that the demons would take advantage of it, so they stole the pot and hid it in the four places on earth where the mela is held. During the act of hiding, a drop of immortal nectar spilled from the pot at each of the four places. Kumbh Mela is held at the time when, according to astrological calculations, the immortal nectar is most readily available to those who bathe in the sacred rivers.

I journeyed to Prayagraj with a small group of other devotees who were interested in attending the festival. Approaching the festival site, we pulled over at a hill that provided a panoramic view of the mela. The magnitude of the site testified to the pilgrims' enthusiasm to be liberated from the material world through contact with the nectar of immortality. Witnessing the vast landscape of tents, I was fascinated by the thought that so many people were coming simply for spiritual purposes.

Prabhupada said: 'At the Kumbh Mela, millions of people come to take bath in the Ganges because they are interested in how to become spiritually liberated from this material world. They travel thousands of miles to take bath in the Ganges at the holy place of Prayag.'[7]

From our vantage point on the hill, I could see thousands upon thousands of people pouring into the mela. These people were prepared to travel long distances and tolerate many discomforts, including sleeping in austere conditions in very cold weather. Some arrived on overcrowded trains. Others came by bus, car and even ox carts. While the rich and famous flew into Prayagraj on chartered flights, the multitudes came on foot carrying all their necessities—food and a couple of changes of clothes—in bundles on their heads. But whether rich or poor, everyone had the same agenda: to bathe in the rivers at the auspicious moment and attain passage back to the spiritual world. I could hear many people glorifying the Ganges with cries of 'Ganga Ma ki jai! All glories to Mother Ganges!'

I knew that we, as Westerners, would be a tiny minority at the mela but we were not the first foreigners to take part by any means. A seventh-century diary written by Hiuen Tsiang from China mentions the Kumbh Mela. He writes that he witnessed half a million people gather on the banks of the Ganges at Prayagraj to observe a celebration for seventy-five days. He even mentions that a king was present with his ministers, scholars, philosophers and sages, and that he gave away huge amounts of gold, silver and jewels to acquire pious credit and assure himself a place in heaven.

The current rulers of India, likewise, were taking part in the mela by facilitating many of the logistical details. The government had been working on the services and accommodations for an entire year, and the statistics were mind-boggling. Over 6,000 religious and cultural organizations had been allotted land, including our ISKCON. The mela site sprawled over fifty-two square kilometres, an area equivalent to a large town.

There were 4,200 premium tents, 300 kilometres of roads, 122,000 toilets, 20,000 dustbins, 10,000 policemen and 30,000 military personnel. They had provided a veritable city of simple tents for free accommodation. There were lost-and-found centres dotted throughout the mela, intended mainly for helping people find their lost family members and friends. In 2013, thousands of people—mostly women and children—went missing in the huge crowds. The entire cost of this year's Kumbh Mela was estimated at 400 million US dollars.

There were many ashrams and camps distributing free food throughout the mela, including our ISKCON camp. Overall, 5,384 tonnes of rice, 7,834 tonnes of wheat, 3,174 tonnes of sugar, 767 kilolitres of kerosene were allocated to the food distribution centres, and 160 dispensers of clean drinking water made available throughout the mela.

A 100-bed hospital and ten smaller hospitals staffed by 200 doctors and 1,500 health professionals were set up throughout the event. Eighty practitioners of Ayurveda, India's traditional medicinal system, were also available. There were elaborate plans for waste management too. Every one of the 122,000 toilets was geo-tagged to help tackle any problems. Talk about organization!

Meeting India's Spiritual Leaders

It is generally very difficult to meet famous spiritual personalities in India due to strict security policies, but luck was on my side. My good friend, Pundrik Goswami of the Radha-Raman temple in Vrindavan, invited me to stay with him at a camp where many of the principal spiritual dignitaries would be staying. It was called Guru Karishni Camp and was run by Swami Sharanandaji Maharaja, a prominent figure in Vrindavan. I considered this to be a golden opportunity to network with these personalities, most of whom would be unlikely to visit our ISKCON camp at the mela or ISKCON temples elsewhere in India.

Once I arrived at the camp, Pundrik Goswami lost no time introducing me to the spiritual leaders present. His introduction followed a standard format: he would begin by glorifying Srila Prabhupada and explaining how he took Krishna consciousness to the West and how ISKCON has become a worldwide spiritual organization. Then he would introduce me and share some of the results of my service in different parts of the world. His introduction acted as an endorsement whereby India's spiritual leaders gained confidence and respect for my humble self and, through me, Srila Prabhupada's movement.

Over several days I had enlightening talks with numerous personalities, including Sri Ravi Shankar, the head of the Art of Living Foundation; Keshav Prasad Maurya, the deputy chief minister of Uttar Pradesh; Swami Avdeshanand, the leader of one million Naga Babas and head of the Juna Akhada; Sri Rajendra Das Ji Maharaja, a well-known sadhu with a big ashram in Vrindavan; and Lokesh Muni, leader of the Jains in India.

Lost at the Mela

Going anywhere outside the Guru Karishni Camp was a challenge because there was an unstoppable flood of humanity beyond its confines and an estimated sixty-four million people were expected to descend upon the mela to bathe on 4 February, the most auspicious bathing day.

I woke up early that morning which was an austerity in itself. It was mid-winter and it was cold in the tent where I was staying. I bathed quickly in an improvised bathroom which was without hot water and then went out into the cold foggy morning.

'How in the world are sixty-four million people going to bathe along the river bank?' I wondered. And then a doubt entered my mind. 'Will I actually be able to bathe in the river myself?'

The previous night I had searched the internet for all the information I could find on the three sacred rivers, the Ganges, Yamuna and Saraswati. A recent BBC article described the Ganges as the world's sixth most polluted river. It said that 3 billion litres of untreated sewage were pumped into the river every day; the figure didn't include the industrial waste poured into the Ganges as it descended from the Himalayas to the Bay of Bengal. By the time it reached Prayagraj, a city that also contributed untreated sewage to its waters, the Ganges, the article said, became a sewer.

Indian Prime Minister Narendra Modi claimed that cleansing the Ganges was nothing less than a mission from God.

'Ma Ganga has called me,' he told the crowd at his victory celebration some years ago when he was swept to power in a landslide. 'She has decided some responsibilities for me. Ma Ganga is screaming for help; she is saying "I hope one of my sons gets me out of this filth". It is possible it has been decided by God for me to serve Ma Ganga.'

He pledged serious money to his Clean Ganga Mission—more than three billion dollars.

This was sobering and disturbing information. I turned away from Google to the writings of my spiritual master for guidance. I found a passage where Srila Prabhupada wrote:

In India, one can actually see that a person who takes a bath in the Ganges waters daily is almost free from all kinds of diseases. A very respectable brahmana in Calcutta [Kolkata] never took a doctor's medicine. Even though he sometimes felt sick, he would not accept medicine from the physician but would simply drink Ganges water, and he was always cured within a very short time. The glories of Ganges water are known to Indians and to ourselves also. The Ganges flows by Calcutta. Sometimes within the water there are many stools and other dirty things which are washed away from neighbouring mills and factories, but still thousands of men

take baths in the Ganges water, and they are very healthy as
well as spiritually inclined. That is the effect of Ganges water.
The Ganges is glorified because it emanates from the toes of
the lotus feet of the Lord. Similarly, if one takes to the service
of the lotus feet of the Lord, or takes to Krishna consciousness,
he is immediately cleansed of the many dirty things which have
accumulated in his innumerable births.[8]

Elsewhere, Rupa Goswami, another prominent teacher in our line,
writes that the Ganges is always pure, regardless of its seeming
pollution: 'The waters of the Ganges are sometimes during the rainy
season full of bubbles, foam and mud. The Ganges waters do not
become polluted. Those who are advanced in spiritual understanding
will bathe in the Ganges without considering the condition of the
water.'[9]

After reading all of this information, I could see that there was
a discrepancy between the material condition of the river and what
the scriptures described as its eternal spiritual character. Considering
everything, I decided to follow the advice of my spiritual masters.

'I'm going,' I said to myself out loud, with full conviction.
'Whatever it takes, I will bathe at the Triveni Sangam, the meeting
place of the three rivers at the auspicious time.'

The arrangements to travel to the sangam were made by Pundrik
Goswami.

'Maharaja,' he said to me, 'you'll come with me and the spiritual
leaders in a van, and your assistants, Narottam das, Vikram das and
Kartamashi das, can go in another. It will take us around four hours
to reach the sangam.'

'That's a long time,' I said. 'How far away is it?'

'It's twelve kilometres from here,' Pundrik Goswami said.

'So, we'll be travelling at a rate of three kilometres an hour?' I asked.

'Remember there are sixty-four million people vying for that little space at the sangam,' he said. 'The police say that since midnight last night thirty-two million people have bathed. But we'll make it. We have a police escort.'

I sat on the floor of the van, relinquishing the seats to six elderly sadhus who were joining us on the journey. Wanting to focus on the purpose of our journey, I read aloud a verse from the scripture Sri Chaitanya-charitamrta which describes the glory of the Ganges:

Mahattvam Gangayah satatam idam abhati nitaram
Yad esa Sri Vishnos charana kamalotpatti subhaga
Dvitiya Sri Lakshmir iva sura narair archya charana
Bhavani bhartur ya sirasi vibhavaty adbhuta guna

(The greatness of Mother Ganges always brilliantly exists. She is the most fortunate because she emanated from the lotus feet of Sri Vishnu, the Personality of Godhead. She is a second goddess of fortune, and therefore she is always worshipped both by demigods and by humanity. Endowed with all wonderful qualities, she flourishes on the head of Lord Shiva. [Sri Chaitanya-charitamrta Adi-lila 16:41])

When the sadhus heard me chanting the Sanskrit glorifying Mother Ganges, they all smiled broadly.

'May Mother Ganges bless you today!' one said, placing his hand upon my hand.

Our van crawled through the dense crowds. Seeing the sadhus inside, people folded their hands in respect, and some touched the van and then touched their heads. When they saw me crouched on the floor of the van, many smiled and called out, 'Hare Krishna!'

'You Western Vaishnavas are keeping our spiritual culture alive,' one of the sadhus said to me.

We finally arrived at the river confluence hours later. The bank seethed as people tried to move towards the water while others tried to move back after bathing.

'Alright! We're here!' Pundrik Goswami called. 'Everybody out!'

I hesitated. 'Out where?' I thought. There was not a centimetre of free ground.

I quickly changed into a small red gamcha (thin cotton waist towel) and slung a small towel around my neck. Kicking off my sandals, I grabbed my cell phone and placed it in a small plastic bag. 'Just in case!' I thought. Finally, I tucked my bag containing my passport and money safely under the seat. For a moment I contemplated taking a sweater because it was so cold outside.

'No,' I decided. 'I'll just take the bare minimum. The river is only metres away and we'll be back in a flash!'

Without warning, the sliding door I was leaning on opened and I fell out of the van onto the ground.

'I'm going to get trampled!' I thought. The crowd surged over me and around me. I pushed myself upwards to gasp for air, all I could see was waves of people for kilometres in every direction. When I finally managed to steady myself on my feet, I saw I was twenty metres behind the sadhus. They were intrepidly pushing their way towards the water, the policemen guarding them on all sides. The crowd was squeezing me and it was hard to breathe.

'Wait for me!' I yelled, trying to recover the distance between us. My cries merged into the tumultuous noise created by the pilgrims as they strained forward to bathe in the nectar of immortality.

I managed to rejoin the sadhus just a few metres from the Triveni Sangam where the Ganges flows alongside the Yamuna and the mystical Saraswati joins them from beneath the ground. We were also joined by Vikram and Kartamashi, the latter of whom was trying to take photos in the midst of it all. His face was ashen.

'I thought I was going to be crushed to death!' he blurted out.

The roar of the crowd at the sangam was deafening as thousands of people simultaneously achieved their goal of bathing. Cries of 'Ganga Ma ki jai! All glories to Mother Ganges!' reverberated everywhere.

Far away in the river, separated from the throng, I saw a small group of four sadhus standing motionless in the water, their hands folded in prayer. Their long, matted hair was tied up in topknots on their heads. Though thin, they were not emaciated; in fact, they were effulgent, almost glowing. Seeing their gravity and obvious devotion, the hair on my arms stood up for a moment.

'That's the mood I'm seeking,' I thought. I remembered a verse that encapsulated my aspirations:

Tvayi me 'nanya-visaya
Matir Madhu-pate 'sakrit
Ratim udvahatad addha
Gangevaugham udanvati

(O Lord of Madhu [Krishna], as the Ganges forever flows to the sea without hindrance, let my attraction be constantly drawn unto You without being diverted to anyone else. [Srimad Bhagavatam 1:8:42])

As if they'd heard the verse I had just recalled, the sadhus I was with sat down together to do puja, their attention single-pointed on the sacred sangam, oblivious to anyone else.

'Here and now?' I thought. I watched in disbelief as they took out all sorts of worship paraphernalia and, in a peaceful reverie, began twirling lit incense sticks in offering to the three rivers. Hundreds of people directly behind us were straining to see the sadhus do their worship, while the build-up of people farther back caused the line to bulge. People fell to the ground because of the weight of the crowd behind them.

I heard Vikram calling, 'Maharaja! Maharaja!' Over to my right, the intense pressure of the crowd was pulling him away. Then he simply disappeared into the mass of people.

Suddenly the crowd surged forward with such force that all of us were thrown into the river. I clutched my phone in the plastic bag as I fell into the cold water. I swam up to the surface, gasping for air. There was transcendental chaos everywhere as people splashed each other in great joy. The glorification of Mother Ganges reached a frantic pitch: 'Ganga Ma ki jai! Ganga Ma ki jai! Ganga Ma ki jai!'

Surrendering to the moment and remembering the four effulgent sadhus, I stood with my hands folded and prayed to Mother Ganges for loving devotion to the Supreme Lord. Then, following the prescribed method for bathing, I dunked three times into the cold water. When I came up the last time, one blissful sadhu jumped on me and we both tumbled back into the water. Coming up, he again pulled me under, this time going deeper into the water. We splashed each other in great fun, and more sadhus joined our little melee.

'Maharaja,' I heard a voice shout. I saw Vikram swimming towards me. 'I finally found you!' he said. 'Our group is back on the bank of the river and is preparing to leave. You must come now.'

As I prepared to get out of the water, I saw Kartamashi on the bank taking photos. I raised my arms in bliss, and he took a last photo before being pushed from behind. He and his camera just escaped falling into the river.

I glanced back to catch a last glimpse of the four sadhus. They were nowhere to be seen.

'How is that possible?' I wondered. 'There's no way they could have moved through all the people bathing in the sangam back to the bank. It's very peculiar.' I remembered something I had read a few days before wherein Srila Prabhupada said that a number of the saints and sadhus present at Kumbh Mela were inauthentic. But others were perfect yogis, some of them 300 and 400 years old. He said that these yogis, from remote parts of India, would come out for the mela and then return to seclusion.

Prabhupada described how yogis were said to take their bath in the Ganges and then come up in another of India's sacred rivers, such as the Godavari more than a thousand kilometres away. He said that we should give respect to everyone who attends the mela, because we cannot know who the sadhus are and what kind of spiritual advancement or perfection they have attained.

It took me a good half an hour to make it back to the van. Somehow, we had acquired a number of additional sadhus for the ride back to the camp, so I offered to ride in the smaller car with Narottam, Vikram and Kartamashi. Always concerned about my welfare, Pundrik Goswami reluctantly agreed. I started to push through the crowd away from the van when I realized I had forgotten my bag with my passport in it.

'I left my bag under the seat,' I called to Pundrik Goswami. 'I'll get it when we're back.'

'Sure, Maharaja,' he called. He held the bag up so I could see it. 'I've got it.'

Confident that the smaller car was nearby, I made my way bit by bit to where I had seen it parked some distance away. But to my astonishment, it was gone. I went as quickly as I could back to where the van was parked, only to find it had left as well.

I stood there, momentarily bewildered. I was alone in this multitude, dressed only in a small wet cotton cloth around my waist with a damp towel around my neck. I didn't have my robes or shoes, and perhaps most alarmingly no jacket to protect me from the cold. I had no clear idea where I was. All I knew was that the camp I was staying in was in Sector 7, and that was twelve kilometres away through the mass of humanity pressing its way along the 300 kilometres of roads crisscrossing the mela site. I had no map, and there were no signs giving directions in Hindi, much less English. I glanced at my watch. It was 4 p.m. Sunset was imminent.

Then I remembered I had my phone clutched in my hand. I unwrapped it from its plastic-bag covering and turned it on. To my dismay I saw there was no service available and my battery had only three per cent left in it. How could that be? I was sure it was fully charged. I hurriedly turned it off.

'How in the world do people know where they're going?' I wondered. Then, laughing to myself, I thought, 'I'm probably the only person in this teeming crowd who doesn't know where he's going!'

Knowing for sure that the direction to proceed was not behind me, I started walking forwards through the thick crowds surging towards the river. An hour later, I made it to a crossroads, turned left and began walking along a dirt road with a myriad of shops and ashrams on either side. Each ashram was festooned with colourful banners advertising the resident guru and his teachings. Speakers blared music from inside. As it was now getting dark, bright lights illuminated the temporary city built on the sandy banks of the Ganges.

People gawked at me curiously, and I understood why. I was the only white person to be seen, and I was practically naked. Several times I was approached by Naga Babas, who thinking me to be one of them pulled me into their tents and offered me a chillum of hashish to smoke. Each time I declined they seemed perplexed.

I knew I needed to get directions, but to my dismay I couldn't find a single person who spoke English. There were many different languages being spoken around me because there were pilgrims from every part of India, but not one of those pilgrims was speaking English. There were policemen on every street corner, but they too could make no sense of what I was saying. On a couple of occasions, they literally pushed me away apparently thinking me to be insane.

A real blow came when I heard a young Indian man say to his friend, 'Isn't that Indradyumna Swami?' But before I could say anything, his friend pulled him away saying, 'Come on! Are you crazy? That's not Indradyumna Swami!' They disappeared back into the crowd before I could confirm my identity and ask for their help.

Every now and then I would turn my phone on to see if I was in range. Each time I wasn't, and each time the battery drained a little more.

By 8 p.m. it was quite cold. From time to time when I got too cold to continue, I slipped into an ashram where a programme was going on and sat amongst the crowd for warmth. On one occasion, while sitting in a chair and watching a bhajan on stage I was approached by one of the ashram leaders.

'Are you in need of anything?' he asked.

'Yes!' I replied enthusiastically, surprised and relieved that I had found someone who spoke English. 'I am lost in the mela and trying to find my way back to my camp. It's in Sector 7. Can you help me to get there? I have been wandering around for four hours now. Is it far away?'

'Yes, it is,' he said. 'It's about twelve kilometres away at the far end of the mela site. At the moment you are fifty metres from the bathing spot at the sangam.'

My jaw dropped. I had walked in a big circle, coming back to the exact place I had started. The ashram leader could see my disappointment.

'Why don't you rest here for a while?' he said. 'I'll get you a blanket.'

'Thank you,' I said. Once I was wrapped in the blanket, I succumbed to my exhaustion and started to drift off to sleep in the chair. I awoke with a start when my entire body began to itch. The blanket was full of some kind of insects, perhaps fleas, and they were ruthlessly biting me. I threw the blanket to the side and quickly left the ashram, determined to reach my destination.

I started out in a different direction. Two hours later, around 10 p.m., I realized that I couldn't keep going unless I had something to eat. I had learned the hard way not to eat food that I wasn't 100 per cent sure of in India, but this was an emergency. I joined a line of pilgrims waiting to be served at one of the food kitchens. It took forty-five minutes for me to reach the front of the line. I was given a leaf plate and two leaf cups and was served khichari (stew made of rice and dal), a vegetable sabji, two warm chapatis and a cup of tea. Some smiling pilgrims waved at me to join them as they ate their meal in a circle on the ground. Several times I heard the word 'Angreji,' which means English person. They were kind and sympathetic to me, probably because of my paltry attire.

Hungry, cold and tired I devoured the meal. 'This is some of the tastiest food I ever had!' I thought, laughing to myself. Once I finished, I thanked the pilgrims and continued on my way with renewed vigour.

I began wondering what Pundrik Goswami, Narottam, Vikram and Kartamashi were thinking.

'Surely, they realized quite quickly that I had been left behind,' I thought. 'They must be frustrated and worried, being unable to contact me or find me. But actually, I'm fine,' I realized. 'There's no real danger and it's only a matter of time until I get back to the camp, whether it's today or tomorrow. And I am meeting so many nice people! Krishna played a little trick on me just so I can see how the mass of people experience Kumbh Mela. He's also teaching me how to fully depend on Him. Wonderful!'

Just then I felt a rock whiz past my ear. Then another and another. Looking back, I saw a group of children laughing at me.

'Pagal baba! Pagal baba! Pagal baba!' they yelled. I knew what the phrase meant: Crazy sadhu!

I walked quickly away but they followed me and continued throwing stones.

'I can't blame them,' I thought. 'I must look pretty crazy—a barefoot white guy wandering around half naked.' Then one of the rocks hit my elbow causing me to yell out in pain. A policeman saw what was happening and yelled at the group of children to leave me alone. Then he came over and spoke to me in Hindi.

'Only little Hindi,' I said, 'English', and I got down on my hands and knees and wrote 'Sector 7' in big letters in the sand.

'There,' I said, pointing. 'I need to go there.'

He looked puzzled and took me by the arm to an ashram just a few metres away. He sat me down on a mat and disappeared. Ten minutes later he came back with a man who offered me a hot cup of tea. I gladly accepted it and then both of them went on their way. I curled up on the mat and fell asleep. When I jolted awake, I checked my watch; I'd slept for ten minutes. I got up and continued on my way, first checking to make sure the group of children was not around.

At 11:30 p.m. I checked my cell phone again. I was in range! But I was alarmed to see there was only one per cent battery power left.

'I have enough power for one phone call,' I thought. 'If the person doesn't answer, I won't be seeing any of my friends tonight.'

I chose to call Narottam. He picked up immediately.

'Hello! Hello! Gurudeva, is that you? Hello!' Narottam sounded both excited and worried.

'Yes, it's me!'

'Good Lord! We've been so worried. What happened? Where are you? I've been out looking for you for hours!'

'I'm not sure where I am. I've been walking around in circles since we were separated. But I'm fine. Just a little cold and tired. Can you find a car and come to collect me?'

'It's almost impossible to find a car at this hour, but I'll try,' he said. 'The main thing is that we need to figure out where you are.' He was silent for a moment, thinking. 'Okay, here's an idea. Take a photo of where you are and send it to me on WhatsApp. I'll go to a police station and ask for their help in finding your location.'

'Brilliant idea!' I agreed. And without even saying goodbye I hung up and quickly took a picture of the scene in front of me. I sent the photo on WhatsApp and my phone immediately died.

It took Narottam just thirty minutes to find me. It turned out that his search had led him quite close to where I was, and the nearby police kiosk was quickly able to identify the junction where I was waiting. When he finally arrived, I jumped into the car and sat as close as I could to the heat coming out of the vents on the dashboard. Just as the car was pulling away there was a loud bang and it stopped in its tracks.

'What was that?' Narottam asked.

'The driver dropped his transmission,' I said with a wry smile.

'What does that mean?'

'Basically, it means we aren't going anywhere in this car,' I said as I got out.

'Now what?' Narottam asked.

'Lots of walking.' I replied. 'Let's go!'

'Where are we going?' he said.

'Sector 7 of course!' I replied.

With Narottam at my side, we were in a much better position to make it back to our camp, simply because he spoke fluent Hindi. He asked people for the directions to Sector 7 and after a short time he had a good idea how to get there.

'How long will it take to walk there?' I asked.

'Through this crowd, maybe two or three more hours,' he replied

I looked at my watch. It was 12 a.m. At that moment I became a bit despondent—and then a taxi came around the corner.

'Narottam, stop that taxi!' I yelled. He literally jumped in front of the taxi, surprising the driver who screamed at him in Hindi.

'What did he say?' I asked.

'He's not working now,' Narottam said. 'No way.'

'Yes, he is. Give me 1,000 rupees, I said.'

I opened the back door of the taxi and jumped in. The taxi driver looked shocked.

'Out!' he screamed in Hindi.

'Bhai sahib, brother! This is for your trouble,' I told him.

He smiled when he saw the money. 'No problem!' he said in English.

At 1 a.m. we pulled into our camp. Everyone was sound asleep, but I saw the light was still on in Pundrik Goswami's room. I knew he would be worried about me. His eyes opened wide when he saw me standing there barefoot in my red waist cloth, the cold wet towel still around my neck.

'Maharaja, I am so sorry!' he said.

'Nothing to be sorry about,' I said with a big smile. 'On the spiritual path everything is auspicious, even apparent adversity is a blessing. Tonight, I experienced Kumbh Mela first hand, much like Hiuen Tsiang from China probably did in the seventh century. But whereas he walked amongst half a million people for seventy-five days, I walked amongst sixty-four million people for nine hours. It was one of the most wonderful experiences of my life! I feel as though that sadhu's benediction has come true: I was blessed by Mother Ganges today.'

On this path there can be no loss or disappointment. Even a little progress on this path will free you from great fear.

—Lord Krishna in the Bhagavad Gita (2:40)

Among rivers, I am the Ganges.

—Lord Krishna in the Bhagavad Gita (10:31)

21

India

Return to Krishna's Home—Vrindavan

Editor's Note

Vrindavan is the Indian village in which Krishna spent his childhood 5,000 years ago. It is regarded by devotees and scholars as the most important place of pilgrimage for Krishna's devotees. With 5,000 temples within its 135-kilometre circumference, Vrindavan is visited annually by thousands of people who journey from all over the world to go to the sites associated with Krishna's childhood pastimes. The ancient scriptures assert that the village of Vrindavan is non-different from the spiritual world and that Krishna is eternally present there. Therefore, to visit or reside in Vrindavan is to be in direct contact with the divine.

Geographically, Vrindavan is situated in Mathura district of the Indian state of Uttar Pradesh, and lies 160 kilometres south of Delhi. It has a population of about 70,000 and has become increasingly modernized and populated in recent decades, fuelled in part by the influx of foreign Vaishnava pilgrims that started when Hare Krishna began to spread around the world. It was from Vrindavan that Srila Prabhupada planned his journey to America to introduce Krishna consciousness to the Western world and it was to Vrindavan that he returned at the end of his life. It is the aspiration of every Krishna devotee to spend their final days in Vrindavan, for it is said that any living creature who dies in Vrindavan is transported to Krishna's eternal spiritual abode.

Indradyumna Swami began visiting Vrindavan in the mid-1970s when the presence of Western devotees there was still new. He was there for the official opening of the Krishna-Balaram Mandir, ISKCON's Vrindavan temple. Throughout the '70s and '80s, his visits were always short—a few days to a week—owing to his responsibilities in Europe where he was leading missionary activities.

In 1994, there occurred a shift. A Russian student of Indradyumna Swami, nineteen-year-old Vraja-lila dasi, died of leukemia in Vrindavan after a short battle with her illness. Although he was on the road with the Polish festival tour, Indradyumna Swami answered her plea for him to come to see her before she died. Vraja-lila died chanting the names of Krishna a few hours after he arrived, with him sitting beside her. He oversaw her funeral rites, her memorial service, her cremation and the scattering of her ashes in Vrindavan's holy Yamuna River. It was a life-changing event for him, seeing how his student's passing had unfolded as if directly guided by the hand of the Lord. Her name itself means 'servant of the Lord's pastimes in Vraja' (Vrindavan).

Vraja-lila's passing coincided with a time in the Hare Krishna movement's history when devotees were becoming interested in knowing more about the holy places and in studying the scriptures more deeply. Then ISKCON established the Vaishnava Institute for Higher Education in Vrindavan which offered short-term, in-depth courses on the scriptures and on the holy places situated in the very place where the institute itself is located. The passing of his student and the overall thrust of the movement's increasing interest in Vrindavan affected Indradyumna Swami. After seeing out the remainder of the Polish festival tour in the autumn of 1994, he returned to Vrindavan to spend the month of Kartik (the holiest month of the year for Krishna's devotees). He wanted to know more about the sites of Krishna's pastimes, the temples, the historical saints who had lived in Vrindavan, their writings and their deities. It was in 1994 that he first joined the Vraja Mandala Parikrama—a walking pilgrimage around Vrindavan.

Since 1994, he has returned to Vrindavan every Kartik month, initially with just a few close friends and students, but later with many devotees who were interested to go on pilgrimage with him. As with his Polish festival tour, his Vrindavan pilgrimage months became major annual events. Indradyumna Swami is someone who likes to share his joy, and there were hundreds of devotees who were only too willing to share it.

Due to the travel restrictions brought in by the pandemic, Indradyumna Swami spent most of his time in Vrindavan over a period of two years. He established a thrice-weekly video lecture series on the pastimes, history and scriptures associated with Vrindavan. He also began playing a pivotal role in the work of the Vrindavan Institute, an organization that works to preserve and translate the original writings of pre-eminent Vaishnava scholars, including disciples of Chaitanya Mahaprabhu—the incarnation of Krishna who inaugurated the chanting of the holy names in the late fifteenth and early sixteenth centuries.

What follows is a handful of Indradyumna Swami's writings on Vrindavan. They have been chosen to give a sense of the significance of Vrindavan for him, and indeed all Hare Krishna devotees.

Travelling through Rajasthan and Vrindavan

In 2001, I spent five days or so travelling in Rajasthan with my son, Gaura Shakti, and two of his business associates, Mickey and Sherry Goldman. They were in India on a trip that combined business and recreation. Mickey and Sherry were both older than me and came from conservative Jewish backgrounds. I could sense they felt a little uncomfortable around a Hare Krishna devotee in saffron robes.

Our plan was to start in Rajasthan and then take them to Vrindavan. I have been interested in Rajasthan for a long time because of its connection to Vrindavan. Many of the most prominent Vrindavan deities were moved to locations in Rajasthan, such as Jaipur, Udaipur, Karauli and Nathdwara to save them from the wrath of India's Moghul rulers, such as Emperor Aurangzeb who ordered the destruction of all sacred Hindu images and temples in the late seventeenth century.

Mickey and Sherry were interested in visiting tourist sites like the City Palace in Udaipur and the fortresses in Jaipur, the Pink City constructed by Maharaja Jai Singh II for the protection of the idols of Radha-Govinda (Krishna and His consort, Radharani) that had belonged to Rupa Goswami, one of the pre-eminent teachers in our line. Radha-Govinda are loved to such a degree by the people of Jaipur that ever since their arrival, the idols have never returned to Vrindavan. Four-hundred years on, they continue to remain in a grand temple that is at the heart of Jaipur city. There are also many other Vrindavan deities in temples around Jaipur, but they receive less attention than Radha-Govinda.

Temples featured prominently on our itinerary, so I decided to try to explain the principles behind deity worship to Mickey and Sherry. As we sat waiting for a car to take us to Nathdwara, I asked them if in the Jewish faith a material object could be accepted as spiritual due to its association with God. I gave the example of the holy cross in the Christian faith and the wine and wafers given to the faithful in the Catholic Church. Although obviously material by nature, those items are accepted as having taken on a spiritual quality due to their being used in God's service. Mickey and Sherry couldn't think of any such example in their faith until I suggested the Torah, the sacred book of the Jews. I said it was only paper, but it was revered by the faithful and given a special place in any home or synagogue because of its spiritual content. When they agreed, I explained that in the Vedic tradition the deity is carved from stone, marble or wood and after installation according to authorized scriptures is accepted as non-different from the Lord.

At first Mickey and Sherry seemed confused. Mickey said, 'We were taught that worshipping such statues is idol worship.' Then to my surprise, Sherry said that because God is present everywhere, there is no reason He couldn't be in the deity while at the same time not being limited to that form. Mickey nodded in agreement.

Having been introduced to our faith in Rajasthan, Mickey and Sherry arrived with us in Vrindavan the next week. Gaura Shakti and I had talked a lot about Vrindavan already, so Mickey and Sherry were prepared as scenes unique to them unfolded before their eyes. Bullock carts lumbered slowly through the small streets loaded with clay pots, vegetables, hay and cow patties. Sadhus, their faces decorated with markings that signalled their belonging to various sampradayas (spiritual lineages), walked happily on their way to see Krishna in any one of Vrindavan's 5,000 temples.

Monkeys scampered here and there, engaged in their eternal mischief. The atmosphere was vibrant, with the bright cloth of the markets, the sounds of bells ringing from the temples, and the villagers greeting each other with Jai Radhe! (Glory to Sri Radha!)

Our scriptures reveal to us that Vrindavan is a spiritual abode, but I was anxious that Mickey and Sherry would perhaps focus on the thin veil of matter covering Vrindavan to keep ordinary tourists away. Pigs and dogs were everywhere, overflowing sewers created a filthy stench, dust covered everyone and everything, and the loud noises of tractors, cars and three-wheeled scooters competed with Vrindavan's sweet, transcendental sounds.

Depending upon one's consciousness, one can see either matter or spirit in Vrindavan. One time Srila Prabhupada was walking in Vrindavan with his disciples and describing its spiritual glories. His description was so detailed, so vivid, that the devotees felt he was seeing Krishna before him. At one point, a disciple politely interrupted and said that despite the wonderful description, he could see only rickshaw drivers, old buildings, sewers, pigs and dogs. Srila Prabhupada smiled and said that his disciple could not see the spiritual nature of Vrindavan because there was a 'speck' in his eye. The devotee responded by rubbing his eyes, causing Srila Prabhupada to laugh.

'No, not like that,' he had said. 'The speck is your material ambitions and desires. When you remove those desires from your heart, then you will see Vrindavan as it is.'

In a sense, Mickey and Sherry had come to Vrindavan as pilgrims, although they had begun their trip to India as tourists. On the way to Vrindavan from Rajasthan, they had taken a side trip to India's ultimate tourist destination, the Taj Mahal, but upon entering Vrindavan they could immediately perceive the difference.

'The Taj Mahal was dead compared with Vrindavan,' Mickey said
the morning of our arrival.'There's a special atmosphere here!'

The first place we visited in Vrindavan was Srila Prabhupada's
samadhi tomb. Most devotees are cremated but when a spiritual
master leaves this world he is entombed and his place of burial
becomes a site of worship for his disciples. In Vrindavan, Srila
Prabhupada's samadhi is an intricately designed marble building, the
first building one encounters when entering the ISKCON temple
grounds. While Mickey and Sherry looked around, I sat before the
large brass deity-idol of my spiritual master as I always do upon first
entering Vrindavan, and I gave him a report of my service since I had
last been there. I spoke of my successes and failures and of my plans
for service until this time the following year, when I would return to
Vrindavan once again.

Next, we entered ISKCON's Krishna-Balaram temple. This
temple is dedicated to Krishna and His brother, Balaram, because
it is situated in the area of Vrindavan where the two divine brothers
herded their cows.

Our next stop was the Radha-Damodar temple, which is a short
rickshaw ride from the ISKCON temple. Srila Prabhupada lived
at the Radha-Damodar temple for several years before he made his
journey to America to bring to Westerners knowledge of Krishna.
We sat in the small rooms where he had planned his trip, and we held
a kirtan. Mickey and Sherry enthusiastically sang along with the rest
of us.

That evening we visited the temple of Vraja Mohan, the deity that
belonged to Narottam Das Thakur, a hero of mine who had been a
travelling monk in the sixteenth century.

'I understand this deity is special to you,' Mickey said.

'Yes,' I replied. 'I'm doing what I can to help reconstruct the temple in honour of Narottam Das Thakur and his deity. When I first found this temple five years ago it was in a bad state. My students and I have been able to offer some financial help, and things are improving. For example, one of my Russian students recently donated about $1,000 and that funded the painting of the temple and three new sets of clothes for the deities. We've talked about deity worship, and this is what it gives us: the chance to render personal, intimate service to the Lord.'

'I think I understand now,' Mickey said. He gazed at Vraja Mohan.

When we left the temple Mickey wasn't around, so I went back inside to find him. From a distance, I saw him with the priest. He was handing him a $100 bill, pointing to the deity and indicating that it was for His service.

I offered a prayer to Vraja Mohan, amazed by Their potency to transform the hearts of my guests:

Pratimā naha tumi
Saakshaat Vrajendra-Nandana

(My dear Lord, You are not a statue; You are directly the son of Maharaja Nanda. [Sri Chaitanya-charitamrta Madhya-lila 5:96])

The following day was the appearance day of Lord Shiva, the demigod responsible for the destruction of the universe. I decided to spend the day alone at Govardhan hill, the hill that Lord Krishna lifted on His finger like an umbrella to protect the residents of Vrindavan during a devastating rain storm. I was particularly eager to visit Chakaleshvara Mahadeva, a Shiva temple on the banks of the

Manasi Ganga lake at Govardhan. It is one of the five principal Shiva temples in Vrindavan. As devotees of Krishna, we don't worship Lord Shiva in his capacity as a demigod, but rather we take shelter in him as the greatest devotee of the Lord. Specifically, we ask him to allow us to enter and remain in Vrindavan as he is the guardian of that holy place.

When I reached the temple, I found more than a hundred Brijbasis (Vrindavan locals) sitting in front of the Shiva deity, absorbed in an enthusiastic kirtan. One man was singing the glories of Shiva while playing harmonium, another was wildly beating a mridang drum, and many more were playing kartal cymbals. They were all dressed in colourful clothing as a way of marking the occasion. The men had on either white or yellow dhotis, with wide red, blue or green sashes around their waists. The ladies wore colourful saris and danced joyfully on the perimeter of the group. Upon seeing me, the men beckoned me forward and sat me down in their midst. Although I didn't know any of the words, I remained among them for well over an hour, fascinated by the atmosphere and praying to Lord Shiva for his blessings.

I spent the rest of the afternoon chanting and reading at Radha kund, a lake on Govardhan hill which is said to be the holiest of all holy places. When I arrived back in Vrindavan to prepare for my departure to South Africa the next morning, Mickey and Sherry came to see me and asked me where I had been all day.

'I went out to a place called Govardhan hill and I spent a lot of the day at Radha kund,' I said.

'You went to Govardhan hill without us?' Mickey said.

'Wait, you know about Govardhan hill?' I asked.

'Sure,' said Sherry. 'The hill that Krishna lifted on His little finger. We heard the story today.'

'I'm so sorry we won't be able to see Govardhan hill!' Mickey said. 'We're so close, but we missed it.'

I did a quick calculation. 'If we leave early,' I said, 'I think we'll have just enough time to make a stop at Govardhan hill and Radha kund and still make it to Delhi airport for our flights.' Rising early the next day, Gaura Shakti, Mickey, Sherry and I packed our belongings into the Tata Sumo van that would be taking us to the airport. I was already missing Vrindavan. We had a quick glimpse of Govardhan hill and then proceeded to Radha kund.

Radha kund can be truly appreciated only by those advanced souls who are truly in love with God. Beginners like me can have some appreciation of this place by studying the scriptures, but outsiders can only be bewildered as to why someone would be eager to visit a small pond at the foot of Govardhan hill.

But I could see that I didn't have to worry about Mickey and Sherry. They were so eager to see Radha kund that we made it there on the morning of our departure. I could see that they felt it was special for them to go there. They had been preparing for this moment through the mercy of the Lord. They had begun as tourists but had visited the most important temples of Krishna, had lived for ten days on food that had been offered to Krishna and had offered their hard-earned money in the service of the deity of Krishna. The cumulative effect of all of those experiences was seen in the awe and reverence Mickey and Sherry displayed when they approached Radha kund and placed Her sacred waters upon their heads.

On the way back to the van, Mickey said, 'You've been so kind to us these ten days here in India. You have answered all of my questions, but I have one question left and this time I'm afraid that you won't be able to answer it!'

'What's that question, Mickey?' I asked.

'How will I be able to explain all of this to my friends back home? How can I put into words the wonders of what we've seen and done? How do you explain Vrindavan to people who've never been here?'

'It's not easy Mickey, but devotees of Krishna carry Vrindavan in their hearts and wherever they go they share that mercy with others. My spiritual master in particular, took Vrindavan to the West. If people read his books, they'll get an idea of the special mercy that is available here.'

We drove away from Radha kund, and I felt a great emptiness that we were leaving, as if we were leaving our real home. It looked like Mickey and Sherry felt the same, because they looked out the back window until Radha kund could no longer be seen. From the look in their eyes, I knew they'd return.

I Return to Vrindavan

For most people the new year begins on 1 January. For me it comes in early October, when my yearly travels and festivals end and I head to Vrindavan for spiritual rejuvenation. Although I have visited Vrindavan many times in the past thirty-eight years, I still feel a sense of mystery and expectation whenever I begin another trip there. As I boarded a flight from London to Delhi in early October, I was so excited it was as if I were going to Vrindavan for the first time. This year I would be leading 250 devotees on pilgrimage visits in Vrindavan.

I thought about what India had been like in the 1970s and '80s. In those days India was still considered a third-world country. When our flight reached cruising altitude and the seat belt sign was turned off, I reached for a copy of the *International Herald Tribune* in the seat next to me and saw an article about President Bush signing an agreement to trade nuclear technology with India, ending a thirty-year ban.

The agreement would give India access to civilian nuclear technology and fuel and would clear the way for American and European nuclear corporations to bid for contracts worth $27 billion to build eighteen to twenty nuclear reactors in India.

'How times have changed,' I thought.

Unfortunately, India's rise to a world power has affected even places like Vrindavan. The sleepy little town I went to in 1973 has grown into a small metropolis with guest houses, homes and businesses being built at an alarming rate. Gone are the peaceful, quiet days when a person could walk through Vrindavan without getting lost in huge crowds and having to dodge motor-rickshaws, buses and cars. Nevertheless, Vrindavan remains and will always be a pure and sanctified place, untouched by material contamination.

After landing, I caught a taxi to Vrindavan. When we crossed the boundary of Vrindavan, I asked the driver to stop and I got out of the car and rolled in the dust, as is the tradition, much to the surprise of tourists passing by in another car.

The next day, we began our Vrindavan pilgrimage by visiting temples near the Yamuna River.

I decided to duck away to visit the Vraja Mohan temple. It is one of the places in Vrindavan where I go for spiritual shelter and inspiration. When I was paying my respects to the deity, the temple priest saw me. 'I have been waiting for you all year,' he said. 'I have a wonderful surprise. Come to my room.'

I sat on the floor of his simple quarters and he reached up on a shelf and brought down a small wooden box. He opened it and took out a beautiful salagrama-sila. Salagrama-silas are worship stones from the Kali Gandaki River in Nepal. The stones are considered to be deities in themselves and come with natural carvings and indentations that indicate which form of Krishna they are. He put the salagrama-sila in my hand.

'We were digging the foundation for the new guest house behind the temple,' he said. 'We broke into the remains of an ancient temple five metres underground and discovered this in one of the rooms. I'm giving it to you as gratitude for all the help you and your students have done in restoring our temple.'

Two days later, I took the devotees on pilgrimage to Govardhan hill. We walked slowly, chanting the names of the Lord and describing each holy place as we stopped there along the path. When we arrived at the sacred Govind kund, a lake where a Surabhi cow bathed Lord Krishna with her milk, my friend, Chaturatma das, told the story of the place. When we reached Uddhava kund near the end of the day, I was happy to see my old Vrajavasi friend, Giriraja das. He has been the priest at Uddhava kund for over fifty years. We rushed forward to greet each other. As we hugged, I thought of my good fortune to be holding a pure devotee like him.

After we sat down, I spoke to the devotees for over an hour about the importance of Uddhava kund. Giriraja sat patiently by my side. He does not know a word of English, but his face would light up every time I said the name of Krishna.

The day after we concluded our Govardhan pilgrimage, we visited Uchagaon, the birthplace of Lalita devi, a great devotee of Radha and Krishna, and Radha's closest friend. For days I had prepared myself by reading about Lalita devi—her personal qualities, her special mood, and her service to Radha and Krishna.

There were hundreds of us walking along the dusty road leading to the hill where Lalita's village was located. I thought about my spiritual master, Srila Prabhupada, and once again realized that it was only by his grace that any of us were here. As we crossed a bridge over a small river, I noticed two devotees speaking to a farmer on the other side. The farmer was an older man, dressed in a simple white dhoti, old shoes, a vest and an old shawl. I thought it odd that the devotees were speaking with him for so long.

'They certainly don't speak the local dialect,' I thought, 'and surely a poor farmer like him doesn't speak English.'

But when I reached the group, I was surprised to hear the farmer speaking English fluently. I listened for a moment and then spoke to him. 'Sir,' I asked, 'how is it that you speak such good English?'

He smiled. 'When I was very young,' he said, 'I had a desire to learn English. Many of Radha and Krishna's pastimes took place in this area.' He extended his arm and pointed. 'Up on the hill is the place where Lalita devi was born. She is the leader of all of Radha's friends. And just over there the cowherd girls declared Radharani to be Queen of Vrindavan. And on that side, just behind those trees, Radharani performed the marriage ceremony of Lalita and Krishna.' He chuckled. 'Radharani became so happy that her veil fell off and landed on a rock. You can still see the impression of that veil on the rock. It is called the chitra-vichitra-sila.'

'You know a lot,' I said.

He laughed. 'Everyone out here knows these things,' he said. 'This is all we talk about.' His expression became serious. 'But it's quickly changing,' he said. 'With progress and Western influence, our culture here in Vrindavan is being negatively affected. Now people are more interested in watching television and Bollywood videos. Even out here.'

'I'm sorry to hear that,' I said. 'Will you come up the hill with us to the Uchagaon temple?'

'Yes,' he said, and we began to walk. 'I'm happy being a farmer. With my knowledge of English, I could have had a good job in a city, but that would have meant leaving Vrindavan. And this, I would never do.'

When our party reached the temple on top of the hill, I gave a talk about Lalita devi, recounting a number of her transcendental pastimes. My respected guest sat next to me and seemed to enjoy the talk. But as I spoke, I felt increasingly embarrassed. 'This man was born in Vrindavan,' I thought, 'and he has been living here his whole life. He knows these things better than I do. Who am I to speak in front of him?'

After my talk, the farmer and I sat down to eat together and I noticed he was carrying a small bag.

'What's in the bag?' I asked.

He smiled, opened the bag and took out an English edition of the 'Krishna book', the book in which Srila Prabhupada has written about Krishna's pastimes in Vrindavan.[10]

'Wherever did you get that?' I asked him. 'This book was written by my spiritual master, Srila Prabhupada.'

'I found it on a bus two years ago,' he said. 'I've read it seventeen times. It's my favourite book. It's all about Vrindavan. I've heard about how your spiritual master went to the Western countries and helped so many people. I want to read more of his books, but I can't afford them.'

Here was an opportunity to serve a genuine Vrajavasi.

'If you give me your address,' I said, 'I'll send you the entire collection of Srila Prabhupada's books.'

'Please do,' he said, 'and in English.'

'Of course,' I replied.

'But don't wait too long,' he said. 'I'm over fifty now and I want to start travelling. It is the Vedic way: to travel to the holy places at the end of one's life.'

'Will you go to all the holy places in India?' I asked.

'No, no,' he said. 'I will never leave Vrindavan. I plan to travel around Vrindavan and share with everyone what I've learned from your spiritual master.'

'Really,' I said.

'Yes,' he said. 'If people in these villages were to know his message, Vrindavan could be saved from the onslaught of Western culture. Just as your spiritual master went to the West and helped so many people, so his teachings can restore Vrindavan's culture to its original glory.'

I hugged him. 'Thank you,' I said. 'Thank you for increasing my faith in Vrindavan and my spiritual master and in his transcendental books.'

Letter to Srila Prabhupada

The following is a letter Indradyumna Swami wrote to his spiritual master, Srila Prabhupada, on his Vyasa-puja (celebration of his birth) in 2020 in the midst of the pandemic.

My dear Srila Prabhupada,

This year I have no tales to share with you of adventures in foreign lands, of festivals so grand that a million souls heard the holy names and tens of thousands received vegetarian meals, or of your temples around the world where I was witness to your faithful followers sharing with others the knowledge you gave them.

For exactly fifty years to the day, I have traversed this planet sharing your message wherever I go and with whomever I meet. It was the joy of my life and I thought it would never end! Then suddenly the entire world came to a screeching halt, and I with it. From where I was stationed in Vrindavan, India, I watched in disbelief as an invisible foe forced the entire human race to their knees and a lockdown sent the world spiralling downwards like nothing within living memory.

As the world struggled with the viral pandemic, I, like every other human on the planet, was forced to adjust to a new reality. The driving force in my life has always been your instruction to me: 'Preach boldly and have faith in Krishna's holy names.' I contemplated the alternatives for continuing my service from behind closed doors. How could I sit tight in Vrindavan for months—maybe even for years—and not become restless?

Traditionally, Vrindavan is the place where devotees retire to engage in solitary bhajan (glorification) day in and day out with a fixed routine of basic studying and chanting. Although you have many times warned that junior devotees should not try to take up solitary bhajan, there appeared to be no alternative for me.

This was not the vision I had for myself when I reached my present age of seventy-one years. I had dreamt of continuing to travel and share Krishna until my last breath, dying on the battlefield 'with my boots on,' so to speak. But any doubts that remained about sitting tight in Vrindavan doing 'solitary bhajan' were dispelled as I began to read your books. You stressed time and again that being in Vrindavan to chant and study was the greatest engagement, but not one to be taken up artificially.

Your written words lent credence for my new-found fate. The very next day I started following a strict regime of rising early, chanting, worshipping my deities and memorizing Sanskrit verses. I began eating frugally only once a day. I cut my sleeping down to four or five hours a night and spent ten to twelve hours a day on studying. I began giving classes online three times a week for my students on the glories of Vrindavan dhama.

As the weeks turned into months, I felt I was making a little progress in coming closer to a goal—or rather a challenge— you had once given me to go 'higher and higher' in order to understand the deeper mellows of devotional service.

And so, I spend my time here in Krishna's home in thoughtful contemplation. There are days when I miss my colleagues, friends and students terribly! And I miss the people too. I really do; all those hundreds and thousands of inquisitive souls who visit our festivals year after year in Poland, America, India, South Africa, Australia—the list goes on and on. Without them my life is empty, no matter what I do. I think it's the hardest part of this situation. I pray to the Lord to watch over and protect them too.

Forever your servant,
Indradyumna Swami

Epilogue
Poland, 2022
Phoenix of the Baltic Sea

I had been religiously following Covid restrictions from my base in Vrindavan, India, for two-and-a-half years. After travelling as a monk for almost fifty years before the 2020 lockdown began, I suddenly found myself confined to a small apartment. The situation conflicted with my nature, but I devoted myself to research, study and lecturing. However, when there opened a window of opportunity to begin travelling and teaching again, I was ready to go.

My top priority was to re-establish the annual festival I had been leading along the Baltic Sea coast since 1990. There were many challenges to overcome. During the pandemic, many of the festival's core group had faced life changes and were no longer able to be a part of the two-month event. There also had been changes in the Polish government; local officials who had long supported us and allowed us to hold our festivals in prominent locations in their towns were no longer in office. Some of the new leaders were unaware of or disinterested in our festivals. Finally, many of our funding sources had dried up due to the economic impact of the pandemic on our donors.

It took hard work, some luck and, no doubt, the Lord's grace, but we somehow overcame the obstacles. And at the beginning of July, 110 devotees, most of them brand new to the tour, assembled in Poland to witness the Festival of India rise like a phoenix on the Baltic Sea coast.

The day of the first festival dawned and I went with all the devotees on Harinam sankirtan in the streets of Niechorze to advertise the event. I had been chanting every summer on the Baltic Sea coast since the inception of our festival thirty years ago, but this time I felt even more joyful and excited, no doubt due to two years of separation from my most treasured service.

I quickly noticed that I was not the only one who had missed the tour. It was obvious by the way people responded that they had missed us too: their eyes lit up upon seeing us, they smiled and waved, they literally grabbed the colourful invitations we were giving out, and eventually when we stopped to chant in one place, they came forward and chanted and danced along with us.

That evening before the festival began, I kept looking towards the street that led to our site with the large stage and the numerous colourful tents and exhibits. An hour before the festival began, I noticed a woman standing in the restaurant tent watching the devotees put the finishing touches on the displays of vegetarian food. When she saw me, she waved as if she recognized me.

'I've waited two long years for this day!' she called to me. 'Your food is unlike any other in this world. I don't know how I survived!'

Soon the crowd started arriving and quickly filled the many benches we provide for our audiences. There was a palpable sense of excitement in the air as everyone waited for the show to begin. And when it finally did, both the audience and the devotees cheered. We were back in action!

One of my all-time favourite things is to watch people's reactions as they arrive at the festival and get their first glimpse of a Hare Krishna festival. I saw the bright eyes, the surprise, the joy, the astonishment!

I watched people browse through the different tents and exhibits. In some places, the crowd was so large I couldn't move. A family in the crowd insisted I take a photo with them. The people around the family moved back and a stranger snapped the photo with the family's camera. Then the family showed me a photo of the living room in their home. On the wall was a large photo of all of them posing with me eighteen years ago.

'We've been waiting for you to come back for two years. Thank you so much for coming to Niechorze!'

I walked on to the book tent, where an older gentleman asked me to sign two Bhagavad Gitas. 'One is for me,' he said. 'I was thinking of buying one years ago when I attended one of your festivals, but I hesitated. During the pandemic I lamented I hadn't done so, because I believe it would have helped me through those difficult times.'

'And the other Bhagavad Gita?' I asked.

'It's for my granddaughter,' he replied. 'Only God knows what she'll go through in her lifetime. She needs to have this book to help her.'

A woman in the book tent approached me. 'Can you please write a dedication in this book?' she asked, handing me a Bhagavad Gita. 'I have attended at least one of your festivals each summer for thirty years. When I saw your poster in town, I decided I should finally try to understand the philosophy behind your movement and so I am buying the book you always hold up when you speak on the stage!'

'This is all the mercy of God,' I thought. In my heart, I passed the gratitude of the people on to my spiritual master.

'Srila Prabhupada,' I said softly, 'are you watching? Surely you must be, for without your mercy none of this would be happening.'

Later, about halfway through our two-month festival tour, I wrote a letter of gratitude to my spiritual master:

Dear Srila Prabhupada,

It is mid-August in the midst of our summer festival tour in Poland, and I am surprised to see that many trees are already turning to their autumn colours. Generally, they don't change colour until mid-September. I know that they will start losing their leaves soon.

Yesterday, I watched as the bright colours blurred together through my window as we sped towards our next festival site. Two thoughts came to mind. First, I thought about how I am in the autumn of my life and soon you will call me to another service, somewhere here in the material world or perhaps even in the spiritual world. The second thought I had was that I am fortunate to have lived as long as I have!

You said on a morning walk on 21 February 1975, in Caracas, Venezuela, 'Instead of contemplating what will happen to this world, you have got a short duration of life, say fifty, sixty years. You chant Hare Krishna and go back to home, back to Krishna.'

Fortunately, I've lived thirteen years past the sixty-year deadline, but unfortunately, I have yet to develop love of God.

I am not discouraged. I don't doubt that I will see Krishna one day, and I'm certain that that will happen only by your grace. Thus, whatever time I have left in this body I will fully dedicate to the mission of sharing Krishna with others. There are lots of excuses I could use to stop travelling: I'm too old, I'm too tired, I've done my part. But nothing I've done can equal even one iota of what you've done for me. My dear spiritual master, my debt to you can never be repaid.

I will try my best to serve the Lord until my last breath, whether it comes today or tomorrow. If I am to be remembered, let it be for my service to you. The Samurai warriors had a code: 'Don't ask me how he died. Ask me how he lived!'

As the sun sets on my life, I am not afraid of what lies ahead, for it can only be more service. I have experienced in this life that I am happy serving your mission in any condition, at any time, in any place—in the jungles of the Amazon, the freezing steppes of Siberia, the deserts of Mongolia, the favelas of Rio di Janeiro, the ruins of Sarajevo, and the concrete jungles of New York, London and Paris. I have always been happy sharing your message with others.

This is especially true when I am on the Baltic Sea coast with our festival, where for the last thirty years thousands of guests have been attending every summer evening. When the audience gives us a resounding standing ovation, tears come to my eyes and I look up to the sky and wonder, 'Srila Prabhupada, are you watching?'

I hope that you are and I feel that you must be. Please know that by holding these festivals in my remaining years, I want to reciprocate with your tireless efforts in establishing this movement in the pioneer days of ISKCON. My life is coming to a natural conclusion and I often dream of where I will serve you next. I still have time left: a few days, a few months or perhaps even many years. I will use this time to become like you, to serve with the same determination as you did.

I am early in my awakening as a servant of the Lord, so I can't claim to know Krishna. But I am confident that I will reach the goal because I know you.

Your servant,
Indradyumna Swami

Acknowledgements

I wish to acknowledge the contributions of the panel of advisers who met regularly over a year and a half to discuss, rally and strategize about how to bring this book into existence: Advaita Chandra of Torchlight Publishing, who has envisioned this volume for a decade or more; Sitala dasi, whose enthusiasm and commitment to the project was an inspiration; and Sri Prahlada das (Ace Simpson) who provided ideas, feedback and historical insight.

Thank you to Yogesvara das who met with our team early on in the process to give suggestions about publication and framing of the project. Thank you to Ranchor Prime for his poetic rendering of Bhagavad Gita verses in his book *Talks Between the Soul and God;*[11] I use his wording of the verses at the end of each chapter. Thank you to Colin Campbell who generously agreed to be interviewed about his experiences in Sarajevo in 1996. Thank you to Ken White for his meticulous proofing of the final pre-publication draft and the final proofs of the book.

I am also grateful to Gauranga das (ISKCON Chowpatty and Govardhana Ecovillage) for his abundant support in linking me to his publishing contacts in India. Thank you to my agent Dipti Patel, and to Sachin Sharma, my editor at HarperCollins, for their enthusiasm and effort in taking this book from its manuscript state to the bookshop shelf. Finally, thank you to my disciple Mandira-Mani dasi (Mandala White) who has been my editor for fifteen years and who led the project of bringing this book to publication. She has served above and beyond the call of duty and I am eternally grateful.

Notes

Scan this QR code to access the detailed notes

About the Author

Indradyumna Swami is a travelling monk and spiritual teacher in the bhakti yoga tradition. His profound compassion and zest to share the spiritual culture of India has inspired him to traverse the globe for the last fifty years. He is an innovative and visionary leader who has transformed the lives of thousands worldwide, enriching and inspiring people on their spiritual journeys.

To connect with Indradyumna Swami, you may follow him on the following social media handles:

Official website: www.travelingmonk.com
Instagram: indradyumnaswami
YouTube: IndradyumnaSwamiOfficial
Facebook: Indradyumna Swami

HarperCollins *Publishers* India

At HarperCollins India, we believe in telling the best stories and finding the widest readership for our books in every format possible. We started publishing in 1992; a great deal has changed since then, but what has remained constant is the passion with which our authors write their books, the love with which readers receive them, and the sheer joy and excitement that we as publishers feel in being a part of the publishing process.

Over the years, we've had the pleasure of publishing some of the finest writing from the subcontinent and around the world, including several award-winning titles and some of the biggest bestsellers in India's publishing history. But nothing has meant more to us than the fact that millions of people have read the books we published, and that somewhere, a book of ours might have made a difference.

As we look to the future, we go back to that one word—a word which has been a driving force for us all these years.

Read.

Harper
Collins

HARPER
FICTION

HARPER
NON-FICTION

HARPER
BUSINESS

HarperCollins
Children'sBooks

HARPER
DESIGN

Harper
Sport

HARPER
PERENNIAL

HARPER
VANTAGE

हार्पर
हिन्दी

three

Hymn

There in the garden of tears,
my heavy load he chose to bear;
his heart with sorrow was torn,
'Yet not my will but yours,' he said.

This is our God, the Servant King,
he calls us now to follow him,
to bring our lives as a daily offering
of worship to the Servant King.

V.   I am spent and utterly crushed:
R.   **I cry aloud in anguish of heart.**
     (cf. Psalm 38:9)

1. agony

Scripture Reading (Luke 22:41-44)

Jesus knelt down and prayed, 'Father, if you are
willing, take this cup away from me. Nevertheless,
let your will be done, not mine.' Then an angel
appeared to him, coming from heaven to give him
strength. In his anguish he prayed even more
earnestly, and his sweat fell to the ground like
great drops of blood.

Meditation

No wonder you prayed in the garden,
'Take this cup away from me.'

This cup of suffering that humanity has inflicted on
itself by turning away from you: persecution,
destruction, injustice, calumny, war, pride, abuse.

This burden that weighs you down.

This weight that is crushing you.

'Can you drink the cup that I am going to drink?'
you asked those disciples who wanted to sit with you
in your kingdom. And today you ask us that same
question. Are we prepared to accept whatever comes
to us in your name, as we strive to bring about your
kingdom here on earth?

Response (Psalm 118:26; cf. Matthew 21:9 etc.)

V.   Blessed is he who comes in the name
     of the Lord:
R.   **Hosanna in the highest.**

Hymn

Father, hear the prayer we offer;
Not for ease that prayer shall be,
But for strength that we may ever
Live our lives courageously.

Be our strength in hours of weakness,
In our wanderings be our guide;
Through endeavour, failure, danger,
Father, be thou at our side.

V.   I bear shame and insult:
R.   **because of your name.**
       (cf. Psalm 69:8)

Scripture Reading (John 15:18-21)

2. judgement

Jesus said, 'If the world hates you, you must realise that it hated me before it hated you. If you belonged to the world, the world would love you as its own; but because you do not belong to the world, because my choice of you has drawn you out of the world, that is why the world hates you. If they persecuted me, they will persecute you too; if they kept my word, they will keep yours as well. But it will be on my account that they will do all this to you, because they do not know the one who sent me.'

Meditation

Innocent, you heard yourself condemned.

We hear of people locked up for years for crimes they did not commit.

We know of prisoners of conscience, punished for their political or religious views.

I wonder where we would stand if we faced trial for our faith in you. As someone said, 'would there be sufficient evidence to convict us?'

Are we known, and seen, to be Christians, not just when we are in church, but in our homes, our workplace, among our friends; or do we avoid owning up to being your disciples for fear of ridicule or abuse?

If we do, are we not as guilty as Pilate, who was willing to deny the truth for the sake of an easy life?

Response

V.   Blessed are you when people abuse you and persecute you:
R.   **your reward will be great in heaven.**

A purple robe, a crown of thorn,
a reed in his right hand;
before the soldiers' spite and scorn
I see my Saviour stand.

He bears between the Roman guard
the weight of all our woe;
a stumbling figure bowed and scarred
I see my Saviour go.

V.   The proud have risen
       against me,
R.   **brutal gangs seek my life.**
       (cf. Psalm 86:14)

3. mocking

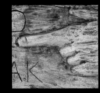

Scripture Reading (John 19:1-3)

Pilate then had Jesus taken away and
scourged; and after this, the soldiers
twisted some thorns into a crown and
put it on his head and dressed him in
a purple robe. They kept coming up
to him and saying, 'Hail, king of the
Jews!', and slapping him in the face.

Meditation

What can we tell you about bullying,
Lord?

You have been the victim of it
yourself.

As if being condemned to death was
not enough, the soldiers dressed you
in kingly robes and put a crown of
thorns on your head and mocked you.

Yet still we bully one another, in
school, at work, in our families; even
in your church.

It may not be as open as what the
guards did to you, but however
subtle, it is still bullying.

Response

V.   Blessed are you when people
       speak all kinds of calumny
       against you:

R.   **your reward will be great in
       heaven.**

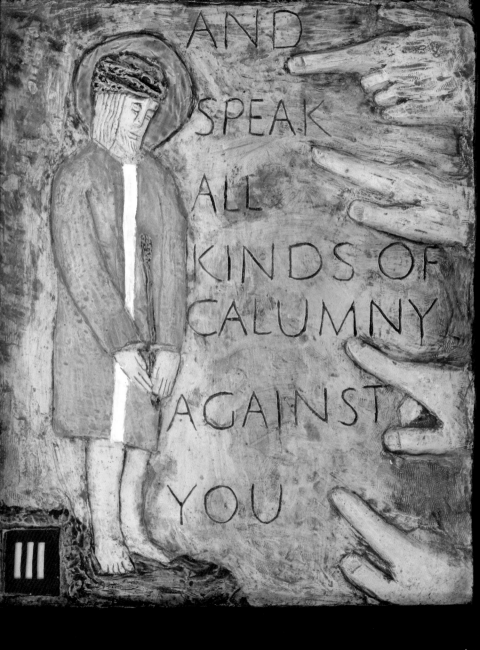

AND
SPEAK
ALL
KINDS OF
CALUMNY
AGAINST
YOU

III

nine

4. cross

Hymn

Peace is the gift of heaven to earth,
softly enfolding our fears.
Peace is the gift of Christ to the world,
given for us.
He is the Lamb who bore the pain of peace.

Peace is the gift of Christ to his Church,
wound of the lance of his love.
Love is the pain he suffered for man,
offered to us:
Oh, to accept the wound that brings us peace!

V.   Mercy and faithfulness meet,
R.   **justice and peace embrace.**
       (cf. Psalm 85:11)

Scripture Reading (Colossians 1:18-20)

Christ is the Beginning, the first-born from the
dead, so that he should be supreme in every
way; because God wanted all fullness to be
found in him and through him to
reconcile all things to him, everything in heaven
and everything on earth, by making peace
through his death on the cross.

Meditation

Christ is our peace.

We say this readily enough at the Eucharist as
we prepare to share the peace.

But here we see what that peace cost you.

You could have called on your father to send ten
legions of angels to save you from arrest, but
you knew that was not the way.

You knew this and told your disciples to put
away their swords.

You knew that violence only leads to
violence, that war only leads to more war.

Peace without justice is no peace worth having.

But fighting is no way to bring about peace.

Response

V.   Blessed are the peacemakers:
R.   **they shall be called the sons of God.**

BL
ESS
ED
ARE
THE
PEACE
MAKERS

IV

Hymn

Look around you, can you see?
Times are troubled, people grieve.
See the violence, feel the hardness;
all my people, weep with me.

Kyrie, eleison. Christe, eleison. Kyrie, eleison.

Forgive us, Father; hear our prayer.
We'll walk with you anywhere,
through your suff'ring, with forgiveness,
take your life into the world.

V.   Lord, I take refuge in you:
R.   **save me from those who attack me.**
    (cf. Psalm 7:2)

5. fall

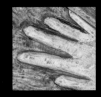

Scripture Reading (from 1 Corinthians 4:9-12)

It seems to me that God has put us apostles on show right at the end, like men condemned to death. Here we are, fools for Christ's sake. To this day, we go short of food and drink and clothes, we are beaten up and we have no homes; when we are cursed, we answer with a blessing; when we are hounded, we endure it passively; when we are insulted, we give a courteous answer. We are treated even now as the dregs of the world, the very lowest scum.

Meditation

Over the years there have been many martyrs for the Christian faith, and even today people are persecuted because of their faith in you.

But what hope is there when even the different religions cannot live together in peace? Look at the land of your earthly life, the so called 'holy' land. Worse still, even Christians cannot always live together in peace.

We recall with shame the events of the Reformation, and the troubles in Ireland.

And what about our own churches, with their factions and power struggles?

Things haven't changed much in two thousand years. You know what it is to be persecuted in the cause of right.

And here you fall under its weight.

Response

V.   Blessed are those persecuted in the cause
    of right:
R.   **theirs is the kingdom of heaven.**

BLESSED THOSE PERSECUTED IN THE CAUSE OF RIGHT

V

Hymn

Brother, sister, let me serve you,
let me be as Christ to you;
pray that I may have the grace to
let you be my servant, too.

We are pilgrims on a journey,
fellow trav'llers on the road;
we are here to help each other
walk the mile and bear the load.

V.   Show your goodness to those who do good:
R.   **to those whose hearts are true.**
(cf. Psalm 125:4)

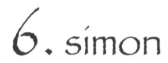

Scripture Reading (Matthew 25:37-40)

'Lord, when did we see you hungry and feed you, or
thirsty and give you drink? When did we see you a
stranger and make you welcome, lacking clothes and
clothe you? When did we find you sick or in prison
and go to see you?'

And the King will answer, 'In truth I tell you, in so far
as you did this to one of the least of these brothers
of mine, you did it to me.'

Meditation

Simon showed you mercy, Lord.

Unwillingly, perhaps.

But he did shoulder your cross and help you on
your way.

Would we have carried your cross in his position?
It doesn't matter, does it, because you aren't here
for us to face that challenge.

But of course you are here, as you reminded us in
this parable.

You are here incarnate in our brother and sister
in need.

You are here as the homeless, the poor, the prisoner,
the sick, the starving.

We see you every day in our streets and on our
televisions, crying out for our help, asking us to
carry your cross.

Can we be a Simon to you today?

Response

V.   Blessed are those who show mercy:
R.   **God will show mercy to them.**

BLESSED ARE THOSE WHO SHOW MERCY

VI

7. mother

Hymn

Sing we of the blessed Mother,
who received the angel's word,
And obedient to his summons,
bore in love the infant Lord;
Sing we of the joys of Mary,
at whose breast that child was fed
Who is Son of God eternal,
and the everlasting bread.

Sing we, too, of Mary's sorrows,
of the sword that pierced her through,
When beneath the cross of Jesus,
she his weight of suffering knew,
Looked upon her Son and Saviour,
reigning high on Calvary's tree,
Saw the price of man's redemption,
paid to set the sinner free.

V.   In the scroll of the book it
is written that I should do
your will.

R.   **Your law is deep in my heart,
O God.**
(cf. Psalm 40:8-9)

Scripture Reading (Isaiah 6:8-9a)

I heard the voice of the Lord saying,
'Whom shall I send? Who will go for us?'
And I said, 'Here am I, send me.'

Meditation

I don't suppose we would be here at all
if at the start of it your mother had not
said 'yes' that fateful day.

I don't suppose your mother really
understood what it was all about when
she said yes to the angel.

But she did say yes.
And as events unfolded and strange
things happened she probably understood
less rather than more as she pondered
these things in her heart.

And now she sees you being led out to
death.

In the normal run of things sons see their
mothers die, not the other way round.

Was this really what she had said 'yes' to
some thirty years earlier?

But Mary remains faithful through it
all and is still there when the others
have fled.

When we hear your call, we often
make excuses.

It isn't the right time; someone else
could do it better; we don't understand
the implications.

But when God's call comes to us, it is
for us.

And like Mary, we must say yes.

Response

V.   Blessed are those who hear the
word of God and keep it:

R.   **blessed is she among women,
and blessed is the fruit
of her womb.**

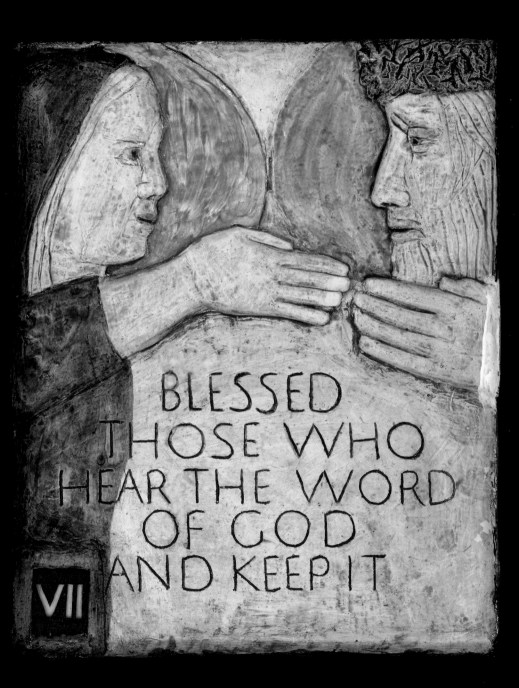

BLESSED
THOSE WHO
HEAR THE WORD
OF GOD
AND KEEP IT

VII

8. women

Hymn

All who love and serve your city,
All who bear its daily stress,
All who cry for peace and justice,
All who curse and all who bless.

In your day of loss and sorrow,
In your day of helpless strife,
Honour, peace and love retreating,
Seek the Lord, who is your life.

V.   How good and how pleasant it is:
R.   **wherever people live as one.**
     (cf. Psalm 133:1)

Scripture Reading (Luke 19:41-42)

As Jesus drew near and came in sight of Jerusalem he shed tears over it and said, 'If you too had only recognised on this day the way to peace! But in fact it is hidden from your eyes!'

Meditation

You came to your city in triumphant procession, but as you drew near you wept over it.

And well you still might.

A city made holy for Jews by David and Solomon.

A city made holy for Christians by yourself.

A city made holy for Moslems by Mohammed.

A meeting place for nations and religions.

A sacred city.

But also a city divided by fear, hatred, and hostility.

Why, Lord, can't these people live together in peace, respecting their differences, rather than fighting over them?

Why, Lord, can't we live together in peace in your church, respecting our differences rather than fighting over them?

Response

V.   Blessed are those who weep:
R.   **every tear will be wiped away**

WEEP FOR
YOURSELVES

AND YOUR
CHILDREN

VIII

Hymn

Word incarnate, truth revealing,
Son of Man on earth!
Power and majesty concealing
by your humble birth:
Yours the glory and the crown,
the high renown, the eternal name.
Suffering servant, scorned, ill-treated,
victim crucified!
Death is through the cross defeated,
sinners justified:

V.   They take what I wore,
R.   **they stare at me and gloat.**
       (cf. Psalm 22:19,18)

9. stripped

Scripture Reading (Philippians 2:5-8)

Make your own the mind of Christ Jesus:
Who, being in the form of God, did not count
equality with God something to be grasped.
But he emptied himself, taking the form of a
slave, becoming as human beings are; and
being in every way like a human being, he was
humbler yet, even to accepting death, death
on a cross.

Meditation

It must have been incredibly humiliating, Lord,
to be stripped in front of the gazing crowds.

To be exposed in your nakedness in front of
these mocking and jeering people.

We cling to our clothes more than just to cover
our nakedness.

They make a statement about us; that we have
the latest fashion or designer label.

Or they are a uniform that gives us a status
that we can hide behind.

But in your eyes we are all equal.

Whatever we look like, whatever we wear.

And so we must be prepared to bare ourselves
to others.

To be seen for what we really are.

Response

V.   Blessed are the poor in spirit:
R.   **theirs is the kingdom of heaven.**

BLESSED THE

IX POOR IN SPIRIT

10. dice

Hymn

Father, I place into your hands
the things I cannot do.
Father, I place into your hands
the things that I've been through.
Father, I place into your hands
the way that I should go,
for I know I always can trust you.

V.   They divide my clothing among them,
R.   **they roll dice for my robe.**
        (cf. Psalm 22:19)

Scripture Reading (Matthew 6:25,33)

Jesus said, 'Do not worry about your life and what
you are to eat, nor about your body and what you
are to wear. Surely life is more than food, and the
body more than clothing! Set your hearts on his
kingdom first, and on God's saving justice, and all
these other things will be given you as well.'

Meditation

As if it wasn't enough to have taken your clothes
from you, the guards now throw dice to share
them out.

There are those who suggest that this is a way of
living life, to make decisions by the throw of dice
or the toss of a coin. It saves them from having
to think.

It can make life easy, and we are all for an easy life
sometimes.

But life isn't easy.

I don't recall you ever telling us it would be.

You did tell us not to worry over material things,
and some Christians see that as meaning that once
we have turned to you everything in life will be
rosy.

But that wasn't what you were saying either.

You were saying that we have to get our
priorities right.

And you should be our first priority, then others,
and finally ourselves.

Response

V.   Blessed are the lowly:
R.   **they shall have the earth for their heritage**

O Lord, all the world belongs to you,
and you are always making all things new.
What is wrong you forgive,
and the new life you give
is what's turning the world upside down.

The world's only loving to its friends,
but you have brought us love that never ends;
loving enemies too,
and this loving with you
is what's turning the world upside down.

V.   Precious in the eyes of the Lord,
R.   **is the death of the faithful.**
    (cf. Psalm 116:15)

11. crucified

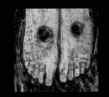

Scripture Reading (John 15:10-13)

Jesus said, 'If you keep my commandments you will remain in my love, just as I have kept my Father's commandments and remain in his love. I have told you this so that my own joy may be in you and your joy be complete. This is my commandment: love one another, as I have loved you. No one can have greater love than to lay down his life for his friends.'

Meditation

You taught us to love our neighbours, Lord.

You taught us to love our enemies.

You taught us to love even those who hate us.

You taught us to forgive those who sin against us, even seventy seven times.

And this is your reward for it all.

Hanging there, dying on the cross.

What love is this, that you lay down your life for your friends.

Response

V.   Blessed are the pure in heart:
R.   **they shall see God.**

BLESSED
THE
PURE
IN
HEART

XI

Hymn

Come, my Way, my Truth, my Life:
such a way as gives us breath;
such a truth as ends all strife:
such a life as conquers death.

Come, my Joy, my Love, my Heart:
such a joy as none can move;
such a joy as none can part:
such a heart as joys in love.

V.   Your love is better than life:
R.   **my heart thirsts for you.**
    (cf. Psalm 63:4,1)

Scripture Reading (John 16:12-13)

12. thirst

Jesus said, 'I still have many things to say to you but they would be too much for you to bear now. However, when the Spirit of truth comes he will lead you to the complete truth, since he will not be speaking of his own accord, but will say only what he has been told; and he will reveal to you the things to come.'

Meditation

Lord, I don't suppose you have been given anything much to eat or drink since your arrest. It is no wonder you are thirsty, hanging there on the cross in this heat.

But of course your thirst is not just physical.

Your thirst is for the truth.

Throughout your ministry you tried to lead people to see this truth.

This truth that is important; this truth that will set us free.

Some think we have got the truth, whether it be the Scriptures, or the Councils of the Church. But it isn't as simple as that.

It is being revealed to us all the time, and we must look for it, strive for it.

And we often don't find it because we prefer our certainty to your truth.

Seeking the truth can be hard work; and it can be divisive.

But you did warn us it would be.

Response

V.   Blessed are those who hunger and thirst for what is right:
R.   **they shall be satisfied.**

BLESSED ARE
THOSE WHO
HUNGER
AND THIRST
FOR WHAT
IS RIGHT

XII

Hymn

Now the green blade riseth from the buried grain,
wheat that in the dark earth many days has lain;
Love lives again, that with the dead has been;
love is come again like wheat that springeth green.

In the grave they laid him, love whom men had slain,
thinking that never he would wake again,
laid in the earth like grain that sleeps unseen:
love is come again like wheat that springeth green.

V.   I will praise you, Lord, before all the people:
R.   **for your love reaches heaven, your truth to the skies.** *(cf. Ps. 57:10-11)*

Scripture Reading *(Luke 12:50; John 19:28,30)*

Jesus said, 'There is a baptism I must still receive, and what constraint I am under until it is completed!' ...

Jesus knew that everything had now been completed and said, 'It is fulfilled'; and bowing his head he gave up his spirit.

Meditation

Your cross stands bare and empty.

The crowds have gone home - another public execution over. Calvary quiet.

But what was that last word you spoke from the cross that only John recorded?

Did he hear it clearly in his distress? Have we translated it right?

'It is finished' seems hardly right, because, thankfully for us, it isn't.

'It is accomplished' is perhaps better, but still seems a bit final.

It is probably not strictly correct, but the old Vulgate perhaps captures the meaning in its rendering - 'it is consummated'.

Consummation completes the marriage covenant, without which it is neither legal nor valid, and is open to annulment.

But consummation is also only the beginning of the marital relationship.

And so with your death on the cross: it was not the end, but the consummation of the covenant you made with us.

Response *(Revelation 14:13)*

V.   Blessed are those who die in the Lord:
R.   **they can rest for ever since their good deeds go with them.**

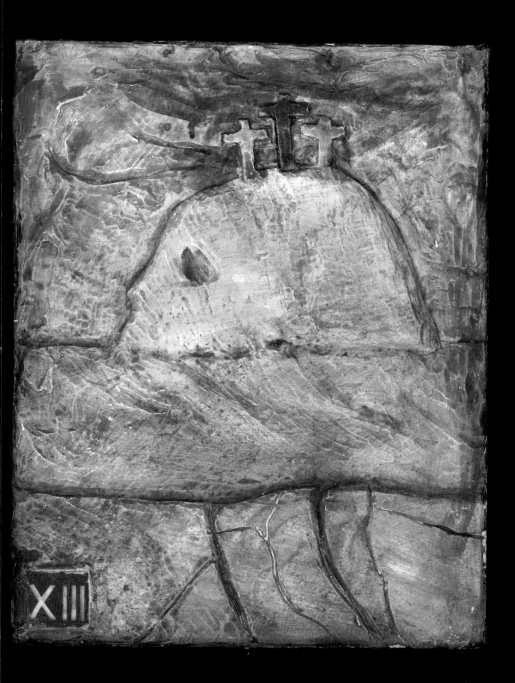

XIII

14. burial

Hymn

Walking in a garden at the break of day,
Mary asked the gardener where the body lay;
But he turned towards her, Smiled at her and said:
'Mary, spring is here to stay, only death is dead.'

V.   You will not abandon your faithful one
     to death:
R.   **you will show me the path of life.**
     (cf. Psalm 16:10-11)

Scripture Reading (from John 19:38-20:1)

Joseph of Arimathaea asked Pilate to let him
remove the body of Jesus. Pilate gave permission,
so they took the body of Jesus and bound it in linen
cloths with the spices, following the Jewish burial
custom. At the place where he had been crucified
there was a garden, and in this garden a new tomb
in which no one had yet been buried, and they laid
Jesus there ...

Very early on the first day of the week Mary of
Magdala came to the tomb. She saw that the stone
had been moved away from the tomb.

Meditation

Your mother held your body one last time, then
gave it up to be laid to rest in the tomb that Joseph
had kindly given.
It was the custom to bury bodies quickly, but yours
had to be done in even greater haste because of
the Sabbath.
They couldn't even complete the usual rituals.
A funeral is always a sad time and no doubt many
tears were shed by those who laid you in the tomb
that Friday afternoon.
But, as that ancient Russian hymn for the departed
reminds us, even as we weep over the grave, our
song must be Alleluia!

Response

V.   Blessed are those who mourn:
R.   **they shall be comforted.**

BLESSED ARE
THOSE WHO
MOURN

XIV

Hymn

Alleluia, alleluia, give thanks to the risen Lord,
Alleluia, alleluia, give praise to his name.
We have been crucified with Christ.
Now we shall live for ever.
God has proclaimed the just reward:
New life for all! Alleluia.

V.   The stone which the builders rejected
has become the cornerstone.

R.   **This is the Lord's doing; a marvel in our eyes.**
(cf. Psalm 118:22-23)

Scripture Reading (1 Corinthians 1:20-25)

Do you not see how God has shown up human wisdom as folly? Since in the wisdom of God the world was unable to recognise God through wisdom, it was God's own pleasure to save believers through the folly of the gospel. While the Jews demand miracles and the Greeks look for wisdom, we are preaching a crucified Christ: to the Jews an obstacle they cannot get over, to the gentiles foolishness, but to those who have been called, whether they are Jews or Greeks, a Christ who is both the power of God and the wisdom of God. God's folly is wiser than human wisdom, and God's weakness is stronger than human strength.

Meditation

Your gospel often seems contrary, Lord.

You said that people who wanted to save their life must lose it.

And you put this into practice by giving your life for us; and God raised you up again.

It is indeed a contrary idea, but then so are these Beatitudes that you taught early in your ministry.

Only now, in the light of your resurrection, can we begin to make sense of these contradictions.

But just making sense of them is not enough.
We must put them into practice.

We must be the people who strive to bring about your kingdom here on earth.

As St. Teresa said, Christ has no body on earth but ours; and it is only through our eyes that he can look with compassion on the world, on our feet that he can go about doing good, and with our hands that he can bless.

V.   Blessed are you when people abuse
     you and persecute you:
R.   **their reward will be great in heaven.**
V.   Blessed are you when people speak all
     kinds of calumny against you:
R.   **their reward will be great
     in heaven.**
V.   Blessed are the peace
     makers:
R.   **they shall be
     called the sons
     of God.**
V.   Blessed
     are those
     persecuted
     in the cause
     of right:
R.   **theirs is the
     kingdom
     of heaven.**
V.   Blessed are
     those who
     show mercy:
R.   **God will show
     mercy to them.**
V.   Blessed are those
     who hear the word
     of God and keep it:
R.   **blessed is the fruit of
     her womb, Jesus.**
V.   Blessed are those who weep:
R.   **every tear will be wiped away.**
V.   Blessed are the poor in spirit:
R.   **theirs is the kingdom of
     heaven.**
V.   Blessed are the lowly:
R.   **they shall have the earth
     for their heritage.**
V.   Blessed are the pure in heart:
R.   **they shall see God.**
V.   Blessed are those who hunger
     and thirst for what is right:
R.   **they shall be satisfied.**
V.   Blessed are those who mourn:
R.   **they shall be comforted.**

Alternative Hymn for use in Lent & Passiontide.

Christ is alive! Let Christians sing.
The cross stands empty to the sky.
Let streets and homes with praises ring.
Love, drowned in death, shall never die.

Christ is alive! No longer bound
to distant years in Palestine,
but saving, healing, here and now,
and touching every place and time.

Christ is alive, and comes to bring
good news to this and every age,
till earth and sky and ocean ring
with joy, with justice, love and praise.

acknowledgements & sources

Hymns

Hymns are listed as follows:
First line (even if the first verse is not used here)

Author and copyright details.
Suggested tune(s)

References to a selection of books, coded as in HymnQuest
AMC - Common Praise
CHE - Celebration Hymnal for Everyone
NEH - New English Hymnal
ONC - Complete Anglican Hymns Old and New
ONL - Liturgical Hymns Old and New

HymnQuest, published by Stainer & Bell in association with the Pratt Green Trust, is an excellent database of hymnody, giving the full text of thousands of hymns, suggested tunes (with the ability to play an incipit), and references to a large number of books among other features. www.hymnquest.com

1. From heaven you came, helpless babe
Graham Kendrick (b.1950) © 1983 Thankyou Music tym@kingsway.co.uk Used by permission
The Servant King
AMC 432, CHE 187, ONC 195, ONL 267

2. Father, hear the prayer we offer
Maria Willis (1824-1908)
Sussex (or alternatives in various hymn books)
AMC 416, CHE 158, NEH 357, ONC 161

3. A purple robe, a crown of thorn
*Timothy Dudley-Smith (b.1926) © Timothy Dudley-Smith in Europe and Africa. Reproduced by permission of Oxford University Press.
All rights reserved.*
A purple robe (or other suitable CM tune)
ONC 39

4. Peace is the gift of heaven to earth
John Glynn (b.1948) © 1976 Kevin Mayhew Ltd. Reproduced by permission of Kevin Mayhew Ltd. Licence Nr. 705001/3
Peace is the gift of heaven to earth
CHE 596, ONL 573

5. Look around you, can you see?
Jodi Page Clark (b. 1941) © 1976 Celebration/kingswaysongs.com tym@kingsway.co.uk Used by permission
Look around you
CHE 376, ONL 440

6. Brother, sister, let me serve you
*The Servant Song by Richard Gillard (b.1953) © 1977 Scripture in Song / Maranatha!Music. Administered by CopyCare, PO Box 77, Hailsham. BN27 3EF UK. Music@copycare.com.
Used by permission*
Servant Song
AMC 393, ONC 88, ONL 186

7. Sing we of the blessed Mother
George B.Timms (1910-1997). Reproduced by permission of Oxford University Press.
Abbot's Leigh
AMC 241, CHE 659, NEH 185, ONC 605

8. All who love and serve your city
Eric Routley (1917-1982) © Stainer & Bell Ltd.
Laus Deo (Redhead)
AMC 373 (tune AMC 392, CHE 108, NEH 343, ONC 288, ONL 196)

9. Christ triumphant, ever reigning
Michael Saward (b.1932) © Michael Saward / Administered by The Jubilate Group. 4 Thorne Park Road, Torquay. TQ2 6RX. UK. copyrightmanager@jubilate.co.uk Used by Permission
Christ Triumphant
AMC 398, CHE 113, ONC 104, ONL 200

10. Father, I place into your hands
    Jenny Hewer (b.1945) © 1975
    Thankyou Music tym@kingsway.co.uk
    Used by permission
    Father, I place into your hands
    CHE 159, ONC 162, ONL 251

11. O Lord, all the world belongs to you
    Patrick Appleford (b.1925) © 1965
    Josef Weinberger Ltd. Reproduced by
    permission of the copyright owners.
    O Lord, all the world belongs to you
    CHE 567, ONC 509, ONL 828

12. Come, my Way, my Truth, my Life:
    George Herbert (1593-1633)
    Come, my way *or* The Call
    AMC 405, ONC 123, ONL 215

13. Now the green blade riseth from the
    buried grain
    John M.C.Crum (1872-1958) From the
    Oxford Book of Carols ©1928 Oxford
    University Press. Reproduced by
    permission.
    Noël Nouvelet
    AMC 153, CHE 513, NEH 115,
    ONC 475, ONL 498

14. Walking in a garden
    Hilary Greenwood (1929-2003) ©
    Society of the Sacred Mission
    Dun Aluinn
    NEH 123, ONC 75

15. Alleluia! Give thanks to the risen Lord.
    Alleluia No.1 by Don Fishel (b.1950) ©
    1973 Word of God Music.
    Administered by CopyCare, PO Box 77,
    Hailsham. BN27 3EF UK.
    Music@copycare.com.
    Used by permission
    Alleluia
    AMC 136, CHE 32, ONC 8, ONL 105

15. *(alternative)* Christ is alive! Let
    Christians sing.
    Brian Wren (b. 1936) © 1969, 1995
    Stainer & Bell Ltd
    Truro
    AMC 140, ONC 96

Responses
The opening responses are adapted from
the Psalms by the author, and are not
necessarily from any particular
translation. The closing responses are
mostly the Beatitude verse as depicted on
the Station, with others by the author,
adapted from Scripture or other sources.

Scripture Readings
Scripture readings are taken from the
New Jerusalem Bible, © Darton Longman
& Todd Ltd., 1985. Occasionally they
have been mildly edited in order to
contextualise the extract used.

Meditations
The Meditations are original compositions
by the author.

This compilation of The Beatitude
Stations is © Bruce Carlin. First published
2007 by the Shrine of Our Lady of
Walsingham.

ISBN 0-9551801-3-9
ISBN 978-0-9551801-3-2

Designed by Adept Design. www.adeptdesign.co.uk

The Beatitude Stations
9780955180132   £3.95

The Shrine of Our Lady of Walsingham
6 Common Place, Walsingham, Norfolk NR22 6BW

For accommodation and general enquiries
Tel: **01328 820255**   Fax: **01328 824206**
Email: **accom@olw-shrine.org.uk**
Website: **www.walsingham.org.uk**